A LAND OF TWO PEOPLES

A Land of Two Peoples

Martin Buber on Jews and Arabs

Edited with commentary by
Paul R. Mendes-Flohr

OXFORD UNIVERSITY PRESS

Oxford New York Toronto Melbourne

OXFORD UNIVERSITY PRESS

Oxford   London   Glasgow
New York   Toronto   Melbourne   Auckland
Delhi   Bombay   Calcutta   Madras   Karachi
Kuala Lumpur   Singapore   Hong Kong   Tokyo
Nairobi   Dar es Salaam   Cape Town

and associate companies in

Beirut   Berlin   Ibadan   Mexico City   Nicosia

Copyright © 1983 by Oxford University Press, Inc.

First published by Oxford University Press, New York, 1983

First issued as an Oxford University Press paperback, 1984

Library of Congress Cataloging in Publication Data

Buber, Martin, 1878-1965.
  A land of two peoples.

  Bibliography: p.
  1. Jewish-Arab relations—1917-   —Addresses,
essays, lectures. 2. Zionism—Addresses, essays,
lectures. I. Mendes-Flohr, Paul R. II. Title.
DS119.7.B75 1983   956.94'001   82-2162
  ISBN 0-19-503165-2   AACR2
  ISBN 0-19-503426-0 (pbk.)

Printing (last digit): 9 8 7 6 5 4 3 2 1

Printed in the United States of America

For
Ernst Akiva Simon
and in memory of
Robert Weltsch

Acknowledgments

The preparation of this volume has been preeminently a collective endeavor. From the very inception of the project I fully enjoyed the moral and intellectual support of Ms. Margot Cohen and Mr. Rafael Buber. With her customary energy and dedication, Margot Cohen—director of the Martin Buber Archive of The Jewish National and University Library in Jerusalem—assisted me, leading me through the byways of Buber's voluminous archive in trace of his writings, many unpublished, on the Arab question. Her intelligent and subtle understanding of Buber also contributed immeasurably to the conception of the volume. I would have surely faltered before the enormity of the task before me were it not for the ever gracious encouragement of Rafael Buber, who has attended to his father's literary estate with imagination and infectious love. His and Margot Cohen's devotion to and manifest belief in this project were a source of constant inspiration. I am profoundly grateful to both of them.

At the embryonic stage of the project, Professor Nahum N. Glatzer provided crucial encouragement and wise counsel. I wish to record my gratitude to him, and for their judicious advice, to my colleagues: Professors Aryeh Goren, Ben Halpern, Alfred Ivry, and Nathan Rotenstreich. I am especially indebted to Professor Jehuda Reinharz for his meticulous and scholarly review of my introduction. In the course of preparing this volume I have not hesitated to impose on my friends. For their patience and indulgence I affectionately thank Janet Aviad, Gordon Fellman, Haim Goldgraber, Galit Hasan-Rokem, Susan Jacoby, Michael Koran, Loraine Obler, Arnold Schwartz, the late Gabriel Stern, Steve Whitfield, and my wife Rita. I should also like to express my profound gratitude to the following people for their intelligent, and often inspired translations: Deborah Goldman, Jeffrey M. Green, Deborah Grenimann, Carol Bosworth Kutscher, Michael Plotkin, Gabrielle H. Schalit, Arnold Schwartz, and Itta Shedletzky.

While working on this volume I had the good fortune to be a visiting scholar at the Center for the Study of World Religions at Harvard University. I am grateful to the director of the Center, Professor John Carman and his wife Ineke for their most attentive hospitality. I am also indebted to the Center for Jewish studies at Harvard University, and to the Department of Near Eastern and Judaic Studies at Brandeis University for the many kindnesses extended me. My sojourn and research in the United States were generously supported by the William and Olga Lakritz Foundation and the Memorial Foundation for Jewish Studies. The Faculty of Humanities and the Institute for Jewish Studies of the Hebrew University have also been generous in their support.

I am also very grateful to the staff of Oxford University Press for their professional and courteous assistance. Working with them has been a distinct pleasure. I particularly wish to thank Mr. Curtis Church for his intelligent and conscientious copy editing. To Nancy Lane, History Editor of Oxford University Press, I wish to express my deeply felt gratitude for her vision and imaginative support.

I am certain that each of the above individuals and institutions joins me in the hope that this volume will make its modest contribution to Arab-Jewish rapprochement.

Jerusalem, Israel   Paul R. Mendes-Flohr
September 1982

Contents

A LAND OF TWO PEOPLES

Introduction

The theologian and philosopher of dialogue, Martin Buber (1878-1965) was a political radical, a humanist socialist actively committed to a fundamental economic and political reconstruction of society as well as to the pursuit of international peace and fraternity. He was profoundly distressed that his commentators and readers often tended to ignore his political concerns or to minimize them by regarding them as distinct and tangential to his religious and philosophical teachings.[1] For Buber, however, politics was an essential dimension of the life of dialogue and service to God; politics, he affirmed, is neither extraneous to the "life of the spirit" nor is it simply an unavoidable task occasionally imposed upon us by the exigencies of history. As the ultimate matrix of interpersonal and everyday life, Buber averred, politics provides the necessary test and gives concrete reality to religious and ethical teachings. Only when brought to bear on politics could the life of the spirit possibly realize its primal task to overcome the insidious dualism between truth and reality, idea and fact, and indeed between morality and politics itself.[2]

Zionism, Buber held, sponsors such a *political* test of Judaism. By seeking the liberation of Jewry from the fractured existence of the Diaspora, Zionism confronts Judaism *qua* religious faith and community with the mundane challenges of a *normal* national life: the importunate reality of social, economic, and political life—riddled as it is by ambiguity and conflict—provides Judaism with the unique opportunity to authenticate its spiritual and moral vision. The so-called Arab question—the fact that the ancestral home of the Jews, Palestine, was also the home of an indigenous Arab population who had their own national aspirations—was according to Buber the preeminent challenge to Zionism and Judaism. Indeed, as a moral touchstone of Judaism and the Zionist enterprise, the Arab question, Buber gravely pointed out, is an innermost Jewish question.[3]

The writings assembled in this volume—culled from numerous speeches, essays, and letters which span the period from the Balfour Declaration of November 1917 to the end of his life in June 1965—poignantly reflect Buber's intense involvement in Zionist affairs, particularly with regard to the Arab question. In these writings we observe Buber and his untiring efforts to alert his fellow members of the Zionist Organization (which he joined in 1898)[4] to the significance of the Arab question and the need to pay heed to Arab susceptibilities and political aspirations. Aside from several programmatic and ideological statements, most of the writings presented in this volume were originally *écrits de circonstance*, pieces written in response to specific issues and incidents. They thus bear eloquent witness to the complex encounter of an intellectual and moral philosopher with the seemingly recalcitrant and morally indifferent reality of politics.

Zionism and the Arab Question

It would be erroneous to view Buber's moral alertness to the Arab question as unique. Buber had no monopoly within the Zionist movement on moral concern for the Arabs of Palestine, nor was his a lone voice. From the very beginning of Zionist settlement in Palestine, there were members of the movement who were aware of the Arab question, appreciating the moral and political implications of the Arab presence in Palestine. Upon returning to Russia from a visit in 1891 to the nascent Zionist community in Palestine, Ahad Ha'am (1856–1927), the revered founder of cultural Zionism, reported his impressions in a widely read (and frequently reprinted) essay, "Truth from the Land of Israel":

> Outside the Land of Israel we tend to believe that all the Arabs are wild sons of the desert, a people too dull to see and understand what happens about them. The Arabs, like all Semites, have a keen intelligence.... The Arabs, particularly the townspeople, see and understand what we are doing and what we want in Palestine, but they pretend not to know as long as they do not perceive any danger to their future in what we are doing at the present.... However, as soon as our people's life in Palestine develops so as to encroach upon the rights of the native population, then they [the Arabs] will not yield so easily.[5]

A veritable library of Zionist writings echoes and amplifies Ahad Ha'am's prescient reflections. In every generation of Zionism we find numerous essays, diaries, speeches, manifestoes, and even belles-lettres which address the Arab question. This awareness was prompted by a wide range of attitudes and experiences. In the early generations in particular, there was a romantic adulation of the Arab: after millenia in alien climes the Jews are returning to the Orient where their Arab cousins will reintroduce them to a life of simple beauty and integrity.[6] Disappointed that their reunion with the Arabs was hardly as fraternal as anticipated, these Zionists tended to blame themselves.[7] Moshe Smilansky (1874–1953), who under the affectionate Arabic pseudonym "Hawaja Mussa" wrote Hebrew stories celebrating the pristine humanity of Arab village life, in an essay of 1913 lamented that:

> After thirty years of settlement [in Palestine] we, who are close to the Arabs in terms of race and blood, remain foreign to them, while their enemies, who constantly awaited their downfall in order to take advantage of it, have succeeded in gaining their confidence and being admitted to the most intimate aspects of their life. We were alien to them and their troubles when they were subject to exploitation, and we remained alien to them and their joy when the sun of freedom shone upon them. . . . During the thirty years we have been here it is not they who have remained alien to us but we to them.[8]

Other Zionists confronted the Arab question as a consequence of the practical issues of living with the Arabs: employment, trade, and generally the need for good neighborly relations. Further, various political powers, especially Great Britain during the period of its Mandate for Palestine (1919–1948), recurrently prodded the Zionists to acknowledge the national aspirations of the Palestinian Arabs and to reach mutual accommodation with them.[9] Then, of course, the sheer intensity of Arab opposition to the establishment of a Jewish National Home in Palestine—an opposition which intermittently erupted into violence—obliged Zionism to reckon with the Arab question. The truth is that the Zionists could not ignore the Arab question, even if they were as morally and politically obtuse as some contemporary students of the Middle East now claim. The charge of Zionist evasion of the Arab question is ill-informed. In fact, as we have noted, most Zionists were

painfully aware of the Arab presence in Palestine, and not infrequently
this awareness reflected genuine moral anguish. Moreover, many of
these individuals were by no means marginal to the movement. At the
World Congress for Labor Palestine held in Berlin in September 1930,
David Ben-Gurion (1886–1973)—often portrayed as exemplifying
Zionist myopia with regard to the Arab question—implored his comrades to be conscious of the fact "with all the discomfort that it entails
for us" that:

> ... for hundreds of years large numbers of Arabs have been living in
> Palestine, that their fathers and their fathers' fathers were born here
> and that Palestine is their country, where they want to continue living
> in the future. We must accept this fact with love and draw all the
> necessary conclusions from it. This constitutes the basis for a genuine
> understanding between us and the Arabs.[10]

And Ze'ev Jabotinsky (1880–1940), the founder of the Revisionist Zionist party and the political mentor of Menahem Begin, declared in 1921:

> Today the Jews constitute a minority in [Palestine]; in another twenty
> years they could very well be the vast majority. If we were Arabs, we
> would not agree to this either. And the Arabs are good Zionists too, like
> us. The country is full of Arab memories. I do not believe that it is
> possible to bridge the gap between us and the Arabs by words, gifts,
> and bribery. I have been accused of attaching too much importance to
> the Arab national movement. [Some say] I admire this movement
> unduly. But the movement exists. . . . [11]

The difference between Buber and other Zionists, especially the
leadership of the movement, is thus not moral sensitivity *per se*, but
rather, as we will see, their assessment of the *political* relevance of the
moral aspect of the Arab question. An analytical distinction may be
made between the *epic*, i.e., the existential-biographic dimension of
the confrontation with the Arab question, and the *ideological* dimension of the encounter, i.e., the individual's political evaluation of the
problem and his proffered solution.[12] The emphasis, tone, and considerations of the epic response need not, of course, correspond to the
ideological response. On the epic or existential level one may be overwhelmed by moral perplexity and guilt, yet on the ideological level
different perspectives—i.e., the broad historical, social, and economic

perspectives characteristic of ideological analysis—are brought to bear in the evaluation of the situation and in the establishment of one's *political* priorities and judgments. Most Zionist leaders, whose ideological response to the Arab question we shall presently examine in detail, concluded that Zionist politics, which must serve the needs and interest of the Jewish people first and foremost, unfortunately could not allow the moral dilemmas attendant to the Arab question to affect in any fundamental way the political priorities of the movement. Buber was to dispute this conclusion, and argue that Zionist politics can, and must accommodate a forthright response to the moral issues raised by the Arab question.

As Neil Caplan has cogently shown in his careful study *Palestine Jewry and the Arab Question, 1917–1925*, the Zionist movement, especially in the *Yishuv* (as the Jewish community in Palestine was called prior to the establishment of the State of Israel), was preoccupied with the Arab question.[13] The regnant position among the Zionist leadership of the Yishuv, however, was in public debate to minimize the issue and not to highlight the intensity and extent of Arab opposition to Zionism. When Arab opposition was discussed publicly, it was generally treated as episodic or as a manipulation of unscrupulous elements in the Arab community. This tactical decision, as Caplan emphasizes, was prompted by the view of the Zionist leadership that, at least initially, the goals of the Zionist movement were politically incompatible with the aspirations of the Arab population of Palestine. This consensus was given forceful expression by Berl Katznelson (1887–1944), one of the founders of *Achdut Ha-Avodah*, the Socialist Zionist Labor Party of Palestine. Addressing the Twelfth Zionist Congress—an *in plenum* assembly of the leaders of the World Zionist Organization, which met in September 1921 in Karlsbad, Czechoslovakia, and discussed at length the Arab question, especially in light of the violent Arab riots of May 1921 against the Yishuv—Katznelson impassionately contended:

The quest for peaceful co-existence with the Arabs is not new. The Jewish worker has [always] sought to foster humane relations between Jews and Arabs. . . . For the time being, however, there is still a great distance between us. Before we can draw the Arab [masses] close to us in peace, [we must acknowledge] that our life is in danger. Moreover, we must secure life and property; only then will we be able to negotiate an understanding with the Arabs. To those who preach morality [to the Yishuv], we have only one thing to say: Come to *Eretz Israel* and prove that you could establish more amicable relations with the Arabs than we have. . . . It is clear to us that the movement's important political work in the present is: renewal of Jewish immigration to Palestine, the fostering of *Halutziut,* that is, the pioneering spirit, the strengthening of our self-defense, and the consolidation of our position in Palestine.[14]

Zionist priorities cannot be compromised, Katznelson insisted, and certainly their realization cannot be made contingent on the chimerical hope of Arab consent to the Zionist enterprise. Earlier in 1918, another leader of the Yishuv, Yitzhak A. Wilkansky (1880–1955), put the political issue posed by Arab opposition in purposefully stark, disquieting terms:

[If it would achieve the urgent goals of Zionism] I would commit an injustice against the Arabs. . . . There are those among us who are opposed to this from the point of view of supreme righteousness and morality. Gentlemen, . . . if one wants to be a "preventer of cruelty to animals," one must be an extremist in the matter. When you enter into the midst of the Arab nation and do not allow it to unite, here too you are taking its life. The Arabs are not dried fish; they have blood, they live, they feel pain with the entry of a "foreign body" into their midst. Why don't our moralists dwell on *this* point. We must be either complete vegetarians or meat-eaters: not one-half, one-third, or one-quarter vegetarians.[15]

Zionism would have to make some harsh, morally painful political decisions.

At this juncture, most Zionists, especially in the Socialist-Zionist camp, were not prepared to endorse Wilkansky's somber evaluation; most preferred to entertain, as Ben-Gurion did for instance, the hope that the Arab masses would eventually recognize the material benefits brought by Zionist settlement in Palestine, and under the aegis of their own socialist leadership, recognize an affinity of interests with Zionism as a movement of the Jewish workers.[16] Nonetheless, the consensus remained that overtures to the Arabs, as important as they might be, were of secondary political significance.[17] Yitzhak Ben-Zvi (1884–1963; the second president of the State of Israel)—an individual given to a romantic affection for the Arabs—in a debate of the National Council of the Yishuv in 1922 observed that a sustained moral solicitude for the feelings and interests of the Arab population of Palestine might, alas, be incompatible with promoting the needs and priorities of Zionism, that is, free, unbounded Jewish immigration and settlement in Palestine.[18] As believers in the right of national self-determination, the Zionists—such as Katznelson, Ben-Gurion, and Ben-Zvi—could not but be confounded by the fact that in pursuit of this right the Jewish nation came into conflict with another people, the Arabs of Palestine, claiming the same elemental right. "In an analogous fashion," the historian Jacob L. Talmon points out, "though fundamentally anti-imperialistic and passionately democratic, the Zionists had [or felt they had] no choice but to look for help to imperialistic powers." Zionists, Talmon continues, "stood bewildered in the cross-fire of those days between the demands of the religious [i.e., moral] conscience and those of secular power politics, between messianic nationalism on the one side, and messianic universalism on the other."[19] The Zionist leadership made a political choice—for many, a morally agonizing choice—to pursue Zionist priorities, regardless of their sympathy for Arab national aspirations.

Demographically, Palestine was overwhelmingly Arab. According to a British census of 1922 there were 660,641 Arabs in Palestine as compared to 83,790 Jews.[20] Even without the statistical data provided by His Majesty's assiduous bureaucrats, the fact that the Arabs constituted a majority of the population of Palestine was incontrovertible. Yet this fact did not undermine the Jews' resolve to establish their National Home in Palestine. For most Zionists the connection between the Jews—the People of Israel—and the *Eretz Israel* (the Land of Israel) was self-evident. This attachment, tenaciously maintained throughout Israel's millenial sojourn in Exile, was often articulated by Zionists as conferring on the Jews a "historical right" to Palestine, i.e., to *Eretz Israel*. This quasi-legal formulation[21] sought to translate into the language of modern secular politics what for the Jews was a phenomenological and spiritual reality—a reality as incontrovertible as the Arabs' presence in Palestine. The Zionist conviction that the "Jewish problem"—the mounting physical and cultural distress of the Jews in the modern world—could only be solved through the "ingathering of the exiles" in their ancestral homeland rendered the Jews' attachment to Palestine ever more compelling. The recognition of the Jewish people's "right" to Palestine by the Balfour Declaration and its endorsement by the Western powers and the League of Nations only reinforced what seemed to numerous Jews as self-evident.

From this perspective, the assertion of the Jewish "right" to Palestine seemed morally valid to the Zionist leadership. Moreover, it was held, the need of the Jewish people for Palestine, especially with the rise of Hitler to power, was greater and more urgent than that of the Arabs. In light of the overarching need of securing the survival of the Jewish people, Zionism's infringement on Arab rights seemed but an inconvenience: "When the Arabs' claim is confronted with our Jewish demand to be saved, it is like the claims of appetite versus the claims of starvation."[22] Hence, *politically* the immediate challenge for Zionism was to offset the Arab demographic superiority—which gave "superficial" justification to the demand to establish Palestine as an Arab state—by creating as rapidly as possible a Jewish "majority" in Palestine.[23] Accelerated Jewish immigration, or *aliyah* in Zionism's Hebrew parlance, thus became the supreme political strategy in the movement's response to the Arab question.[24] Parallel to promoting *aliyah* and the formation of a Jewish majority—a policy which in the twenties was shrouded in deliberate ambiguity but from the thirties on became increasingly explicit[25]—work proceeded apace on the creation of an economically and socially self-contained, autonomous Jewish community in Palestine: an independent school system, a self-defense corps (the *Haganah*), the institutions of self-government, and a network of agricultural settlements. The intention was to present the Arabs (and the British) with a *fait accompli* of a Jewish majority entrenched in a prosperous economy and vibrant social structure. It was hoped that the Arabs would acquiesce in this situation, and accepting it seek to live with the Jews in fraternity and peace.

The dominant Zionist position, borne by a militant resolve not to concede what were regarded as basic Jewish rights, was eloquently summarized by the president of the World Zionist Organization, Chaim Weizmann (1874–1952)—an advocate of conciliation and political moderation, who possessed a profound sensitivity to the Arab question.[26] In a reply, dated 17 January 1930, to a letter by an American Jew, inquiring whether the Arabs did not indeed have a legitmate case against Zionism, Weizmann conceded that Palestine is a country of two nations, each with equal rights:

But equality in rights between partners as yet very unequal in numbers requires careful thought and constant watching. Palestine is to be shared by two nations: one is there already in full strength, while of the other so far a mere vanguard has reached it. The Arabs are the *beati possidentes* [blessed in possession]. While we have to defend the rights of those *qui ont toujours tort* [who are always wrong]. The force of inertia works in favour of the Arabs, and thoughts which run in the customary grooves cut across and undermine the foundations of that thing to come, our National Home in Palestine. While we accept the principle of equality between Jews and Arabs in the future Palestinian State, the Arabs press for having that State constituted immediately, because circumstances would enable them to distort it into an Arab dominion from which no path would lead back to real equality.

We do not require political dilettantes, or adventurers, like [St. John] Philby keen on showy "argosies in the Pacific," to teach us how desirable it is for us to come to a friendly understanding with the Arabs, and it is downright mean on their part to try to create the impression that we were not aware of the need for such an understanding, or not anxious to reach it. . . .

All the Arab objections to what we have done in Palestine during the last ten years, ultimately boil down to one single thing: that we have come, are coming, and mean to come in increasing numbers. In 1848 a leading Italian said to the Austrians: "We do not ask you to govern us well, but to go." The Arabs, when they speak out the truth, say to us: "We do not ask you to deal fairly with us, but not to come;" and so long as they do not bolster up that demand by mendacious allegations of wrongs suffered at our hands, I can both understand and honor their point of view. Whoever thinks that our claim to a National Home—to one spot on the face of the earth—is unjustified, that we alone among all nations must for ever be wanderers, driven out from one land, refused access to another, and despised and treated as inferiors where we remain; whoever thinks that the Mandate was a mistake and an injustice to the Palestinian Arabs, let him say so. If any Jews feel that way, let them say so too. All I can say to people who have suddenly been converted to that view is that in honesty they should have thought of that twelve years ago, before so many hopes were raised, so many sacrifices made, and so much labour spent on what we have thought, and the world has acknowledged, to be an honorable and just ideal.

If ever there is to be our National Home in Palestine, if the right of free access to the country is to be maintained, if the idea of the rights of both nations is valid, clearly that half of the future population which is on the spot and is determined to keep out the other half, must not be given a free hand, nor conceded powers which are due to the whole population only.

... I say it clearly and with a full consciousness of my responsibility: I shall not for a shibboleth give up our national hopes or abandon the foundations of our national existence. We have to look to the end; we have no right to commit national suicide. We had much rather see ourselves abandoned by superficial or half-sincere friends among the non-Jews, we had much rather re-start our wanderings in the desert and renounce the idea of seeing our oldest hopes realized in our time, than give up our fundamental right to freedom and equality in Palestine, our birthright in *Eretz Israel.* We must not sin against the right nor betray the future of our people.[27]

Implicit in this letter, only recently published, is what may be called the "tragic" view of the problem of Palestine: a conflict of two just claims, which, regrettably, are irreconcilable. With the ascendance of the Nazis and the heightened need to provide Jewry with a haven, and, concomitantly, the increasing determination of the Arab opposition to Zionism, there was a growing and deepening conviction among Zionists that the gap between the Jews and Arabs was indeed utterly unbridgeable.

Buber and the Arab Question

The tragic view of the conflict between Jew and Arab in Palestine became a familiar refrain in Zionism. Buber vigorously rejected this view with its implied resignation to an ever intensifying conflict, and the assumption that in the face of the trenchant opposition of the Arabs, the only viable option remaining to Zionism was a persistent self-assertion bolstered by the politics of power. Buber's rejection of the concept of a tragic conflict—and its moral and political conclusions—provides the leitmotif of his writings on the Arab question and Zionist policy assembled in this volume.

By assuming that the differences between the Zionist and Arab positions are irreconcilable by means other than the politics of power, the tragic view of the conflict, Buber contends, in effect brackets and suspends the moral issue. It is insufficient, he insisted, simply to acknowledge the problem, however sincerely. The Zionist movement must live with the problem; the movement must allow the problem to gnaw at its conscience until a *morally* equitable solution is found, that is, a mutually just and agreeable reconciliation of the contending claims of the Arabs and Jews. The moral issue, Buber tirelessly argued, must be placed at the center of the movement's political imagination and agenda. Although he did not hesitate to make specific policy recommendations—he was a vigorous proponent of the idea of a bi-national state in which Jews and Arabs would enjoy political and national parity[28]—the substance of Buber's challenge to the Zionist leadership was not that he had a more judicious policy to offer, but rather his demand that it introduce into its political thinking a moral tension or, as he preferred to call it, "direction" *(Richtung)*—a moral direction which he deemed necessary to quicken the insights leading to a more judicious policy.

Buber's criticism of the Zionist leadership was, of course, also directed against the general tendency in political thinking to bifurcate morality and politics as distinct and separate realms of judgment and behavior. Specifically he detected a frightful hypocrisy in the tendency of most political leaders, regardless of ideology, to include moral issues in their litany of pious concerns, and yet, because of the insidious assumption that "our cruel and complex world" is not amenable to ethical principles, they nevertheless proceed along the beaten path of national self-assertion and *Realpolitik*. This cynicism, only thinly veiled by platitudinous homage to the ideals of morality and justice, constitutes, according to Buber, a forfeiture of the promise of those very ideals.

Buber was associated with a vocal and vigorous minority within Zionism which regarded the Arab question as the central issue confronting the movement. Because it threatened to vitiate the moral and spiritual core of Zionism, in their judgment, the Arab question could not be deferred or neutralized by the tactics of power politics. Moreover, they held, by its mere deferral and political containment the moral challenge posed by the Arab question would not in the least be eliminated. The Arab opposition to Zionism, in the view of these Zionists, was prompted by a fundamental fear that their rights and land would be usurped and that the Jewish "interlopers," with the countenance of the British, would dominate them and their country. This was, in the opinion of Buber and like-minded Zionists, a genuine and understandable fear. It is from this perspective that they urged the Arab question be considered. The moral challenge, accordingly, was to allay Arab anxieties without conceding those Zionist priorities, grounded in authentic Jewish need, deemed to be morally compelling.

Zionists who shared this perspective advanced various formulas to harmonize Arab and Jewish political-*cum*-moral needs.[29] These formulas all involved mutual compromise and accommodation, and a willingness to reduce the aspiration of the respective national movements to the minimum necessary to secure the basic and morally tenable interests of the Jewish and Palestinian Arab people. These advocates of what has been called a "pacifist Zionism" recognized that their distinctive approach to the Arab question posited, and indeed ultimately required, the same good will and political altruism on the part of the Arabs that they were exacting from the Zionist movement.[30] Should there not be a significant number of Arabs who would respond to their call—as, in fact, there was not[31]—then, as they also admitted, their "pacifism" suffered from a discreditable asymmetery. But, as Buber repeatedly emphasized, the requisite political altruism assumes mutual trust, and thus as the "interlopers"—the intruding, invading party—the burden of creating this trust is, nonetheless, on the Zionist movement. To acquire the trust of the Arabs, Jews must nurture it by both small and bold political gestures: Jews must develp a genuine respect for the culture and sensibilities of the Arabs; the Zionist movement must avoid placing itself under the tutelage of an imperialist power, especially one inimical to Arab interests; Zionism must put forth a credible "peace plan," adumbrating the possible ways of harmonizing the interests of the Arabs of Palestine and the Jewish people. Arab trust, it was affirmed, could only be acquired by such gestures which manifestly indicated Zionism's willingness for mutual accommodation, respect, and fraternity. This approach was eloquently summarized by a close friend of Buber's, Robert Weltsch (1891–1982), editor of the prestigious German Zionist weekly, *Jüdische Rundschau*. On the eve of the Fourteenth Zionist Congress in August 1925, Weltsch wrote a widely discussed editorial in which he exclaimed:

> [We] may be a people without a home, but, alas, there is not a country without a people. . . . Palestine has an existing population of 700,000, a people who have lived there for centuries and rightfully consider this country as their fatherland and homeland. That is a fact which we must take into account. Palestine will always be inhabited by two peoples, the Jewish and the Arab. . . . Palestine can only prosper if a relationship of mutual trust [*Vertrauen*] is established between the two peoples. Such a relationship can only be established if those who are

the newcomers—and such we are—arrive with the honest and sincere determination to live together with the other people on the basis of mutual respect and full consideration of all their human and national rights.... The realization of Zionism is unthinkable if we do not succeed in integrating our movement into the ever stronger nationalist awakening of the neighboring Asian peoples. World public opinion cannot forget the existence of a large native population in Palestine; the growing sympathy with the aspirations toward national self-determination of the native peoples will make Zionism unpopular in many circles, not out of anti-Jewish feelings but out of consideration for the natural rights of the Arabs.[32]

Failure to respond in an imaginative and forthright fashion to the Arab question would thus not only be a moral failing but also impolitic. Buber was one of the principal proponents of this perspective, insisting that the politics of power—so-called *Realpolitik*—was myopic, and hence in the long run bound to undermine the pristine goals of Zionism.

It was not then in the name of abstract ethical principles that Buber opposed the official Zionist policy, but rather in the name of what he held to be a greater realism. Consonant with this greater realism, he rejected the policy of creating a "Jewish majority" in Palestine which, as we have seen was the guiding strategy of response to the Arab question. Buber allied himself with a minority of Zionists—a minority even within the "pacifist" camp—who for the sake of accommodation with the Araɒs were prepared to limit *aliyah*.[33] In terms of the fundamental principles of Zionism, this was an extremely radical position, for free immigration of Jews into Palestine was from the founding moment of Zionism deemed the *conditio sine qua non* for the realization of the movement's supreme moral purpose, namely, the solution of the Jewish question. Moreover, by rendering *aliyah* subject to Arab sensibilities and consent, Buber and his comrades contradicted the most passionate vision of Zionism to reconstitute the Jewish people as a sovereign nation invested with the dignity and freedom to determine its own destiny.[34] Buber recognized these sentiments, but he argued that, as much as he appreciated and even shared them, it would be politically injudicious to make them inflexible ideological doctrines. It was, he felt, sheer fantasy to assume that a politically sovereign Jewish commonwealth would solve the Jewish problem; for one, it was highly unlikely that world

Jewry would heed the call to Zion. The assurance of large Jewish immigration quotas to Palestine, preferably voluntarily regulated by the Zionist movement, would be sufficient to provide a haven for Jews who need it. "Many, not a Majority"—as *many* Jewish immigrants as possible, but not necessarily the creation of a Jewish *majority* in Palestine—struck Buber as an apt slogan for a sound policy. To demand a Jewish majority, Buber felt, was not only unrealistic but reckless, for it would surely exacerbate Arab fears and intensify tensions in Palestine.

The establishment in 1948 of the State of Israel, enjoying a Jewish majority within its truncated borders, rendered Buber's criticism of Zionist policy irrelevant. Nonetheless, he remained convinced that the pursuit of political sovereignty was a fatuous, unwarranted extravagance, and hence the war which witnessed the birth of the Jewish state—to be sure, initiated by the Arabs, but foreseen as the ineluctable consequence of the State's declaration of independence—was to Buber's mind avoidable. Buber, however, reconciled himself to the new reality, and as a Zionist and citizen of the State of Israel maintained his vigilance, as is amply documented in this volume, for what he regarded as the moral and political errors of his government, especially with respect to the problems that came in the wake of Israel's War of Independence: the Arab refugee problem and the ambiguous status of the Arabs still within the borders of Israel. Despite the distressing complexity of the Arab question, Buber remained sanguine that with moral resolve and political imagination a solution to the Arab-Jewish conflict could be found.

In the course of more than sixty years of ceaseless opposition to *Realpolitik* as the governing mode of Zionist policy, Buber developed a unique conception of politics. He sought to avoid the Scylla of abstract, politically ineffectual moral idealism, and the Charybdis of the cynical ethic of *sacro egoismo:* the view that the egotistic pursuit of the interest of one's own group, even if it involves the disregard and abuse of another group, is "sacred" and hence morally self-sufficient.

Buber's Conception of Politics: The Line of Demarcation

Buber's distinctive approach to politics has its roots in the movement of Religious Socialism that emerged after the First World War. Together with such religious intellectuals as Paul Tillich, Leonard Ragaz, and Eugen Rosenstock-Huessy, Buber contended that the anguish and disunion of modern society was due to the radical polarization of the sacred and the secular sphere.[35] Religion has confined itself to the ecclesiastical precincts of confessional and ritual piety, relinquishing all claim on the "secular" world. But the division between the holy and the profane is not ontological; all of Creation is potentially sacred. The sacralization of all existence requires that faith in God the Creator and Redeemer be extended to our public and political activity—provinces of life hitherto abandoned to pragmatic aims and cynicism. "To believe in God," Ragaz noted, "is easy. But to believe that one day this world will be God's world; to believe this in a faith so firm and resolute as to mold one's life according to it—this requires faithfulness until death."[36] According to the precepts of Religious Socialism, the true challenge of religious faith is to affirm life in the "broken" world of the everyday. "We can only work for the Kingdom of God," Buber writes, "through working in all the spheres allotted to us. . . . [T]here is no legitimately messianic politics, but that does not exclude politics from the sphere of this hallowing."[37]

Religious Socialism, Buber taught, is in consonance with the spirit of authentic or primal Judaism *(Urjudentum)*—echoes of it are found in the pan-sacramentalism of Hasidism, but its pristine expression is found in what Buber referred to as the Hebrew humanism of the Bible. "The men of the Bible are sinners like ourselves, but there is one sin they do not commit, our arch-sin; they do not dare confine God to a circumscribed space or division of life, to 'religion.' They have not the insolence to draw boundaries around God's commandments and say to him: 'Up to this point, you are sovereign, but beyond these bounds begins the sovereignty of science or society or the state.'"[38] The ultimate intent of Zionism, Buber averred, is to herald a renewal of Hebrew humanism. A crucial index of this renewed Hebrew humanism would be the crystalization of a political ethos that would heal the division between morality and politics.

Implicit in Buber's conception of the task of Hebrew humanism is the debate on the relation of ethics to politics—a recurrent theme in German thought, reaching back at least to Johann Gottfried Herder (1744–1803)—which became a focal issue for German intellectuals in the wake of the First World War.[39] The intrigue, cunning, and brute reality of political power that manifestly dominated the course of the War had a sobering effect on many. The historian Friedrich Meinecke (1862–1954), who in his pre-War writings celebrated the institution of the state as marking a grand advance in humanity's ethical refinement, concluded in his historical reassessment of *raison d'état*, *Die Idee der Staatsräson* (1924),[40] that "power politics, Machiavellism, and war can never be banished from the world." But this fact, he counseled, need not lead us to despair, for state egoism *(Staategoismus)* may be morally creative: "In all kinds of ways, good grows out of evil." Undoubtedly the most widely discussed statement on this theme was Max Weber's lecture of 1918, *Politik als Beruf* (Politics as a Vocation).[41] Therein Weber forcefully argued for a fundamental distinction between the ethics dictated by the exigencies of political power *(Verantwortung-sethik)* and the imperatives of individual moral conscience *(Gesinnungsethik)*. From a sociological perspective, according to Weber, those responsible for the public weal are often obliged to employ "morally dubious means" to further ends deemed to be of common good. "He who lets himself in for politics," Weber argued, "that is, for power and force as means, contracts with diabolical powers and for his action it is *not* true that good can follow only from good and evil only from evil, but often the opposite is true. Anyone who fails to see this is, indeed, a political infant." To be sure, Weber did not wish to promote a crass Machiavellian view of politics. He merely sought to indicate that the proponents of *Gesinnungsethik* as a principle applicable to politics are not only naïve but also irresponsible, perhaps even immoral—for given the nature of politics, the "consequences" of a political decision often differ from the intention. The ideal politician, Weber insisted, appreciates "the ethical paradox of politics."

Buber refused to accept Weber's verdict that "the genius or demon of politics lives in an inner tension with the god of love." It would be the sublime task of Zionism—Buber and his disciples seem to say—to prove Weber and Meinecke wrong. If we are really Jews, Buber told a Zionist conference in 1932, we must affirm that "in historical reality we do not set ourselves a righteous goal, choose whatever way to it an auspicious hour offers, and, following that way, reach the set goal. If the goal to be reached is like the goal which was set, then the nature of the way must be like the goal. What is accomplished through lies can assume the mask of truth; what is accomplished through violence can go in the guise of justice, and for a while the hoax may be successful. But some people will realize that lies are lies at bottom, violence is violence, and both lies and violence will suffer the destiny history has in store for all that is false." The teaching of the prophet Isaiah shall guide us in our task: "Zion will be redeemed with justice" (Isaiah 1:27).[42]

In the face of the exigencies of building the Jewish National Home, however, some of Buber's disciples and friends despaired whether Zion would indeed be redeemed with justice, whether in the restoration of its patrimony to its ancestral land Jewry would eschew the cunning and ruthless ploys of power politics. Hans Kohn (1891–1971), a close friend and biographer of Buber, who settled in Palestine in 1925 to assume a senior position in the Zionist Organization, wrote to Buber many tormented letters indicating the difficulties in reconciling his highly refined ethical sensitivities with the *Realpolitik* pursued by the Zionist leadership of Palestine. What distressed him was the failure of this leadership to foster a peaceful co-existence with the Arab population. In a letter of 1929 to Buber, who at the time still resided in Germany, Kohn wrote: "You are fortunate not to witness the details of the Palestinian and Zionist reality, for with Zionism as it is today, the [current] objectives of Zionism can not be affirmed. . . . It is not a matter of Ishmael, but of Isaac. . . . I fear that we support something that we are unable to comprehend. That something drives us, because of misconceived solidarity, ever deeper into the morass. Zionism will either be peaceful or it will be without me. Zionism is *not* Judaism."[43] Shortly afterwards Kohn resigned his position with the Zionist Organization, and left Palestine eventually to assume a successful academic career in the United States.

In the face of the tensions illuminated by Kohn and others—such as his friends in *Brith Shalom* (Covenant of Peace), a Zionist group that Kohn helped to found, and which sought to promote Arab-Jewish understanding[44]—Buber developed a philosophy of ethical action that was to help him deal with the many moral ambiguities confronted by Zionism. Buber, of course, appreciated Kohn's predicament, but he found his friend's basic moral position to suffer from a "doctrinaire" idealism.[45] To Buber, Kohn had taken his point of departure from abstract, *a priori* moral principles, and when confronted with an untenable political situation, decided to withdraw from the battle. In the end, Buber seems to have felt,[46] Kohn proved more committed to the purity of his moral ideals than to the task of redeeming the world. We may not forget, Buber wrote a few months after receiving Kohn's

letter, that "if work is to be done in public life, it must be accomplished
not above the fray, but in it."[47] To be sure, contact with the real world
will vitiate the purity of our moral principles—but "the Word is not
victorious in its purity, but in its corruption—it bears fruit in the *cor-
ruptio seminis.*"[48]

Paradoxically, the real, "corrupting" world provides the only possibility for the actualization of moral principles. And this real world is
a dynamic flux of situations. Each situation is unique, with its special
nuances, anxiety and experience, memory and hope; each situation has
its own contours shaped by discrete historical circumstance. To be
effective and meaningful, ethical ideals must respond to the uniqueness
of each situation, and adjust their demands to the given conditions.
This adjustment of our ethical ideals to the reality of each situation is
not to be construed as an expedient compromise, however. Buber
firmly believed that ontological truth is bound to time, to the existen-
tially evolving reality of human beings and history, and that abstract
ethical principles must be grounded in this truth in order to be genuinely understood, and, *pari passu,* to attain their destiny in concrete
reality. Ethical principles and ideals then function heuristically: they
illumine the path whose exact contours and direction we must survey
through "dialogue," that is, in a spontaneous, undogmatic response to
the "calling" of each situation. "There is no firmly established law, formulated once and for all," Buber observed, "but only the Word of God
and our current situation which we have to learn by listening. We do
not have codified principles that we can consult. But we must understand the situation and the moment."[49]

We descend with our moral principles into the "unclean" reality,
but there we do not merely become dirty: "Our hands, ready to mold,
reach deep into the mud."[50] This molding—the true moral task—
Buber calls drawing "the line of demarcation." Aware of the full
weight of our responsibility, with fear and trembling, we determine
the limits of the ethical command in a particular situation. "I cannot
see the God-willed reality of justice," Buber wrote to Reinhold Nie-
buhr, "anywhere other than in being just, and this means of course:
being just insofar as it is possible here and now, under the 'artful' conditions of actual society. . . . Sometimes, striving to be just, I go into the
dark, till my head meets the wall and aches, and then I know: Here is
[now] the wall, and I cannot go farther. But I could not know it before-

hand."[51] The line of demarcation gains luminosity only within the darkness of each situation. Groping in the dark we marshal all our spiritual strength to reach the line, the line marking the maximal possibilities of truth and justice in that particular hour. The line of demarcation, of course, must be drawn anew in each situation that demands decision, for each such situation, "like a new-born child, has a new face that has never been before and will never be again."[52]

The French philosopher Julien Benda had written in his controversial book of 1927, *La trahison des clercs,* that the intellectuals betray their vocation when they abandon the monasteries of pure thought. On the contrary, Buber protested, to deny the challenge of the line of demarcation because the concrete situation is not readily conformable to our ideals and principles is the real "betrayal of the intellectuals."[53] Between the politician's cynical acceptance of our imperfect world and the vacuous purity of the votaries of abstract principle, Buber wished to point to a third way. Preserving the tension between the absolute moral command and the imperfect world, we enter that world and seek to actualize the command within the limits of the given situation. To be sure, this is a small and unmessianic goal. Yes, "we live in an unredeemed world."[54] But, as the Hasidim teach us, according to Buber, "out of each human life that is unarbitrary and bound to the world, a seed of redemption falls into the world."[55]

The ethic of the line of demarcation thus lends Buber's Religious Socialism a special nuance. Rejecting ecclesiastical seclusion, politics is to be affirmed by the religious individual. This affirmation of politics, however, is not to be expressed by fashioning an ideology and comprehensive platform, based on putatively eternal principles of polity. Religious socialists, Buber taught, should direct their political activity to a particular situation, and establish their "program" in a spontaneous, dialogical manner. In his inaugural lecture at the Hebrew University of Jerusalem in 1938, Buber attributed politics pursued in this spirit to the inspiration of the Biblical prophets. "The Hebrew prophet invariably receives only a message for a particular situation. . . . He sets no universally valid image of perfection, no pantopia or utopia, before men."[56] Significantly, in this, his first public address since having left Germany to settle in Palestine in March 1938—an act that fully attests to his abiding commitment to Zionism—Buber continued to observe that bound to his contingent but ever so real situation, the prophet has no choice "between his fatherland and another land that 'suits him' better; for [the prophet] is directed to the *topos*, to this place, to this people. . . ."[57] Buber's own situation included the Jewish people, and he fully recognized its needs in that particular, fateful hour. "Maintaining our existence is undoubtedly an essential prior condition of all our actions," he told the Sixteenth Zionist Congress, held at Zurich in 1929. The Jewish people and its needs are, so to speak, primordial facts that constitute the individual Jew's existential reality, a reality Buber felt the individual Jew is bound to accept and mold according to the dictates of the Spirit, to "lift up," to use the Hasidic metaphor.[58] "I believe it is possible to serve God and the group to which one belongs if one is courageously intent on serving God as much as one can within the sphere of the group."[59]

A *Believing Realism: The Prospects of Arab-Jewish Rapprochement*

Buber remained firm in his support of his people's return to the Land of Israel. "We could not and cannot renounce the Jewish claim [to Palestine]," he told Mahatma Gandhi.[60] Buber was equally certain, as we have noted, that the Jewish claim need not negate the rights and national aspirations of the Arabs of Palestine. This conviction is not based entirely on rational analysis, however, but on a religious trust. "We have been and are still convinced," Buber wrote the great Indian teacher of *satyagraha* (soul force), "that it must be possible to find some compromise between this [the Jewish] claim and the other; for we love this land and we believe in its future; since such love and such faith are surely present on the other side as well, a union in the common service of the land must be within the range of possibility. Where there is faith and love, a solution may be found even to what appears to be a tragic opposition."[61]

Peace and justice, accordingly, will not be achieved by negating either the Jewish or the Arab claim; to do so would be to forfeit the prospect of genuine justice and peace. To be sure, the situation is fraught with complexity and multiple wounds, but this is the situation we are obliged to work within if we are indeed to serve the cause of justice and peace. As the prophets teach us, it would be wrong to withdraw "into the attitude of a calm spectator [because we feel] ourselves surrounded by wild beasts. [We] must speak our message."[62] Buber was equally convinced that *Realpolitik* is ill-suited to the task. It would only exacerbate mistrust and conflict, and at most it would achieve fragile, pyrrhic victories. Prophetic politics—or Hebrew humanism—is the only "hope for this hour."[63]

Prophetic politics, however, is not messianic politics; it does not, Buber emphasized, lay claim to the power to usher in a realm of unambiguous, absolute justice. He soberly maintained that in confronting and working from within the complexities and often contradictory forces of the political reality, prophetic politics cannot possibly avoid committing a measure of injustice. Hence, Buber acknowledged that even during the early "idealistic" period of Zionist pioneering settlement in Palestine, "the best of us had no hopes of remaining guiltless and unsullied for our future generations, [for we knew] we were reducing the space for the future generations of the Arabs."[64] But in contradistinction to *Realpolitik*, which accepts group survival and interests as morally self-sufficient political objectives, prophetic politics charges us to remain ever cognizant of the effects of our community's actions on others, and, accordingly, to "sin" no more than is absolutely necessary. "What matters is that in every hour of decision we are aware of our responsibility and summon our conscience to weigh exactly how much is necessary to preserve the community, and accept just so much and no more; that we do not interpret the demands of a will-to-power as a demand made by life itself; that we do not make a practice of setting aside a certain sphere of action in which God's command does not hold, but rather regard this action as against His command, forced on us by the exigencies of the hour as a painful sacrifice."[65]

So that the sin we must inevitably commit to endure as a community (or as individuals) may be minimized, Buber taught, we reach out to the other community which confronts us and endeavor to understand its needs and concerns. Empathy and dialogue, we trust—indeed, pray—will indicate the boundaries which both secure our goal and limit as much as possible the pain to be caused the other. "We cannot refrain from doing wrong altogether, but we are given the grace of not having to do more than absolutely necessary."[66] And this is none other than the grace of being human. Buber's varied efforts on behalf of Arab-Jewish rapprochement, testified to by many of his writings included in this volume, gave expression to his resolve to surmount the mistrust between the Jewish people and the Arabs through empathy and dialogue.

Buber remained consistent with his resolve to find a "prophetic" solution to the moral predicament involved in the Zionist settlement in Palestine, a solution not based on cunning, needless violence, and egotistical self-assertion, but on dialogue and mutual accommodation. He was convinced that this approach was not naïve, as it was often accused of being. Prophetic politics is not meant "as a vague idealism, but a more comprehending, more penetrating realism, the realism of a greater reality!"[67] Through empathy and dialogue, Buber firmly believed, Zionism will find the path—a path not at all apparent to so-called political realists—that will lead to genuine peace and justice with the Arabs of Palestine. One may call this position a "believing" realism. Buber would say his trust in the efficaciousness of dialogue is based on a simple faith in God—He who has appointed humankind to be His co-workers in the process of redemption will graciously assist us in our work in the here and now. Philosophically, this faith is akin to the ethical idealism of the neo-Kantians, to whom dimensions of Buber's thought may be traced: the *a priori* conception of the universal good, of the socially desirable, is to be regarded as a categorical imperative regulating our political decisions and actions. In this spirit Buber would have undoubtedly endorsed the neo-Kantian motto dear to his close friend and political mentor Gustav Landauer: "Peace is possible, because it is [morally] necessary."[68]

Notes

1. For a comprehensive discussion of Buber's political thought and its relation to his philosophy of dialogue, see Ernst A. Simon's magisterial Hebrew monograph: *The Line of Demarcation: Nationalism, Zionism and the Arab-Israeli Conflict in the Thought of Martin Buber* (Givat Haviva: The Center for Arab Studies, 1973). This study is based on Simon's earlier German essay, "Nationalismus, Zionismus und der jüdisch-arabische Konflikt in Martin Buber's Theorie und Wirksamkeit," *Bulletin des Leo Baeck Instituts*, 12, no. 33 (1966), 21–84. Also see the sensitive essay by Robert Weltsch, "Buber's Political Philosophy," in Paul A. Schilpp and Maurice Friedman, eds., *The Philosophy of Martin Buber*, The Library of Living Philosophers, vol. 12 (La Salle, Ill.: Open Court, 1967), pp. 435–49. Both Simon and Weltsch were close associates of Buber's, especially in the endeavor to promote Arab-Jewish rapprochement.

2. See M. Buber, "The Holy Way" (1919), trans. Eva Jospe, in Buber, *On Judaism*, ed. N. N. Glatzer (New York: Schocken Books, 1967), p. 141.

3. Simon, *The Line of Demarcation*, pp. 14ff.

4. Having joined the World Zionist Organization shortly after its founding Congress in August 1897, Buber soon assumed a prominent role in the nascent movement. He

was a delegate to the Third Zionist Congress in 1899; in 1901 Herzl appointed him editor of the central weekly of the movement, *Die Welt*. In the same year he was a founding member of the Democratic Faction which sought a fundamental transformation of the World Zionist Organization, both structurally and ideologically. In addition to demanding greater democratization of Zionist institutions, Buber and his comrades urged the movement to give far greater attention to cultural activities than Herzl was willing to allow; they also challenged Herzl's emphasis on *Realpolitik* and his general conception of Zionist priorities. Thereafter Buber, who remained a Zionist until his death, invariably found himself in the ranks of the movement's "loyal opposition."

5. "The Truth from Palestine" (1891), in Ahad Ha'am, *At the Crossroads: Collected Essays* (Tel Aviv: Devir, 1949), part 1, p. 24 (Hebrew). The literature on Zionism and the Arab question is vast, much of it tendentious, however. In recent years a number of judicious studies on various aspects of the subject have appeared. See, e.g., Paul A. Alsberg, "The Arab Question in the Policy of the Zionist Executive before the First World War." *Shivat Zion* (Jerusalem, 1956), vol. 4, pp. 161–209 (Hebrew); Gil Carl AlRoy, "Zionist Attitudes Toward the Arabs in Palestine," in Gabriel Ben-Dor, ed., *The Palestinians and the Middle East Conflict*, Proceedings of the Institute of Middle Eastern Studies, University of Haifa (Tel Aviv: Turtledove Publishing, 1978), pp. 119–25; Mickael Asaf, *Relations Between Arabs and Jews in Palestine, 1860–1948* (Tel Aviv: Cultural and Educational Publications), 1970; Neil Caplan, *Palestine Jewry and the Arab Question, 1917–25* (London: Frank Cass, 1978); Aharon Cohen, *Israel and the Arab World*, trans. from the Hebrew by Y. Abbady and D. Leon, with a preface by Martin Buber (New York: Funk and Wagnalls, 1970); Shmuel Ettinger, ed., *Zionism and the Arab Question: Collected Historical Studies* (in Hebrew) (Jerusalem: The Zalaman Shazar Centre, 1979); Yaakov Goldstein "Were the Arabs Overlooked by the Zionists?" *Forum: A Quarterly on the Jewish People, Zionism and Israel*, 39 (Jerusalem, Fall 1980), 15–30; Yoseph Gorni, "Attitudes to Arab-Jewish Confrontation as Reflected in the Hebrew Press: 1900–1918," in *Zionism* (Tel Aviv University Publication), 1 (1980), 47–81; Neville Mandel, *The Arabs and Zionism Before World War One* (Berkeley: University of California, 1976); Yaakov Ro'i, "The Zionist Attitude to the Arabs: 1908–1914," *Middle Eastern Studies*, 4, no. 2 (April 1968), 198–242. Also see the excellent anthology, in English translation, of various Zionist responses to the Arab question: Eliezer Schweid, ed., *The Confrontation with the Arab Problem*, vol. 5 in *Sources* (of Contemporary Jewish Thought), general editor David Hardan (Jerusalem: World Zionist Organization, Department of Education and Culture, 1975).

6. For a concise and sensitive summary of this aspect of the Zionist "fantasy," see Amnon Rubenstein, *From Herzl to Gush Emunim, and Back* (Tel Aviv: Schocken, 1980), ch. 2 (in Hebrew); also see Yoseph Gorni, "Romanticism and the Second Aliya," *The Jerusalem Quarterly*, 13 (Fall 1979), 73–85; and Ehud Ben-Ezer, "Between Romanticism and a Bitter Reality: The Arab Question in Hebrew Literature," *Shedmot*, 43 (Spring 1972), 11–21, and 44 (Summer 1972), 35–47 (Hebrew). The romantic view of the Jew's return to the Arab world should be understood in the perspective of the recurrent accusation of European anti-Semitism that the Jews were an "alien" Asiatic or Oriental people. Many Zionists sought to turn the stigma into a virtue, urging the Jews to be proud of their Oriental origins. Buber's essay of 1916, "The Spirit of the Orient and Judaism," is an outstanding example of this tendency. Cf. " . . . the Jew has

remained an Oriental. He was driven out of his land and dispersed throughout the lands of the Occident; he was forced to dwell under a sky he did not know and on a soil he did not till; he suffered martyrdom, and worse than martyrdom, a life of degradation; the ways of the nations among which he has lived have affected him, and he has spoken their languages; yet despite all this, he has remained an Oriental. He has preserved within himself [the fundamental spiritual sensibilities of the Orient]. One can detect all this in the most assimilated Jew, if one knows how to gain access to his soul. . . . On this manifest or latent Orientalism, this base of the Jew's soul that has endured underneath all influences, I build my faith in a new spiritual-religious creation of Judaism. In the detachment and dissolution of its Western existence it can succeed only in parts. . . . The Jew is not the same person he once was; he has passed through every heaven and hell in the Occident, and his soul has come to grief. But his original strength has remained unimpared; once it comes into contact with its maternal soil, it will once more become creative. The Jew can truly fulfill his vocation among the nations only when he begins anew, and, with his whole, undiminished, purified original strength [*Urkraft*], translates into reality what his religion taught him in antiquity: rootedness in his native land; leading the good life within narrow confines; and building a model community on the scanty Canaanite soil." Buber, "The Spirit of the Orient and Judaism," trans. E. Jospe, in Buber, *On Judaism*, ed. N. N. Glatzer, pp. 75–77.

7. Typical of this genre of Zionist literature is the essay "The Hidden Question," by Yitzhak Epstein (1862–1943), a leading Hebrew educator in the Yishuv. Published in the prestigious Hebrew journal *Ha-Shiloah* in 1907, this now famous exhortation asserts that: "Among the grave questions linked with the concept of our people's renaissance on its own soil there is one question which is more weighty than all the others put together. This is the question of the Arabs. Our own national aspirations depend upon the correct solution to this question. It has not been eliminated; it has simply been ignored by us Zionists. . . . The lamentable fact that our attention could be diverted from such a fundamental question, and that after thirty years of settlement activity [in Palestine] it is being discussed and talked about as if it is an entirely new issue—all proves that our movement is frivolous and that we still treat such matters in a superficial manner." *Ha-Shiloah*, 17, no. 98 (August 1907), 193. Haim Nachman Bialik, the editor of this monthly issued in Odessa, Russia, was the poet laureate of modern Hebrew, and introduced Epstein's essay with the following note: "Although Epstein's essay was first delivered as a lecture at *Ivriyyah* [a society for the renewal of Hebrew as the language of the Jews] during the Seventh Zionist Congress in Basel, 1905, I fear that the matter to which it addresses itself is still actual. And perhaps precisely now when practical work in *Eretz Israel* has increased it is appropriate that we ponder the issue [raised by Epstein]."

8. M. Smilansky, "Our Deeds," *Ha-Olam* (official Hebrew weekly of the World Zionist Organization), 1913, trans. by D. Shefer in E. Schweid, ed., *The Confrontation with the Arab Problem*, pp. 52f.

9. Immediately after the Arab riots of 1921, the British High Commissioner of Palestine, Sir Herbert Samuel, summoned the leaders of the Yishuv and exclaimed: "There is only one way, and that is an agreement with the [Arab] inhabitants. Zionism has not yet done a thing to obtain the consent of the inhabitants, and without that consent

[Jewish] immigration will not be possible." At a subsequent meeting he admonished them: "You yourselves are inviting a massacre, which will come as long as you disregard the Arabs." Cited from unpublished protocols by N. Caplan, *Palestine Jewry and the Arab Question*, p. 105.

10. Ben-Gurion, "The Foreign Policy of the Jewish Nation," in Ben-Gurion, *From Class to Nation* (Tel Aviv: Ayanot, 1955), p. 107 (Hebrew). Attended by 210 delegates from close to twenty countries, the Congress for Labor Palestine sought to marshal the support of world socialist and labor leaders for the Yishuv. At the Congress such prominent figures in Socialist Zionism as Ben-Gurion, Berl Katznelson, and Arthur Ruppin were joined by such outstanding European socialists as Jean Lonquet of France and Eduard Bernstein of Germany. See "Die Weltkongress für das arbeitende Pälestina," *Jüdische Rundschau,* 1 October 1930, pp. 501f.

11. Z. Jabotinsky, "The Role of the [Jewish] Legion: The Prevention of Violence," *Speeches: 1905-1926* (Jerusalem: Eri Jabotinsky, 1947), p. 198 (Hebrew). These remarks were made during a debate on the security of the Yishuv at a meeting of the Actions Committee of the Executive of the World Zionist Organization, held in Prague, July 1921.

12. I have adapted this distinction from Eliezer Schweid. See his introduction to the anthology, *The Confrontation with the Arab Problem*, pp. 15f.

13. London: Frank Cass, 1978.

14. *Stenographisches Protokoll der Verhandlungen des XII. Zionisten-Kongresses in Karlsbad vom 1. bis 14. September 1921* (Berlin: Jüdischer Verlag, 1922), p. 152. Katznelson's address was delivered in Yiddish.

15. Protocol of a conclave held in December 1918 of representatives of all factions of Palestinian Jewry which formulated the Yishuv's "national demands" to be presented at the forthcoming Paris Peace Conference. Cited in Caplan, *Palestine Jewry and the Arab Question*, p. 29.

16. For Socialist-Zionist views on the Arab question, see Esco Foundation for Palestine, Inc., *Palestine: A Study of Jewish, Arab, and British Policies* (New Haven: Yale University Press, 1947), vol. 1, pp. 573–78. For a representative collection of Socialist-Zionist writings on the subject, see Enzo Sereni and R. E. Ashery, eds., *Jews and Arabs in Palestine: Studies in a National and Colonial Problem* (New York: Hechalutz Press, 1936).

17. The Yishuv's leadership continued to promote so-called "Arab Work"—that is, the support of moderate Arab political organizations (often through surreptitous funding); the extension of the Yishuv's social and economic services, particularly agricultural and medical, to the Arab population; assistance in the organizing of Arab labor unions, and the like. Efforts were also made to disseminate among the Jews a knowledge of Arab culture and language. The energy and resouces devoted to these endeavors were, however, limited. Cf. Caplan, *Palestine Jewry and the Arab Question*, pp. 127–45, 189ff.

18. *Ibid.* p. 137.

19. Jacob L. Talmon, *Israel Among the Nations* (London: Weidenfeld and Nicolson, 1970), p. 132.

20. Esco Foundation, *Palestine*, vol. 1, pp. 320f. For a comprehensive documen-

tation and analysis of the population question of Palestine, see Dov Friedlander and Calvin Goldscheider, *The Population of Israel* (New York; Columbia University Press, 1979), pp. 53–82.

21. Although he spoke often and passionately of Jewry's unique affinity to the Land of Israel, Buber loathed talk of a Jewish historical "right" to Palestine, rejecting it as a specious legalism. See his "The National Home and National Policy in Palestine"—in this volume. For a detailed exposition of his conception of Jewry's relationship and claim to Palestine, see Buber, *On Zion: The History of an Idea*, trans. S. Godman, with a forward by N. N. Glatzer (New York: Schocken Books, 1973), *passim*.

22. Ze'ev Jabotinsky, *Evidence Submitted to the Palestine Royal Commission*, House of Lords, London, 11 February 1937 (London: New Zionist Press, 1937), p. 13.

23. See Caplan, *Palestine Jewry and the Arab Question*, pp. 5–7, and *passim*.

24. *Ibid.*, pp. 200ff.

25. How best to pursue the strategy of creating a Jewish majority in Palestine engaged much of the passion and imagination of the Zionist movement. The equivocations of Britain with regard to the Balfour Declaration and its commitment to foster the Jewish National Home, and the fluctuations in the rate of *aliyah* posed severe problems. In the twenties the Zionist leadership deemed it tactically wise to proceed cautiously and to upbuild the Yishuv in an "organic" manner, "person by person, farmstead by farmstead," while seeking to defer the decision on the political future of Palestine as long as possible. Provocative rhetoric was to be avoided, as well as a precipitous disclosure of the *Endziel*, the movement's ultimate goal of establishing a politically sovereign Jewish state. The "bracketing" of the *Endziel* allowed many Zionists, like Buber, to consider political sovereignty as not essential to the attainment of the movement's immediate objectives. From the thirties on, however, with the increasingly desperate plight of European Jewry, and the corresponding increase of *aliyah*, there was an emphatic shift in Zionist policy. Not only did the objective of creating a Jewish majority in Palestine become more explicit, but political sovereignty was no longer regarded as the distant *Endziel*, rather it was now increasingly deemed the *conditio sine qua non* assuring the realization of the movement's principal objective of providing a haven for the persecuted Jewish masses. Cf. Ben Halpern, *The Idea of the Jewish State* (Cambridge: Harvard University Press, 1961), pp. 20–51, esp. pp. 35–38.

26. Cf. Weizmann's remarks at the Fourteenth Zionist Congress, August 1925, during a debate on Jabotinsky's proposal for a Jewish Legion to protect the Yishuv against the "riotous" Arabs. "The key [to securing the tranquil development of the Yishuv] lay in establishing at Jewish initiative a genuine friendship and cooperation with the Arabs of the Near East. (Enthusiastic applause.) Palestine must be built without violating one iota the legitimate rights of the Arabs. The Zionist Congress should not limit itself to 'Platonic' formulas. The Congress must learn the truth that Palestine is not Rhodesia, and that 600,000 Arabs live there, who, according to the world community's sense of justice, have exactly the same right as we have to a National Home. (Applause.) ..." *Protokoll der Verhandlungen des XIV. Zionisten Kongresses vom 18. bis 31. August 1935 in Wien* (London: Zentralbureau der Zionistschen Organization, 1926), p. 328.

27. Weizmann to James Marshall, 17 January 1930. *The Letters and Papers of Chaim Weizmann*, vol. 14, ed. Camillo Dresner (Rutgers University Press and Israel University Press, 1979), pp. 208–11. Weizmann's approach to the Arab question exem-

plifies our distinction between the "epic-existential" or moral response and that of an ideological nature (cf. p. 6f, above). As a leader of the World Zionist Organization, his judgments were preeminently ideological, and by them he astutely sought to adjust Zionist priorities to the dictates of pragmatic politics. Thus at times when the moral considerations corresponded with those of the immediate political situation, Weizmann espoused a position close to that of Buber's; at other times their respective positions diverged considerably. Cf. Jehuda Reinharz, Introduction, *The Letters and Papers of Chaim Weizmann*, vol. 9, series A (Rutgers University Press and Israel University Press, 1977)., pp. xxix f.; and Y. Goldstein, "Were the Arabs Overlooked by the Zionists?" pp. 24–26.

28. Cf. selections 10, 13, 25, 31, 34, 38, and 40.

29. Cf. Susan Lee Hattis, *The Bi-National Idea in Palestine During Mandatory Times* (Haifa: Shikmona Publishing, 1970), *passim.*

30. Puah Meroz, "Pacifist Zionism: Its Greatness and Weakness. Brith Shalom in the Struggles of the Yishuv and Zionism." *Basha'ar: Social and Cultural Review* (Tel Aviv), 21, no. 6 [142] (Nov.–Dec. 1978), 554–64; 21, no. 7 [143] (Jan.–Feb. 1979), 60–81 (Hebrew). The term "pacifist" in this context points not so much to a doctrinal or ideological eschewment of violence as to the conviction that the attainment of a peaceful and amicable understanding with the Arabs must be a paramount concern of Zionist policy.

31. Cf. selection 49, esp. note 2. For Arab responses to Zionism and, specifically, "pacifist" Zionism, see: David-Ben Gurion, *My Talks with Arab Leaders*, trans. by A. Rubinstein and M. Louvish (Jerusalem: Keter Books, 1972), pp. 21–23, 152–82; S. L. Hattis, *The Bi-National Idea in Palestine*, pp. 62f., 99ff., 122ff., 187ff., 272ff., 303ff.; Yehoshua Porath, *The Emergence of the Palestinian Arab National Movement, 1919–1929* (London: Frank Cass, 1974), pp. 31–69; and Yoseph Nevo, "The Attitude of the Arabs of Palestine to Jewish Settlement and Zionism," in S. Ettinger, ed., *Zionism and the Arab Question*, pp. 163–72.

32. Robert Weltsch, "Zum XIV. Zionistenkongress. Worum es geht?" *Jüdisch Rundschau*, 30 nos. 64/65 (Berlin, 14 August 1925). pp. 549f. On the intense debate on the Arab question which took place within German Zionist circles, see *Dokumente zur Geschichte des deutschen Zionismus: 1882–1933*, ed. with intro. by Jehuda Reinharz (Tübingen: J. C. B. Mohr/Paul Siebeck, 1981). pp. xiii f., and documents 180–91, 196, and 197; Jehuda Reinharz, "Ideology and Structure in German Zionism: 1882–1933." *Jewish Social Studies*, 42, no. 2 (Spring 1980), pp. 139–41; and Donald L. Niewyk, *The Jews and Weimar* (Baton Rouge: Louisiana University Press, 1979), pp. 132–36, 155–56.

33. Commitment to the cause of Arab-Jewish understanding did not necessarily imply a willingness to compromise the ideal of a mass, unlimited Jewish immigration to Palestine. Indeed, most members of the "pacifist" camp were "maximalists" on the issue of *aliyah:* there were likewise many "minimalists" who were less sanguine about the prospects of Arab-Jewish amity. Cf. Israel Kolatt. "The Zionist Movement and the Arabs," in S. Ettinger, ed., *Zionism and the Arab Question*, p. 10.

34. In his classic study of the ideological perspectives governing Zionist politics, Ben Halpern identifies the quest for sovereignty as the overarching "myth" animating the movement's passion and fundamental commitments. To be sure, the conceptions of

sovereignty were often modified by tactical and political considerations (see above, note 25). Cf. Ben-Gurion's criticism of Brith Shalom and its demand that for the sake of peace with the Arabs Zionism undertake to limit the growth of the Yishuv: "The masses of Israel will never relinquish their burning and firm desire to be a free people which determines alone and by itself its destiny like all free nations; to be a people which is dependent neither on the grace nor on the wrath of another nation. There is no power in the world that could extirpate this desire from the heart of our people. . . ." From a speech at the World Congress for Labor Palestine, September 1930, Ben-Gurion, *From Class to Nation*, p. 107.

35. See Renate Breipohl, ed., *Dokumente zum religiösen Sozialismus in Deutschland: Mit einer historisch-systematischen Einführung* (München: C. Kaiser, 1972); also see Markus Mattmüller, *Leonard Ragaz und der religiöse Sozialismus, eine Biographie* (Zollikon: Evangelische Verlag, 1957); also see the proceedings of the conference on religious socialism which Buber helped organize: *Sozialismus aus dem Glauben, Verhandlungen der sozialistischen Tagung im Heppenheim a.d.B., Pfingstwoche 1928* (Zürich/Leipzig: Rotapfel Verlag, 1929). On Buber's Religious Socialism, see the aforementioned proceedings, pp. 90ff., 121ff., 217ff. Also see his "Three Theses for a Religious Socialism" ("For Leonard Ragaz on his sixtieth birthday"), in Buber, *Pointing the Way: Collected Essays*, ed. and trans. by Maurice Friedman (New York: Schocken Books, 1974), pp. 112ff. For a concise overview of Buber's relation to the movement of Religious Socialism, see Hans Kohn, *Martin Buber: Sein Werk und seine Zeit*, 2nd ed. (Köln: Joseph Melzer, 1961), pp. 217ff.; also cf. Richard Falk, *Martin Buber and Paul Tillich: Radical Politics and Religion* (New York: National Council of Protestant Episcopal Churches, 1961).

36. Cited in S. H. Bergman, *Thinkers and Believers* (Tel Aviv: Devir, 1959), p. 171 (Hebrew). Bergman, one of Buber's closest friends in the Yishuv, devoted a long Hebrew essay to the Religious Socialism of Ragaz, entitled "Leonard Ragaz: Fighter for the Kingdom of Heaven," in *ibid.*, pp. 176–95.

37. Buber, "Gandhi, Politics, and Us" (1930), in Buber, *Pointing the Way*, p. 137. A comprehensive of Buber's conception of politics would have to consider the impact that his close friend, Gustav Landauer (1870–1919), the anarcho-socialist, had on his thought. Cf. Hans Kohn, *Martin Buber, passim;* Robert Weltsch, "Buber's Political Philosophy," pp. 438–40; Eugene Lunn, *Prophet of Community: The Romantic Socialism of Gustav Landauer* (Berkley: University of California Press, 1973), *passim;* Ruth Link-Salinger, "Friends in Utopia: Martin Buber and Gustav Landauer," *Midstream* (January 1978), pp. 67–72; and Bernard Susser, *Existence and Utopia: Martin Buber's Philosophy of Politics* (Rutherford, N.J.: Fairleigh Dickinson University Press, 1981), *passim.*

38. Buber, "Hebrew Humanism" (1941), trans. Olga Marx, in Buber, *Israel and the World: Essays in a Time of Crisis*, 2nd ed. (New York: Schocken Books, 1963), p. 247.

39. Cf. Ernst Troeltsch, "Privatmoral und Staatsmoral," in Troeltsch, *Deutsche Zukunft* (Berlin, 1916), pp. 61–112; Alfred Vierkandt, *Machtverhältnis und Machtmoral*, Kant-Gesellschaft, Philosophische Vorträge. (Berlin, 1916); Otto Baumgarten, *Politik und Moral* (Tübingen, 1916); Heinrich Scholz, *Politik und Moral: Eine Untersuchung über den sittliche Charakter der modernen Realpolitik* (Gotha, 1915); Erich

Franz, *Politik und Moral: Über die Grundlagen politischer Ethik* (Göttingen, 1917); and Friedrich Wilhelm Förster, *Politische Ethik und politische Pädogogik*, 3rd ed. (Munich, 1918).

40. F. Meinecke, *Machiavellism: The Doctrine of Raison d'État and Its Place in Modern History*, trans. by D. Scott of *Die Idee der Staatsräson* (New Haven: Yale University Press, 1957), pp. 429ff. The challenge to the statesmen, according to Meinecke, is to ensure that good will indeed emerge from evil by striving to achieve as much harmony as possible between *raison d'état* and "the universal moral law."

41. "Politics as a Vocation," *From Max Weber: Essays in Sociology*, trans., ed., and introd. by H. H. Gerth and C. Wright Mills (New York: Oxford University Press, 1949), pp. 121ff. For a critique of Weber's thesis, see Ernst Akiva Simon, "Are There Two Ethics?" (a contribution to an international Goethe centennial symposium, "Ethics and Politics," held in 1949 at Aspen, Colorado), in Arnold Bergstrasser, ed., *Goethe and the Modern World* (Chicago: Henry Regnery, 1950), pp. 374–78. Simon, Professor Emeritus of Education, Hebrew University of Jerusalem, who is perhaps Buber's most consistent disciple in the Zionist movement, protests "Max Weber's invention of a special conscience, made for statesmen alone. There is only *one* good, and only *one* ethics." *Ibid.*, p. 377.

42. Buber, "And If Not Now, When?" (1932), selection 16 in this volume. Cf. "What is wrong for the individual cannot be right for the community" ("Was für den Einzelnen unrecht ist, kann nich für die Gemeinschaft recht sein"), *ibid.*

43. Kohn to Buber, 21 September 1929, in Martin Buber, *Briefwechsel aus sieben Jahrzehnten*, ed. by G. Schaeder (Heidelberg: Lambart Schneider, 1974), vol. 2, p. 353. Kohn's relationship to Buber is discussed at length in the introduction to selection 15.

44. On Brith Shalom, see introduction to selection 10. Also cf. Susan L. Hattis, *The Bi-National Idea in Palestine*, pp. 35–62; Aharon Kedar, "Brith Shalom: The Early Period: 1925–1928," in Y. Bauer, M. Davis, I. Kolatt, eds., *Studies in the History of Zionism. Presented to Israel Goldstein on his Eightieth Birthday* (Jerusalem: Hassifriya Hazionit, 1976), pp. 224–85; Aharon Kedar, "The World-View of Brith Shalom," in Ben-Zion Yehoshua and A. Kedar, eds., *Zionist Ideology and Policy* (Jerusalem: Zalman Shazar Centre, 1978), pp. 97–114; Aharon Kedar, "Brith Shalom: Documents and Introduction," *The Jerusalem Quartely*, 18 (Winter 1981), 55–85; and Poah Maroz, *op. cit.*

45. Martin Buber, *Briefwechsel*, vol. 2, p. 353.

46. Our discussion of Buber's response to Kohn's resignation from the Zionist movement is in part conjectural, due to the fact that Buber's letters to Kohn are not available. One would assume that they are in the Hans Kohn Archive, Leo Baeck Institute, New York, which by order of his will is closed until 1990. Our reconstruction of Buber's response to Kohn is based on allusions to their exchange in Buber's published letters, and on themes he emphasized in lectures he gave in the period immediately following Kohn's letters to him. I have also consulted with Ernst Simon and Robert Weltsch, who at the time were close to both Buber and Kohn. See introduction to selection 15 of this volume.

47. Buber, "Gandhi, Politics, and Us" (1930), in *Pointing the Way*, p. 137.

48. *Ibid.*, p. 128. At first glance, Buber's strictures about the inapplicability of

abstract morality to politics would seem to render his position akin to the political realism sponsored by Weber and Meinecke. But, in contradistinction to them, Buber consistently refused to acknowledge that good and justice could ever emerge dialectially
from the use of power and violence, no matter how judiciously these classical tools of
politics are employed. The challenge, according to Buber, is to penetrate the realm of
politics with as much morality as possible: "*Quantum satis* means in the language of
lived truth not 'either-or,' but 'as-much-as-one-can.'" "The Validity and Limitation of
the Political Principle" (1953), in *Pointing the Way*, p. 217.

49. Buber, "Politics Born of Faith" (1933), in Buber, *A Believing Humanism*, trans.
and introd. by M. Friedman (New York: Simon and Schuster, 1967), p. 178.

50. Buber, "Replies to My Critics," in A. Schilpp and M. Friedman, eds., *The Philosophy of Martin Buber*, p. 772.

51. Buber in Sydney and Beatrice Rome, eds., *Philosophical Interrogations* (New
York: Holt, Reinhardt and Winston, 1964), p. 80.

52. Buber, "The Education of Character" (1939), in Buber, *Between Man and
Man*, trans. R. G. Smith and introd. by M. Friedman (New York: Macmillan, 1965), p.
114.

53. "If Not Now, When?", selection 16.

54. Buber, *The Origins and Meaning of Hasidism*, trans. by M. Friedman (New
York: Horizon Press, 1960), pp. 105f.

55. *Ibid.*

56. Buber, "The Demand of the Spirit and Historical Reality" (inaugural lecture,
The Hebrew University of Jerusalem, 1938), in Buber, *Pointing the Way*, p. 190.

57. *Ibid.*

58. Address to the Sixteenth Zionist Congress, 1 August 1929, included in this volume under the title, "No More Declarations!" selection 12.

59. Buber, "The Validity and Limitations of the Political Principle" (1953), in
Pointing the Way, p. 217. Cf. "I have no warrant whatever to declare that under all
circumstances the interest of the group is to be sacrificed to the moral demand, more
particularly as the cruel conflicts of duties and their unreserved decision on the basis
of the situation seem to me to belong to the essential existence of a genuine personal
ethos. But the evident absence of this inner conflict, the lack of its wounds and scars,
is to me uncanny." *Ibid.*

60. Buber, "A Letter to Gandhi" (February 1939), selection 18 in this volume.

61. *Ibid.*

62. Buber, "The Demand of the Spirit and Historical Reality" (1938), in *Pointing
the Way*, p. 190.

63. Cf. Buber, "Hope for this Hour" (1952), in *Pointing the Way*, pp. 220ff.

64. Buber, "Instead of Polemics" (1956), selection 55 in this volume.

65. Buber, "Hebrew Humanism" (1941), trans. Olga Marx, in Buber, *Israel and the
World*, pp. 246f.

66. Buber, "Politics and Morality" (1945), selection 33 in this volume.

67. Buber, "Hope for this Hour" (1952), in *Pointing the Way*, p. 227.

68. This motto ("Friede ist möglich, weil er nothwendig ist.") was actually coined
by the Christian pacifist Moritz von Egidy (1847–1898). Cf. Gustav Landauer, "M. von
Egidy und der sozialistische Akademiker." *Der sozialistische Akademiker* (Berlin), 2

(1896), pp. 186f. In this brief essay, Landauer vigorously defends the logic of the motto. "Egidy's motto on peace is not in the least illogical; it is merely what one usually calls a paradox—a paradox that offends so-called common sense and the appearance of what is correct. . . . Egidy's motto is only an application of the famous Kantian categorical imperative: 'You can, for you will it.' This imperative also is regarded by the common sense of the Philistines as 'illogical'; but for those who wish to think, it is an eminently reasonable proposition: before moral necessity there is nothing impossible [vor der moralischen Nothwendigkeit gibt es keine Unmöglichkeit]." *Ibid.*, p. 187. In this light, we may understand Buber's statement that "politics is the art of the impossible." Cited in Stephen Poppel, "Martin Buber: The Art of the Unpolitical," *Midstream* (May 1974), 61.

1

A State of Cannons, Flags, and Military Decorations?

(February 1918)

(Editor's prefatory note:)

Until the actual establishment of the State of Israel, the nature of the future Jewish community to arise in Palestine divided Zionist opinion: the vision of a sovereign political state was not universally shared. Buber was prominently associated with the trend in Zionism that was wary of the goal of political sovereignty, and he especially feared that this goal would encourage the development of the type of arrogant, narrow nationalism which came to the fore during the First World War.

Like many European intellectuals, Buber emerged from the First World War with a profound distrust of nationalism. In the midst of that protracted struggle with its untold suffering, an ever increasing number of intellectuals, many of whom, like Buber himself, initially responded to the call to battle with patriotic fervor, condemned the war, attributing its madness to the myopia of unbounded national pride and *sacro egoismo*, the attitude of regarding one's nation's interests as sacred and morally absolute. One of the most powerful condemnations of the war and nationalism was Stefan Zweig's play *Jeremiah*, published at the height of the war in 1917.[1] Zweig viewed his immensely popular play as a prophetic tragedy and "a hymn of the Jewish people,"[2] who, suffering eternal defeat, have transformed their fate into a source of a new Jerusalem: a life beyond political nationhood, bearing the vision of brotherhood, mutual tolerance, and universal enlightenment. The selection below is Buber's reply to a letter from Zweig, written in January 1918,[3] inquiring whether, given the sobering experience of the war, the Zionists recognized the message of his play as the true ideal of Judaism; in other words, as he bitingly put it: Has the War disabused the Zionists of their dream, "the dangerous dream of a Jewish state with cannons, flags, and military decorations"? The more reality seems to frustrate the realization of the Zionist dream, Zweig exclaimed, the more "I cherish the painful idea of the Diaspora [and] love the Jewish fate more than Jewish well-being." "What is a nation if not a transformed fate?"—Zweig rhetorically asked. "What would

35

remain of it if it escapes its fate? Palestine would be a final point, a return of the circle into itself, the end of a movement that has shaken Europe and the whole world. And it would be a tragic disappointment. . . . "

In his response to Zweig's affirmation of the Diaspora, Buber not only registers his own distrust of nationalism, but also illuminates the nature of his Zionist commitment and his appreciation of the frightful ambiguities of Zionist aspirations—ambiguities, however, which are to be accepted as a creative challenge if Judaism is to cease to be an ethereal, disembodied spirituality and find expression in concrete, living community. On the very same day that he wrote to Zweig, however, Buber confided in a letter to his friend and fellow Zionist, Shmuel Hugo Bergman (a Czech philosopher who emigrated to Palestine in 1920), his fear that the danger of Zionism's debasement into an unalloyed nationalism may not be so remote. He nonetheless concludes his letter to Bergman, also reproduced here, with a resolute decision to renew the struggle against this tendency within Zionism.

Notes

1. Stefan Zweig, *Jeremias* (Leipzig: Insel Verlag, 1918).
2. See Stefan Zweig, *The World of Yesterday: An Autobiography* (New York: The Viking Press, 1943), pp. 252–54.
3. See Martin Buber, *Briefwechsel aus sieben Jahrzehnten,* ed. by Grete Schaeder (Heidelberg: Verlag Lambert Schneider, 1972), vol. 1, pp. 524–25.

A STATE OF CANNONS, FLAGS, AND MILITARY DECORATIONS?

4 February 1918

Dear Stefan Zweig, .

. . . Today only this: I do not know anything about a "Jewish state with cannons, flags, and military decorations," not even as a dream.

What it will become depends on those who create it. And precisely for this reason people like me, who are of human and humane disposition, must take a decisive part *here, where* human beings are once again granted the opportunity of building a community. I cannot accept your historical conclusions in reference to the *new* nation evolving [in Palestine] out of ancient blood. If a Jewish Palestine is doomed to be the end of a movement which existed only spiritually, it will be the beginning of another movement that wants to realize the spirit concretely. You say the former movement [characteristic of the Diaspora] shook the whole world, but it was legitimate only in the realm of the spirit. . . . I for my part prefer to participate in the extraordinary venture of something new, in which I do not see much "well-being" but quite a good deal of great sacrifices. I prefer this, rather than to go on enduring a Diaspora, which for all its beautiful and painful fertility, passes on the nourishing substance of that movement piece by piece to [a whirl of] inner decay. I even prefer a tragic disappointment to a not at all tragic but constant degeneration without any prospect. . . .

[Martin Buber][1]

3/4 February 1918

Dear Mr. Bergman,

. . . A few days ago I had a discussion with Dr. [Victor] Jacobson[2] about what should happen in Palestine; at the end of it I was close to depression. "We must create by all means a majority [of Jews] in the country as soon as possible"—an argument which makes one's heart stand still; and what can one answer on this level? We must face the fact that most leading Zionists (and probably also most of those who are led) today are thoroughly unrestrained nationalists (following the European example), imperialists, even unconscious mercantilists and idolators of success. They speak about rebirth and mean enterprise. If we do not succeed to erect an authoritative [Zionist] opposition, the soul of the movement will be corrupted, maybe for ever. I for my part am determined to commit myself totally to this cause, even if this should affect my personal plans. . . .

With heartfelt greetings,

Martin Buber

Notes

1. The draft of this letter does not include the salutation or closing.
2. Victor Jacobson (1869–1935) was a Zionist leader and diplomat. At the time he was a member of the Executive of the World Zionist Organization.

2

Toward the Decision

(March 1919)

(Editor's prefatory note)

After the armistice concluding the First World War the alliance among the Western nations was severely strained by an intense rivalry for control of the Near East. These imperialistic motives, however, flagrantly contradicted the purported moral idealism of the Allies, who hailed their struggle against Germany and the Axis powers as a war of freedom and the defense of the principle of national self-determination. A formula reconciling their imperialistic interests and the principle of self-determination was worked out at the Paris Peace Conference, which convened in January 1919: a League of Nations would be established which would assign to the principal Western nations a trusteeship or mandate to guide the *gradual* self-determination of the new states to be created out of the territories and colonies of the conquered Axis powers.

The fate of Palestine, formerly within the domain of the Ottoman Empire, was the subject of lengthy negotiations at the Paris Peace Conference. Both the Arabs and the Zionists were invited to send delegations and to submit memoranda to the Conference. The representatives of the Zionist Organization, who appeared before them at the end of February and in early March 1919, were accorded a cordial and attentive hearing. This initial reception instilled the Zionist movement with great hope, although at this juncture the Conference made no decisions. Indeed, it was only in April 1920 that the Allies, meeting at San Remo, agreed to grant Great Britain a mandate to administer Palestine with the explicit charge of fulfilling the commitments she undertook in the Balfour Declaration of November 1917.[1]

In the following essay—published in *Der Jude*, the prestigious journal which he founded in 1916 and edited—Buber indicated a keen awareness of the disguised imperialistic motives of the Paris Peace Conference. He cautions his fellow Zionists not to be beguiled by the slogans and moral posture of the Allies. The courtship with imperialism, no matter how humanitarian its pretensions, can only vitiate the moral claims and character of Zionism. The moral *and* political viability of Zionism, Buber concludes, can only be assured through the establishment of a genuine alliance with the Arab peoples. This remained his life-long conviction.

Note

1. The Balfour Declaration noted that Great Britain viewed "with favour the establishment in Palestine of a national home for the Jewish people, and will use their best endeavors to facilitate the achievement of this object. It being clearly understood that nothing shall be done which may prejudice the civil and religious rights of the existing non-Jewish communities of Palestine, or the rights and political status enjoyed by Jews in any other country."

Toward the Decision

The representatives of the Great Powers who are presently gathered in Paris to deliberate over a new order in the territorial relations of Europe and the Near East have accepted in principle, so it has been reported, the demands formulated in the Zionist memorandum. Everywhere where the Jewish people or a will toward Jewish peoplehood lives, these three things are a source of joy and pride: that we have been recognized as a nation by the present configuration of powers in

the civilized world; that our right to Palestine has been confirmed; and
that from now on our settlement work in Palestine can be pursued
more extensively, no longer under the Turkish yoke, but in the free
atmosphere of the British Empire, with the explicit and
[internationally] acknowledged goal of developing the Yishuv into an
autonomous communal entity. . . .

Yet as I contemplate under which circumstances this recognition has
been accorded us my joy ceases. . . . This is not the day of our [national]
self-determination, but only one of newer and perhaps deeper
[political] entanglements. It is a day on which the alleged representatives of the nations have raised the flag of distributive justice over their
tents, a day on which they exchange guarantees of illgotten increases
in power, without, at the same time, forgetting the now indispensable
cloak of morality [viz., the slogan of national self-determination], for
today general moral concerns have arisen which may not be neglected
in any peace conference, in contrast to previous ones. Like every idealistic movement, Zionism (which, if it did not exist, would have been
invented by the Allies) also adapts itself to such a cover [the moral
slogans of the imperialistic powers]. But can it see its fulfillment
therein? If this were the day of Zionism, Zionism would not be a movement of Jewish liberation. Can Jewry be truly liberated so long as Judaism's unswerving demand for justice and truth for *all* nations is shoul-
dered out of the way?. . .

I hear the "politicians of delusion" [*Fiktivpolitiker*], who regard
themselves as realistic, as experts in *Realpolitik* (for they cursorily survey the reality of the day, the ephemeral reality of political entanglements), saying angrily: "Look at that hopeless ideologue! He would
have us give Palestine back to the Great Powers because we disagree
with their morality!"

Take it easy! I do not believe we should do any such thing, even if
we could. If, at the start of the war, it appeared that we could remain
outside of the web of malice and error, fate has decreed that it was
impossible to steer clear of it, and we were drawn into it. No nation
that has been caught in that web can free itself by its own efforts alone.
Furthermore, it was our inevitable duty to stand up for our right to
Palestine from the moment it appeared that the fate of Palestine was
now to be decided. (This is not the place to discuss the proper means
of standing up for our right.) From then on we were obliged to defend
our right forcibly and clearly before those institutions which achieved

authority over it. The main issue, however, is what we will do with that right once it has been acknowledged. This depends on, among other things, whether we will be able to defend our right successfully before a High Court which has greater authority than this peace conference. Not only that: for us everything depends on whether, as a result of a process which does not bear the countenance of redemption can nevertheless arise. . . .

In no way do I speak against the concept of Palestinian Jewry's playing a mediating role between the Occident and the Orient. We, who are both Orientals *and* Europeans, have both the capacity and the vocation to become a gateway for the spirit and for life through the wall erected by history between the exalted mother continent and its teeming and divided peninsula. However, we must not undertake this task as the servants of a mighty and doomed Europe, but rather as the allies of a weak Europe full of future promise, not as middlemen for a decadent culture, but as collaborators of a creative young one. . . .

The loyalty of our movement and our settlement [in Palestine] to the League of Nations and its agents is understandable. We must, however, make it clear that we have nothing to do with its present system of values, with imperialism masquerading as humanitarianism. We must therefore abstain from all "foreign policy" except for those steps and actions which are necessary for the achievement of a lasting and amicable agreement with the Arabs in all aspects of public life, indeed, only those steps which would bring about and sustain an all embracing, fraternal solidarity with the Arabs.

3

At This Late Hour

(April 1920)

(Editor's prefatory note:)

The collapse of the Ottoman Empire during the First World War quickened the nascent Arab nationalism of the Near East.[1] The Allies, particularly the

French and the British, appealed to these sentiments in order to gain the support of the Arabs against the Turks and, at the same time, to secure a position of influence in the Arab world. Various and often contradictory secret agreements ensued between the Allies, who occasionally worked against one another, and the contending Arab leaders.

This spiral of intrigue was partially halted by the Paris Peace Conference of 1919, which had on its agenda to coordinate the Allies' respective arrangements in the Near East and to determine the disposition of the Arab territories freed from the Turkish yoke. With respect to Palestine, the situation was immeasurably complicated by the conflicting claims of the indigenous Arab population who constituted an indisputable majority in the area called Palestine (at the time Palestine was not a distinct geo-political entity) and of the Zionists whose claim was endorsed by the Balfour Declaration. At the initial sessions of the Peace Conference, however, it seemed that an amicable solution between the Zionists and the Arabs might be reached, as the Feisal-Weizmann agreement of January 1919 gave evidence. After several meetings in Palestine, London, and finally in Paris, Emir Feisal, the recognized leader of the Arab nationalists, and Chaim Weizmann, leader of the Zionist delegation to the Peace Conference, signed a public document which spoke of the compatability of Zionism and Arab nationalism and the possibility of cooperation between the movements.[2] Alas, the agreement was stillborn. At this juncture, the Allies were not in a position to promote it, because of their failure to agree among themselves concerning the division of their zones of influence in the Near East. In any event, the Feisal-Weizmann accord was quickly repudiated by other Arab leaders.

In the Arab world there was mounting resistance to the Balfour Declaration and the prospect of a Jewish National Home in Palestine.[3] While delegations were dispatched to the capitals of Europe to plead the cause of an Arab Palestine, a series of demonstrations and rallies was organized in Palestine itself. The Arab campaign against the implementation of the Balfour Declaration was encouraged by what seemed to be the weakening of Great Britain's resolve to obtain a mandate for Palestine. The Military Government of Palestine, established by Great Britain upon its conquest of the region and administered by it officially on behalf of the Council of Allied Nations until the final disposition of Palestine could be agreed upon, was clearly indifferent, even hostile to Zionist aspirations. Although we now know that the actions of the Military Government were not in accord with the instructions from London, the Arabs took these actions to signal Great Britain's loss of interest in the Zionist cause. Hence, they sought to exert ever greater pressure on His Majesty's government to abandon its commitments to Zionism. The Arabs' tactics took a violent turn. Shortly before the San Remo Conference of mid-April 1920 at which the Allies were *inter alia* to make a final decision about the future of Palestine, murderous attacks were launched against Jewish settlements in Palestine, culminating in a frenzied assault on Jews in Jerusalem on April 4–5, 1920. The Zionists, however, did not sit by idly. They orchestrated a counter-campaign to marshal world opinion in support of the Balfour Declaration. Further, several governments were induced to intercede with Great Britain on behalf of the Zionist cause. Finally, the Zionist Organization sent to San Remo its most forceful spokesmen to press their case. In the end, the Zionists prevailed. On April 24, the Allies meeting at San Remo decided that the Balfour Declaration would be the legal basis of the Mandate for Palestine and that the Mandate should be entrusted to Great Britain. On July 1, 1920, a little over a month after this monumental decision, the military government of Palestine came to an end and the civil administration of the Mandate was instituted.

In the following essay, written just after the publication of the San Remo accords, Buber offers a socialist analysis of the initial Arab opposition to Zionism. He argues that the Arab hostility to Zionism is but a cunning contrivance of the *effendis*, the wealthy Arab landowners. Threatened by the socialist values of the Zionist pioneers, the *effendis* falsely seek to portray the Zionists as a danger to the interests of the Arab peasant masses, the *fellahin*. But Zionism, Buber affirms, is not intrinsically inimical to the *fellahin*—that is, if Zionism remains unencumbered by chauvinism and imperialististic patronage. Reliance on the bayonets of an imperialistic mandatory power, i.e., Britain, will not protect Zionism from Arab nationalism. On the contrary, it will only intensify and justify the wrath of the Arabs. To be sure, "the hour is late," for it seems that Zionism has been irrevocably harnassed to the chariot of British imperialism, but Buber nonetheless calls upon the Zionist leadership to have the courage to eschew Britain's patronage and to forge an alliance with the Arab masses. Indeed, Buber concludes, there is no alternative if the moral integrity and political future of Zionism are to be secured.

Notes

1. See Y. Porath, *The Emergence of the Palestinian-Arab National Movement: 1918-1929* (London: Frank Cass, 1974), pp. 20–30.

2. The agreement between Emir Feisal and Chaim Weizmann, signed on 3 January 1919, is cited in Walter Laqueur, ed., *The Israel-Arab Reader: A Documentary Hisory of the Middle East Conflict* (New York: Bantam Books, 1969), document 8, pp. 18–20.

3. For a detailed and perceptive discussion of this development, see Porath, *The Emergence of the Palestinian-Arab National Movement: 1918-1929*, pp. 31–69.

At This Late Hour

... When the representatives of the victorious powers assembled in Paris, there was hardly any noteworthy national movement among the Palestinian Arabs, at least none with aggressive tendencies. Such a movement arose only in Versailles, Paris, and London because the sight of a fight over the spoils of war was visible from afar. That fight makes the negotiations over the disposition of former Turkish territories in particular into a task like Penelope's weaving. The Arab representatives in Europe found, instead of unambiguous instructions, voices speaking at cross purposes and in opposition to one another. Their awe before the rulers of the planet was immediately extinguished. Like the Turks, they right away discovered how to scurry back and forth from one power to another, how to play one off against another, and how to use their relations to both to their own advantage. This new behavior ... necessarily found its way back to the Arab population, which realized that, contrary to their prior opinion, no new play had begun, merely another act of the old play with new scenery and a new director. Ultimately, the Palestinian Arabs were also affected.

When news of the Balfour Declaration reached the Land of Israel in the autumn of 1917, the only ones who were openly displeased by the news were the large landowners among the Arabs. However, for our part, we forfeited the opportunity of explaining to the *fellahin* that they could expect an improvement in their standard of living as a result of Jewish immigration. Nonetheless, the *fellahin* generally regarded the Jews favorably, in a somewhat instinctive manner, and they were willing to live with them in peace. In contrast, the *effendis* felt, and rightly so, that their property was endangered. Extensive holdings cannot subsist forever in opposition to planned national settlement. But what could they do against the Balfour Declaration, especially considering that the [British] conquest of Palestine was complete? They certainly could have done very little if the [Military] Government had thought about the matter seriously. But, in fact, the *effendis* did succeed in doing all sorts of things. In particular, they were able to depict the dangers posed to their class [by the socialism of the Zionist pioneers] as a threat to the existence of the *fellahin*. Exploiters have taken this path, thinking to "rescue" the exploited from international solidarity by means of nationalism.

Hitherto, no one took the Balfour Declaration seriously. Neither the so-called League of Nations nor the Supreme Council of Allied Powers nor even the British government issued any statement to the Palestinian Arabs in order to explain the situation to them clearly, to describe the economic and cultural benefit that would accrue to them as a result of large and well-planned Jewish imigration. On the part of Europe, nothing was done to strengthen the understanding between the Arabs and the Jews. In the Land of Israel itself every effort was made by circles within the mandatory administration to interfere with such an accord. For the administration wished to do what occupying powers since the time of Napoleon have always striven to do: only to secure the present situation, never to prepare for a future one (the governing administration of Palestine did not grasp, nor did it learn from London, to what extent bringing about an improved situation was in the interest of the Empire). Because unambiguous instructions from the central authorities were lacking, naturally action was taken against the interests of the future.

Given the unholy and disturbing influence of the Versailles treaty on the Orient, and the growing fear for their property on the part of the great Arab capitalists (to speak in European terms), it was this action [taken by the administration] that caused the recent riots [of 1920] and also the pogrom in Jerusalem.

These developments soon had their effect on the British government. The position of those politicians and generals was strengthened who had opposed the [Balfour] Declaration for all sorts of reasons. When, in addition, the differences of opinion with France became sharper, the dangerous moment came when it appeared that England might declare its lack of interest [in Palestine]. We overcame that danger, and we must credit that principally to our political representatives [who were in San Remo]. However, that action will be to their eternal credit only if they learn the lesson and draw the proper conclusions from the developments of the last eighteen months, from the events of the last three months, from the crisis of the past two weeks: the lesson and implications of inner freedom.

We would dangerously delude ourselves if we assumed that the evil has been averted because a single mandatory power is replacing the Council of Allied Powers and civil administration is replacing military rule. . . . Are we permitted to believe that the authority of England

alone will suffice to extinguish the movement [of Arab nationalist opposition to Zionism] which has already arisen? On the contrary, [this
opposition] will persist in varied and chronic forms if we are unable to
erase it by more powerful means [than the authority of England], powerful but non-violent means, for violence could never be of permanent
assistance to us. Should we believe that any existing European government or a similar one which might follow in its footsteps would be
capable of finding the correct means and applying them? Would it be
capable, in this critical moment for the Orient, of administering a
moderate, well-founded, and *internal* Eastern policy?. . .

We, who intend to serve as intermediaries between Europe and Asia
in the Land of Israel, must not appear before the East, which is awakening from its dull slumber, as agents of a West which is doomed to
destruction, lest justified suspicion fall upon us. We were called to herald an Occident in the process of regeneration. We must help our
brothers in the Orient, on the basis of a covenant with that Occident,
and on the basis of their own strength, to lay the foundations of a true
social existence. Granted, until now the *effendis* of both East and West
have succeeded in suppressing the very aspiration for such an existence. However, it is in our power, on the basis of our socialist principles, to build the bridge that the evil genius of Versailles will never
succeed in erecting. By bringing the call for liberation to the suppressed classes of the peoples of Asia, we shall redeem them from the
false rule of nationalism, aggression, and the thirst for power. Their
exploiters, the talented pupils of the Europe of Versailles [namely, the
effendis], endeavor to divert their awakening aspirations from their
natural aims by means of nationalism. But we shall only be able to do
so if we ourselves achieve the highest expression of national self-reali-
zation, if we save our own souls from the snatches of false nationalism,
if our socialism is neither tactics nor propaganda, but rather a genuine
aspiration and a creative will. These are the "more powerful means"
at our disposal of which I previously spoke. This is the highest defense
of our soul which alone will save us from the constant spiritual pogrom
that threatens us in the Land of Israel. It depends on us whether we
shall appear before the awakening East as hateful agents and spies or,
rather, as beloved pioneers and teachers.

4

Nationalism

(September 1921)

(Editor's prefatory note:)

The establishment of the British Mandate in Palestine with the blessings of the principal Western powers was a momentous achievement for Zionism: the opportunity to build the National Home for the Jewish people had arrived. In a duly exultant mood, the first Zionist congress to be held since the war was convened in Karlsbad, Czechoslovakia, and lasted from September 1 to 14, 1921. As this the Twelfth Zionist Congress proceeded, it was quickly beset by bitter controversy over organizational and financial matters. Buber, who was a delegate representing the *Hitachdut*— a newly formed coalition of non-Marxist socialist Zionist parties[1]—called upon the Congress to pause and to transcend its immediate concerns and to ponder what he deemed to be the truly exigent task confronting the movement.[2] This task, he maintained, was to guard the spiritual and moral integrity of Zionism in the face of the political complexities of building a National Home under the aegis of an imperialistic power and, especially, in the face of the resolute opposition of the Arab population of Palestine. In his long, almost academic address, Buber reminded the Congress that there are distinct types of national self-assertion, and that in attending to the just needs of the Jewish people, Zionism should be wary of assuming the posture of a self-righteous, egocentric nationalism. Such a posture, which he dubs "hypertrophic" nationalism, he warns, would vitiate the very cure—the restoration of national dignity and spiritual renewal—that Zionism seeks to offer the ailing Jewish people. Moreover, a myopic preoccupation with the problems of one's nation invariably narrows one's moral consciousness, obscuring the humanity of other peoples, especially of one's adversaries. The resultant exaltation of nationalism as morally self-sufficient principle distorts the original purpose of nationalism: to heal the afflictions of one's nation and thereby enable it to serve the higher ideal of humankind.

Notes

1. *Hitachdut* was a coalition of *Ha-Po'el Ha-Tza'ir* (the Young Worker), a party founded and active in Palestine, and *Tze'irei Tzion* (the Youth of Zion), a loosely knit

body of groups in the Diaspora which drew inspiration from *Ha-Po'el Ha-Tza'ir*. At a
conference held in Prague in March 1920 they joined together—under the name
Hitachdut 'olamit shel Ha-Po'el Ha-Tza'ir u-Tze'irei Tzion (World Union of . . .)—
in order to gain organizational strength in the forthcoming World Zionist Congress to
be held in September of that year. Buber played a prominent role in the founding
meeting of the Hitachdut.

   2. Buber's address was delivered on September 5th at an extraordinary meeting
sponsored by the Hitachdut for the delegates of the Congress. A request that the official
session of the Congress be postponed to allow the delegates to attend Buber's address
was rejected by the Congress's executive. See *Protokoll des XII. Zionisten Kongresses*,
pp. 256f.

NATIONALISM

I am addressing you at a very troubled moment in this congress and
do not know how much attention you will be able to give me at this
point. Nevertheless, I have decided not to postpone what I have to say.
A consciousness of my responsibility urges me to speak before the confusion increases. What I am going to deal with is the unambiguous
demarcation of a kind, a degenerate kind, of nationalism, which of late
has begun to spread even in Judaism.

An unambiguous demarcation. I need not retract anything I have
ever said against a-national Jewry, against those Jews for whom—when
it comes to public life—the concept of Judaism has less reality than the
concept of nation. But now we must draw a new, no less ambiguous
line of demarcation within our own national movement.

We have passed from the difficult period of the World War into a
period which outwardly seems more tolerable, but on closer examina-
tin proves still more difficult, a period of inner confusion. It is characteristic of this period that truth and lies, right and wrong, are mingled
in its various spiritual and political movements in an almost unprecedented fashion.

In the face of this monstrous and monstrously growing phenomenon, it is no longer enough to draw the usual distinctions according to
general, currently accepted concepts. For in every such concept, the
true and the false are now so intertwined, so tangled and meshed, that

to apply them as heretofore, as though they were still homogeneous, would only give rise to greater error. If we are to pass out of confusion into new clarity, we must draw distinctions *within* each individual concept.

It is a well known fact that, *sociologically* speaking, modern nationalism goes back to the French Revolution. The effects of the French Revolution were such that the old state systems which had weighed so heavily on the peoples of Europe were shaken and the subject nations were able to emerge from under the yoke. But as they emerged and grew aware of themselves, these nations became conscious of their own political insufficiencies, of their lack of independence, territorial unity, and outward solidarity. They strove to correct these insufficiencies, but their efforts did not lead them to the creation of new forms. They did not try to establish themselves *as peoples*, that is, as a new organic order growing out of the natural forms of the life of the people. All they wanted was to become just such states, just such powerful, mechanized, and centralized state apparatuses as those which had existed in the past. They looked back into past history rather than forward into a future nationally motivated in its very structure.

We shall understand this more readily if we review the *psychological* origin of modern nationalism. European man became more and more isolated in the centuries between the Reformation and the Revolution. United Christendom did not merely break in two; it was rent by numberless cracks, and human beings no longer stood on the solid ground of connectedness. The individual was deprived of the security of a closed cosmic system. He grew more and more specialized and at the same time isolated, and found himself faced with the dizzy infinity of the new world-image. In his desire for shelter, he reached out for a community-structure which was just putting in an appearance, for nationality. The individual felt himself warmly and firmly received into a unit he thought indestructible because it was "natural," sprung from and bound to the soil. He found protection in the naturally evolved shelter of the nation, compared to which the state seemed man-made, and even the Church no more than the bearer of a mandate. But since the strongest factor in this bond he had just discovered was awareness that it had evolved naturally, the horizon narrowed and—even worse—the fruitfulness of the national element was impaired. In the individual, the original feeling of allegiance to a people, alive in the depth of his soul long before modern national awareness, changed from a creative power to the challenging will-to-power of the individual as a member of the community. The group-egosim of the individual emerged in its modern form.

A great historian [Jacob Burckhardt] has asserted that power is evil. But this is not so. Power is intrinsically guiltless; it is the precondition for the actions of man. The problematic element is the will-to-power, greedy to seize and establish power, and not the effect of a power whose development was internal. A will-to-power, less concerned with being powerful than with being "more powerful than," becomes destructive. Not power but power hysteria is evil.

In the life of human beings, both as individuals and in groups, self-assertion can be genuine as well as false, legitimate as well as illegitimate. A genuine person too likes to affirm himself in the face of the world, but in doing so he also affirms the power with which the world confronts him. This requires constant demarcation of one's own right from the rights of others, and such demarcation cannot be made according to rules valid once and for all. Only the secret of hourly acting with a continually repeated sense of responsibility holds the rules for such demarcations. This applies both to the attitude of the individual toward his own life, and to the nation he is a member of.

Modern nationalism is in constant danger of slipping into power hysteria, which disintegrates the responsibility for drawing lines of demarcation.

The distinction between the two kinds of nationalism I am concerned with depends entirely on the right understanding of this responsibility and this danger. But to arrive at this understanding, we must first analyze the phenomenon of nationalism and its relation to peoples and nations. Or to be more exact, we must define what "people" means. What, in this relation, is a nation? What is the significance of nationalism in relation to both people and nation?

The word "people" tends, above all, to evoke the idea of blood relationship. But kinship is not the *sine qua non* for the *origin* of a people. A people need not necessarily be the fusion of kindred stems; it can be the fusion of unrelated stems just as well. But the concept "people" always implies unity of fate. It presupposes that in a great creative hour throngs of human beings were shaped into a new entity by a great molding fate they experienced in common. This new "coined form" [*gepraegte Form*], which in the course of subsequent events "develops as a living substance," survives by dint of the kinship established from this moment on; it need not be exclusive, but must retain unquestioned preponderance even in areas where there are strong admixtures of other strains. The physical factor of this survival is the propagation of the species in more or less rigid endogamy; the spiritual factor is an organic, potential, common memory which becomes actual in each successive generation as the pattern for experience, as language, and as a way of life. This people constitutes a particular sort of community, because new individuals are born into it as members of its physical and spiritual oneness, and they are born into it naturally, not symbolically, as in the case of the Church. This people survives biologically, yet it cannot be fitted into a biological category. Here nation and history combine in a unique fashion.

A people becomes a nation to the degree that it grows aware that its existence differs from that of other peoples (a difference originally expressed in the sacral principle which determines endogamy), and acts on the basis of this awareness. So the term "nation" signifies the unit "people," from the point of view of conscious and active difference. Historically speaking, this consciousness is usually the result of some inner—social or political—transformation, through which the people comes to realize its own peculiar structure and actions, and sets them off from those of others. It is decisive activity and suffering, especially in an age of migrations and land conquests, which produces a *people*. A *nation* is produced when its acquired status undergoes a decisive inner change which is accepted as such in the people's self-consciousness. To give an example: the great shift which made ancient Rome a republic made it a nation, too. Not until Rome became a republic did it become a nation aware of its own peculiar strength, organization, and function, differentiating itself in these from the surrounding world. This dynamic state of nationhood can then reach its height in a peculiar formulation of its historic task. The French state-people, for instance, did not attain to complete national existence until in its great revolution it became a missionary for the idea of revolution.

At certain moments in national life a new phenomenon makes its appearance. We call it nationalism. Its function is to indicate disease. Bodily organs do not draw attention to themselves until they are attacked by disease. Similarly, nationalism is at bottom the awareness of some lack, some disease or ailment. A people feels a more and more urgent compulsion to fill this lack, to cure this disease or ailment. The contradiction between the immanent task of the nation and its outer and inner condition has developed or been elaborated and this contradiction affects the feeling of the people. What we term nationalism is their spiritual reaction to it. Being a people may be compared to having strong eyes in one's head; being nationalistic, to suffering in connection with a disease of the eyes from the constant preoccupation with the fact of having eyes. A people is a phenomenon of life, a nation one of awareness, nationalism one of overemphasized awareness [*Überbewusstheit*].

In a people, assertiveness is an *impulse* that fulfils itself creatively; in a nation it is an *idea* inextricably joined to a task; with nationalism, it becomes a *program*.

A nationalist development can have two possible consequences. Either a healthy reaction will set in that will overcome the danger heralded by nationalism, and also nationalism itself, which has now fulfilled its purpose; or nationalism will establish itself as *the* permanent principle; in other words, it will exceed its function, pass beyond its proper bounds, and—with overemphasized consciousness—displace the spontaneous life of the nation. Unless some force arises to oppose this process, it may well be the beginning of the downfall of the people, a downfall dyed in the colors of nationalism.

We have already said at the outset that original nationalism is the indication of a fundamental lack in the life of the nation, a lack of unity, freedom, and territorial security, and that it warns the nation to mend this situation. It is a demand upon the world for what it needs, a demand that the unwritten *droits de la nation* be applied to a people to enable it to realize its essence as a people and thus discharge its duty to mankind. Original nationalism inspires the people to struggle for what it lacks, to achieve this. But when nationalism trangresses its lawful limits, when it tries to do more than overcome a deficiency, it becomes guilty of what has been called *hybris* in the lives of historical personalities; it crosses the holy border and grows presumptuous. And now it no longer indicates disease, but is itself a grave and complicated disease. A people can win the rights for which it strove and yet fail to regain its health—because nationalism, turned false, eats at its marrow.

When this false nationalism, i.e., a nationalism which has exceeded the function it was destined to and persists and acts beyond it, prevails not only in *one* people, but in an entire epoch of world history, it means that the life of mankind, pulsing in its stock of peoples, is very sick indeed. And that is the situation today. The motto which Alfred Mombert, a remarkable German Jewish poet, prefaced to the third part of his *Aeon* trilogy, takes on new significance. It is: *Finis populorum.*

Every reflective member of a people is in duty bound to distinguish between legitimate and arbitrary nationalism and—in the sequence of situations and decisions—to refresh this distinction day after day. This is, above all, an obligation imposed on the leaders of a nation and of national movements. Whether or not they probe deeply into their conscience and do this unremittingly, will determine not only the fate of a movement—which must inevitably disintegrate if it becomes an end in itself—but often that of the nation, its recovery or decline. Thus, drawing this distinction is not a mere moral postulate which entails no other obligations, but a question of life or death for a people which is irreparably impaired when its spontaneity, fed on the primordial forces of natural, historical existence, is thrust aside and strangled by an apparatus activated by an exaggerated self-awareness.

But the criterion which must govern the drawing of this distinction is not implicit in nationalism itself. It can be found only in the knowledge that the nation has an obligation which is more than merely national. He who regards the nation as the supreme principle, as the ultimate reality, as the final judge, and does not recognize that over and above all the countless and varied peoples there is an authority named or unnamed to which communities as well as individuals must inwardly render an account of themselves, could not possibly know how to draw this distinction, even if he attempted to do so.

Peoples can be regarded either as elements or as ends in themselves and can regard themselves either as elements or as ends in themselves.

For him to whom peoples are elements, they are the basic substances which go to build mankind, and the only means to build up a more homogeneous mankind, with more form and more meaning. But such elements cannot be compared to chemical elements which can enter into solution and be separated again. Spiritual elements must maintain themselves because they are threatened with the loss of themselves. But just because they are elements, they are not preserved for their own sake, but to be put to use. A people fully aware of its own character regards itself as an element without comparing itself to other elements. It does not feel superior to others, but considers its task incomparably sublime, not because this task is greater than another, but because it is creation and a mission. There is no scale of values for the function of peoples. One cannot be ranked above another. God wants to use what he created, as an aid in his work. In an hour of crisis, true nationalism expresses the true self-awareness of a people and translates it into action.

He, on the other hand, who regards the nation as an end in itself will refuse to admit that there is a greater structure, unless it be the world-wide supremacy of his own particular nation. He tries to grapple with the problem of the cracked and shattered present by undermining it instead of by transcending it. He does not meet responsibility face to face. He considers the nation its own judge and responsible to no one but itself. An interpretation such as this converts the nation into a moloch which gulps the best of the people's youth.

National ideology, the *spirit* of nationalism, is fruitful just so long as it does not make the nation an end in itself; just so long as it remembers its part in the building of a greater structure. The moment national ideology makes the nation an end in itself, it annuls its own right to live, it grows sterile.

In this day and age, when false nationalism is on the rise, we are witness to the beginning of the decline of the national ideology which flowered in the nineteenth and early twentieth centuries. It goes without saying that it is perfectly possible for this decline to go hand in hand with increasing success of nationalistic politics. But we live in the hour when nationalism is about to annul itself spiritually.

It is an hour of decision, of a decision which depends on whether a distinction will be drawn, and how sharply it will be drawn. We all play a part, we can all play a part in such a distinction and decision.

I need not discuss in detail the application of these ideas to Judaism and its cause.

Judaism is not merely a nation. It is a nation, but because of its own peculiar connection with the quality of being a community of faith, it is more than that. Since Jewry has a character of its own, and a life of its own, just like any other nation, it is entitled to claim the rights and privileges of a nation. But we must never forget that it is, nevertheless, a *res sui generis*, which, in one very vital respect, goes beyond the classification it is supposed to fit into.

A great event in their history molded the Jews into a people. It was when the Jewish tribes were freed from the bondage of Egypt. But it required a great inner transformation to make them into a nation. In the course of this inner change, the concept of the government of God took on a political form, definitive for the time being, that of the "anointed" kingdom, i.e., the kingdom as the representative of God.

From the very beginning of the Diaspora, the uniqueness of Judaism became apparent in a very special way. In other nations, the national powers in themselves vouch for the survival of the people. In Judaism, this guarantee is given by another power which, as I have said, makes the Jews more than a nation: the membership in a community of faith. From the French Revolution on, this inner bond grew more and more insecure. Jewish religion was uprooted, and this is at the core of the disease indicated by the rise of Jewish nationalism around the middle of the nineteenth century. Over and over this nationalism lapses into trends toward "secularization" and thus mistakes its purpose. For Israel cannot be healed, and its welfare cannot be achieved by severing the concepts of people and community of faith, but only by setting up a new order including both as organic and renewed parts.

A Jewish national community in Palestine, a desideratum toward which Jewish nationalism must logically strive, is a station in this healing process. We must not, however, forget that in the thousands of years of its exile Jewry yearned for the Land of Israel, not as a nation like others, but as Judaism (*res sui generis*), and with motives and intentions which cannot be derived wholly from the category "nation." That original yearning is behind all the disguises which modern national Judaism has borrowed from the modern nationalism of the West. To forget one's own peculiar character, and accept the slogans and paroles of a nationalism that has nothing to do with the category of faith, means national assimilation.

When Jewish nationalism holds aloof from such slogans and paroles, which are alien to it, it is legitimate, in an especially clear and lofty sense. It is the nationalism of a people without land of its own, a people which has lost its country. Now, in an hour rife with decision, it wants to offset the deficiency it realized with merciless clarity only when its faith become rootless; it wants to regain its natural holy life.

Here the question may arise as to what the idea of the election of Israel has to do with all this. This idea does not indicate a feeling of superiority, but a sense of destiny. It does not spring from a comparison with others, but from the concentrated devotion to a task, to the task which molded the people into a nation when it attempted to accomplish it in its earlier history. The prophets formulated that task and never ceased uttering their warning: If you boast of being chosen instead of living up to it, if you turn election into a static object instead of obeying it as a command, you will forfeit it!

And what part does Jewish nationalism play at the present time? We—and by that I mean the group of persons I have belonged to since my youth, that group which has tried and will continue to try to do its share in educating the people—we have summoned the people to turn, and not to conceit, to be healed, and not to self-righteousness. We have equipped Jewish nationalism with an armor we did not weld, with the awareness of a unique history, a unique situation, a unique obligation, which can be conceived only from the supernational standpoint and which—whenever it is taken seriously—must point to a supernational sphere.

In this way we hoped to save Jewish nationalism from the error of making an idol of the people. We have not succeeded. Jewish nationalism is largely concerned with being "like unto all the nations," affirming itself in the face of the world without affirming the world's reciprocal power. It too has frequently yielded to the delusion of regarding the horizon visible from one's own station as the whole sky. It too is guilty of offending against the words of that table of laws that has been set up above all nations: that all sovereignty becomes false and vain when in the struggle for power it fails to remain subject to the Sovereign of the world, who is the Sovereign of my rival, and my enemy's Sovereign, as well as mine. It forgets to lift its gaze from the shoals of "healthy egoism" to the Lord who "brought the children of Israel out of the land of Egypt, and the Philistines from Caphtor, and Aram from Kir" (Amos 9:7).

Jewish nationalism bases its spurious ideology on a "formal" nationalistic theory which—in this critical hour—should be called to account. This theory is justified in denying that the acceptance of certain principles by a people should be a criterion for membership in that people. It is justified in suggesting that such a criterion must spring from formal common characteristics, such as language and civilization. But it is not justified in denying to those principles a central normative meaning, in denying that they involve the task—posed in time immemorial—to which the inner life of this people is bound, and together with the inner, the outer life as well.

I repeat: this task cannot be defined, but it can be sensed, pointed out, and presented. Those who stand for that religious "reform" which—most unfortunate among the misfortunes of the period of emancipation!—became a substitute for a reformation of Judaism which did not come, certainly did all they could to discredit that task by trying to cram it into a concept. But to deny the task its focal position on such grounds is equivalent to throwing out the child along with the bath water. The supernational task of the Jewish nation cannot be properly accomplished unless—under its aegis—natural life is reconquered. In that formal nationalism disclaims the nation's being based on and conditioned by this more-than-national task; in that it has grown overconscious and dares to disengage Judaism from its connection with the world and to isolate it; in that it proclaims the nation as an end in itself, instead of comprehending that it is an element, formal nationalism sanctions a group-egoism which disclaims responsibility.

It is true that, in the face of these results, attempts have been made from within the nationalistic movement to limit this expanding group-egoism from without, and to humanize it on the basis of abstract moral or social postulates rather than on that of the character of the people itself, but all such efforts are bound to be futile. A foundation on which the nation is regarded as an end in itself has no room for supranational ethical demands because it does not permit the nation to act from a sense of true supranational responsibility. If the depth of faith, which is decisive in limiting national action, is robbed of its content of faith, then inorganic ethics cannot fill the void, and the emptiness will persist until the day of the turning.

We, who call upon you, are weighed down with deep concern lest this turning may come too late. The nationalistic crisis in Judaism is in sharp, perhaps too sharp, relief in the pattern of the nationalistic crises of current world history. In our case, more clearly than in any other, the decision between life and death has assumed the form of deciding between legitimate and arbitrary nationalism.

5

A Proposed Resolution
on the Arab Question

(September 1921)

(Editor's prefatory note:)

At the Twelfth Zionist Congress Buber was also charged by his party, *Hitachdut*, to deliver its main political statement, which outlined the party's view of Zionism's current priorities and proposed for adoption by the Congress a resolution committing Zionism to a positive attitude toward Arab national aspirations. The Arab question profoundly exercised the *Hitachdut*, especially its parent party, *Ha-Po'el Ha-Tza'ir* of Palestine.[1] As a party that stressed the ethical aspects of socialism and a populist sentiment for the poor, the hostility of the Arab masses—and the obvious hurt and suspicion that animated this hostility—presented a serious ideological and moral challenge. Moreover, as a party that sought to settle in the rural regions of Palestine, the *Hitachdut* had a concrete need to appease the Arabs. Especially after the Arab riots of May 1920, which far surpassed in magnitude similar outbreaks in the past, rapproachement with the Arabs seemed to the *Hitachdut* ever more necessary.[2] Although opinion varied about the feasibility of this goal and the means to pursue it,[3] there was deepening awareness in the ranks of the *Hitachdut*, both in Palestine and in the Diaspora, that Arab opposition was no longer to be regarded simply as the contrivance of the *effendi*, but as the expression of a genuine and powerful national movement. Buber shared in this shift of perception.

Buber's address, an excerpt of which is presented here, faithfully reflects the ideology of *Ha-Po'el Ha-Tza'ir*. Rejecting Herzl's policy of first securing Palestine through diplomacy and *Realpolitik*, *Ha-Po'el Ha-Tza'ir*, which was founded in Palestine in 1905, advocated the immediate immigration of a vanguard of Zionist pioneers (*halutzim*, in Hebrew) to the ancestral homeland to build gradually the institutions and culture of the Jewish workers' commonwealth to arise there. The *halutzim*, who were behind the establishment of the first communal settlements in Palestine, celebrated the ideal of labor—

physical, non-exploitative labor, especially agricultural—as the moral basis for the regeneration of the Jewish nation. The ideal of self-labor was exalted by A. D. Gordon (1856–1922), the revered philosopher of the *halutz* ethos, as an absolute moral and spiritual value. Returning to the *land* of Israel, Gordon taught, Jewry will be transformed into an *am-adam*—"a human people" or rather a people-incarnating-humanity: a people guided solely by ethical commands in its relations with other peoples, as the individual should in his or her relations with other human beings. Not only is the individual created in the image of God, but so is a people. The crucial test for Jewry as *am-adam*, Gordon held, would be in its relations to the Arabs: "Our attitude towards them must be one of humanity, of moral courage which remains on the highest plane, even if the other side is not all that is desired. Indeed, their hostility is all the more reason for our humanity."[4]

Buber, who formally joined the German affiliate of *Ha-Po'el Ha-Tza'ir* in 1919, recognized in the party's teachings, especially as articulated by A. D. Gordon,[5] a great affinity to his own, and hence when he was called upon to speak in the party's name, he did so with alacrity.[6] Although the resolution Buber presented on the Arab question was on behalf of the party, its formulation is clearly his own.[7]

Notes

1. Yoseph Shapira, *Ha-Po'el Ha-Tza'ir: The Idea and Its Actuality* (Tel Aviv: Ayanoth Publishers, 1967), pp. 357–58. (In Hebrew.)

2. *Ibid.* This was not, however, the regnant opinion of the Zionist leadership. In response to the Arab riots of May 1921, the emphasis was on the need to foster "moderate" Arabs and to strengthen Jewish self-defense. Zionist leadership, especially in the Yishuv, was not prepared "to enter a debate over which basic concessions. . . would have to be made in the quest for peace with the Arabs." Neil Cohen, *Palestine Jewry and the Arab Question, 1917–1925* (London: Frank Cass, 1978), p. 105.

3. Shapira, *Ha-Po'el Ha-Tza'ir*, p. 358.

4. "From Without" (1919), *Collected Works of A. D. Gordon* (in Hebrew), ed. S. H. Bergman and E. Shochat (Jerusalem, 1952), vol. 1, p. 480.

5. Buber concludes his Hebrew disquistion on the idea of Zion with a chapter on A. D. Gordon. Buber, *On Zion. The History of an Idea*, foreword by N. N. Glatzer, trans. S. Godman (New York: Schocken, 1973), pp. 154–61.

6. Cf. Martin Buber, *Briefwechsel*, vol. 2, pp. 79–85.

7. Robert Weltsch, who invited Buber on behalf of the *Hitachdut*'s central committee to deliver the party's resolution on the Arab question, submitted a draft of this resolution to Buber for his consideration. Cf. *ibid.*, vol. 2, pp. 81–83. Weltsch's proposal, which is found in the Martin Buber Archive, Jerusalem, has been translated in Susan Lee Hattis, *The Bi-National Idea in Palestine* (Haifa: Shikmona Publishers, 1970), pp. 43–44, n. 35.

A PROPOSED RESOLUTION ON THE ARAB QUESTION

. . . With respect to our political program, we must not consider Europe alone. There is also the Arab question. What can be done in this area with regard to assuring the minimum that we need? The immediate logical consequence of the Balfour Declaration would have been negotiations with the non-Jewish population of Palestine. If, unfortunately, such negotiations have hitherto not been feasible, they must take place as soon as possible. I do not underestimate the enormous difficulties, nor am I misled by the slogan that one should negotiate with people and not with states. I know how hard it is to negotiate with people who are not yet constituted politically as nations and who have no legitimate representatives. Nevertheless, something ought to have occurred that did not. Certainly not negotiations with an Arab notable here and there. Of course, negotiations [with the Arabs] demand two preconditions in order to succeed. The first precondition is that we undertake actual, large-scale, well-planned settlement [in Palestine] which will be visible to the whole world. The second one is that we have a clear, realistic economic and political program which could serve as a basis for negotiations. It seems to me that both preconditions are lacking.

The hour in which we presently find ourselves is, in precisely this sense, a frightfully difficult one. It demands of us awareness and decisiveness. However, it is not on the basis of the passing moment that we are called upon to be aware and decisive; it is on the basis of historical insight and the observation of the permanent realities of the peoples of the Near East, their strivings, and their movements, which are worthy of our national sympathies to the degree that they originate in a pure, truthful, and just will to live. So that the policies I have in mind, still at this late hour, can be inaugurated in view of the whole world, we must clearly and publicly announce our intentions and aspirations. Let whomsoever hear who may! In any case, we must announce it as loudly and clearly as we can. Whether it is heard or not, our word will remain in force. Therefore, in this spirit, I conclude by presenting to you, in the name of the group which I represent here, *Hitachdut Ha-Po'el Ha-Tza'ir u-Tz'eire Tzion*, the following draft resolution with the wish and hope that the Congress will adopt it in the same spirit and without any reservations:

At this hour, in which the nationally conscious representatives of the Jewish people have gathered together again after eight years of separation, we once again declare before the nations of both the West and the East that a strong nucleus of the Jewish people is determined to return to its ancient homeland, there to renew its life, an independent life founded on labor which shall grow and endure as an organic element of a new humanity. No earthly power can shatter this determination, whose strength is found in the lives and deaths of generations of our pioneers. Any act of violence committed against us because of it sets the seal of blood upon the scroll of our national will.

Our national desire to renew the life of the people of Israel in their ancient homeland, however, is not aimed against any other people. As they enter the sphere of world history once more, and become once more the standard bearer of their own fate, the Jewish people, who have constituted a persecuted minority in all the countries of the world for two thousand years, reject with abhorence the methods of nationalistic domination, under which they themselves have long suffered. We do not aspire to return to the Land of Israel with which we have inseparable historical and spiritual ties in order to suppress another people or to dominate them. In this land, whose population is both sparse and scattered, there is room both for us and for its present inhabitants, especially if we adopt intensive and systematic methods of cultivation.

Our return to the Land of Israel, which will come about through increasing immigration and constant growth, will not be achieved at the expense of other people's rights. By establishing a just alliance with the Arab peoples, we wish to turn our common dwelling-place into a community that will flourish economically and culturally, and whose progress would bring each of these peoples unhampered independent development.

Our settlement [in the Land of Israel], which is exclusively devoted to the rescue of our people and their renewal, is not aimed at the capitalistic exploitation of the region, nor does it serve any imperialistic aims whatsoever. Its significance is the productive work of free individuals upon a commonly owned soil. This, the socialist nature of our national ideal, is a powerful warrant for our confidence that between us and the working Arab nation a deep and enduring solidarity of true common interests will develop and which in the end must overcome all the conflicts to which the present mad hour has given birth. Out of the sense of these links there will arise in the hearts of the members of the two nations feelings of mutual respect and goodwill, which will operate in the life of both the community and its individual members. Only then will both peoples meet in a new and glorious historical encounter.

6

Resolution on the Arab Question of the Twelfth Zionist Congress

(September 1921)

(Editor's prefatory note:)

Buber's proposed resolution on the Arab question was sent to committee for discussion and final formulation before being voted upon by the Congress. There in the committee Buber's proposal met with fierce opposition, and after heated debate and much political maneuvering what emerged was a compromise proposal that Buber felt had little in common with his original proposal. Chagrined, he held that it fully emasculated the principal intent of his proposal; its nice-sounding but vacuous phrases, he claimed, were meant solely as a "tactical gesture" to parry the charge that Zionism was hostile to the Arabs.[1] It bore, Buber claimed, no deep commitment to reach an accord with the Arabs. Indeed, the call for peace contained in the compromise proposal is qualified by expressions of anger and defiance. Accordingly, whereas Buber's proposal begins on a positive note, the compromise resolution begins with an expression of indignation. Indicatively, Buber's underscoring of the moral perspective of Zionism and its vision of a "new humanity" was eliminated; likewise his references to Jewry as "a persecuted minority" and Zionism's attendant resolve to reject "domineering nationalism," imperialism, and capitalistic exploitation were deleted. Further, Buber's proposed assurance to the Arabs of an autonomous, independent development was obscured by the vague phrase "an undisturbed national development." Finally, whereas Buber's proposal concluded with an unambiguous vision of peace and fraternity between Jew and Arab, the peroration of the resolution seeks to remind the Arabs that the Balfour Declaration is not negotiable. It may also be noted that the compromise resolution makes no reference to developing a concrete political and economic plan to be brought before the Arabs as the basis of obtaining an "honorable entente." The compromise resolution, which was adopted by the Congress, is presented below.

Note

1. See Robert Weltsch, "Nachwort," Hans Kohn, *Martin Buber, Sein Werk und seine Zeit*, 2nd ed. (Cologne: Joseph Melzer Verlag, 1961), p. 435. On the eve of the Twelfth Zionist Congress, Sir Herbert Samuel, the High Commissioner of Palestine, repeatedly urged the World Zionist Organization immediately to undertake such constructive projects as would indicate to the Arabs that "the success of Zionism will be to their benefit and not result in their destruction," and to issue an official declaration reassuring the Arabs that this indeed is the intention of Zionist settlement activity. See Neil Caplan, *Palestine Jewry and the Arab Question* (London: Frank Cass, 1978), pp. 114f.

RESOLUTION ON THE ARAB QUESTION OF THE TWELFTH ZIONIST CONGRESS

With sadness and indignation the Jewish people have lived through the recent events in Palestine. The enmity of a part of the Arab inhabitants, incited by unscrupulous elements to commit deeds of violence, can weaken neither our resolve to construct a Jewish National Home nor our will to live at peace and in mutual respect with the Arab people, and together with them, to make our common home in a flourishing commonwealth whose reconstruction will assure undisturbed national development for each of its peoples. The two great Semitic peoples, who have already been linked together once before by bond of common culture, shall again, at this time, comprehend the need for uniting their vital interests in common enterprise.

The [Twelfth Zionist] Congress calls upon the Zionist Executive to redouble its efforts to secure an honorable entente with the Arab people on the basis of this declaration and in strict accordance with the Balfour Declaration. The Congress emphatically declares that the work of Jewish settlement shall not infringe upon the rights and needs of the working Arab nation.

7

Notes from the Congress Concerning Zionist Policy

(October 1921)

(Editor's prefatory note:)

Buber fought for his proposal on the Arab question with enthusiasm and conviction,[1] but, as we have seen, his struggle was in vain. The dictates of party
politics had demanded compromise. Buber, of course, acknowledged this fact
of political life, but he insisted that compromise need not vitiate principle.
That the committee reviewing his proposal, which consisted of many individuals whom he respected and whose world-view he shared, deemed political
compromise superior to principle perplexed Buber greatly. His response was
far-reaching. He withdrew from party politics and the precincts of political
bargaining where principle is all to often obscured, if not discarded.[2]
Although he withdrew from party politics, he nonetheless remained intimately and passionately involved in Zionist affairs. After the conclusion of
the Twelfth Zionist Congress, he shared some critical reflections with the
readers of his journal, *Der Jude*. From the perspective of the Congress'
debates on Zionist policy, he ponders the consequence of Zionism's entrée,
through the aegis of the Balfour Declaration and the British Mandate, into
world politics. Lamenting this development, Buber begrudgingly admits that
the die has been cast: there is little choice but to accept the Mandate as an
opportunity to build the Jewish National Home in Palestine. In our "excite-
ment," Buber cautions, "we Zionists" should not be naïve with respect to Britain's primary imperialistic interests. The protestations of good will toward the
Jewish people and the reorganization of the British empire into dominion
states enjoying home rule should not blind Zionists to the basic fact that Great
Britain's policy remains at bottom a self-serving imperialism. As an imperialistic factor in the Near East, Britain is bound to clash with the awakening
Arab nationalism. It thus would be imprudent to say the least for Zionism to
appear as an agent or ally of Britain. Far more important than a "charter"
from the big powers supporting Jewish settlement in Palestine, Zionism
requires the amity and understanding of the Arabs.

Notes

1. Cf. Ernst Simon, *The Line of Demarcation: Nationalism, Zionism, and the Arab-Israeli Conflict in the Thought of Martin Buber* (Givat Havivah: Center for Arabic Studies, 1973), p. 26. (In Hebrew.)

2. Twenty-six years after the Twelfth Zionist Congress, Buber wrote the following recollection of his short-lived, but fateful experience with the wiles of party politics:

> Many years ago, when I fought for the idea of a Jewish-Arab alliance at one of the Zionist Congresses, I had a shocking experience that affected the direction of the rest of my life. I composed a draft resolution that emphasized the two nations' common interests and indicated the path to cooperation between them, the only path than can lead to the redemption of the Land [of Israel] and of the two peoples living in it. Before the draft was submitted to the Congress for approval, it went before a drafting committee that was to determine the final wording. I participated in that committee, of course. It was there that something happened which for any professional politician is an utterly simple and routine matter, but which appalled me to such an extent that I still haven't recovered from the shock. In the drafting committee, which was composed mainly of old friends of mine, first one small change was suggested, then another, and then another. At first glance, each small change was not at all critical, and each change was explicitly justified by the argument that the resolution had to be formulated in such a way that it would be adopted by the Congress. Every so often I would hear the following words: "Do you want something merely for show or do you want the Congress to accept the principle of Jewish-Arab cooperation, to take the issue to its heart, and to be willing to fight for it. If that is what you want, you must agree to these small changes." Of course I didn't want something merely for show, I wanted to make a thoroughgoing change in the Zionist movement's position on the Arab question. Each time, therefore, I fought for the formulation I had suggested, but I also agreed and compromised again and again whenever the passage of the whole resolution depended on my giving in. When the drafting committee finished its work and a clean copy of the agreed-upon version was brought to me in my hotel—I saw beautiful and convincing sentences, but the vigor and power of my original proposal were missing. I accepted the matter and notified them that I agreed to bring the resolution before the Congress. I settled for an oral presentation, before the resolution was read aloud and voted on, in which I explained and elucidated the fundamental change that I was aiming for in my resolution. I felt, however, that my role as a politician, that is, as a man who participates in the political activities of a group, was over. I began something, and it was my duty to finish what I had begun, but I could never begin something now, in which I would again have to choose between the truth and the possibilities of realization. From then on I would have to forego the drafing of resolutions and be satisfied with oral presentations. . . . "

Entitled "Truth and Deliverance," this memoir was addressed to Judah L. Magnes, the moving spirit behind the founding of the Ichud, the association for Arab-Jewish rapprochement which served as the principle framework for Buber's ramified political activity during the last period of his life. (Cf. selections 25–27) In the concluding passage of the memoir, Buber expresses his gratitude to Magnes and the Ichud for renewing his conviction that "political activity need not sacrifice truth." Buber, "Truth and Deliverance" (Hebrew), *Be'ayot*, no. 5–6 (July 1947), p. 189. Magnes' lifelong effort to introduce a "prophetic" dimension into Zionist policy, especially with regard to the Arab question, is richly documented in Arthur A. Goren, ed., *Dissenter in Zion. From the Writings of Judah L. Magnes* (Cambridge: Harvard University Press, 1982).

NOTES FROM THE CONGRESS CONCERNING ZIONIST POLICY

[Zionism] must not abandon its historically determined, supra-party position on account of a momentary conjunction of events. We must not confuse our own claim with that of the strangers [i.e., the British who have conquered Palestine]. That is to say, although we should declare our acceptance of the British Mandate, nevertheless let us not insist on that Mandate in such a way that we must declare ourselves England's unconditional partisans, and be so considered henceforth. . . .

The Land [of Israel] already contains a non-Jewish population without whose expressed or tacit agreement all of our accords with a third party are likely to encounter severe difficulties. We are therefore obliged immediately to begin direct negotiations with this population on social and economic issues, and, insofar as the matter depends on the nation which constitutes the decisive majority of that population, on general political issues as well. . . .

With respect to public opinion we cannot discern political trends better than in the public statements of prominent individuals. Yet what is called "public opinion," that is to say, the articulate public, is frequently the last to be aware of these trends, although the "reticent public" is often the first to get an inkling of them. A political trend is but the change, which does not take place in the open, in the systems necessary for the existence, strengthening, and expansion of the state. When we begin to see that we can no longer depend on the old systems (the "reticent public" often feels this first, but it is unable to give itself any account of it), then a change must take place, and if it does not, the state runs the risk of being limited, weakened, or even destroyed. In general the matter touches upon particular questions of foreign or domestic policy: constitutional details, policy toward a neighboring state, or something of the sort. However, at exceptional moments, at times of crisis, the political trend touches upon a wide area of political activity, and it easily overflows into other areas, sometimes affecting the entire existence of the state, which, because its systems are changing, undergoes itself a change in character. England now finds herself in such a moment. She of all the present European states is the most able to change, the most adaptable, the most capable of altering her positions at the right moment, and thus the best able to resist any opposition. I am astonished not only that our representatives were blind to this development, but that they still fail to see it clearly. Now that it is impossible not to notice this development, they still do not grasp its importance. During a session of the political committee of this Congress, I called the attention of a man who bears responsibility in this area to the changes that are taking place in British imperial methods as an underlying cause for a good deal of friction. He replied that he had heard nothing of it, neither among officials nor in public opinion. Such failure to take note has often occurred in history, and seldom has it had beneficial results.

The change that has begun in British imperial methods is, following the Bolshevik Revolution, the second of the great world-historical events of our time, which from local events had world-wide consequences. Its origin lies in the need to prevent the collapse of the empire, and it essentially consists in the dissolution of the bonds among its parts, that is to say, *centrally administered decentralization* in order to maintain the empire. That change, which like any new political tendency, was censured as "ideology," first took root in the circles of the advocates of the "Round Table" principle. With the beginning of constitutional reform in India the principle proved its real value on a large political scale. It gave rise to the Dominion Conference. Today it determines the course of negotiations with Ireland, which every newspaper reader in 1920 would have considered it mad to predict. It directly affects the relations of the parts of the empire, both among themselves and to the empire. It will also have increasing influence upon its relations to nations which, although they do not belong to the empire, belong nevertheless to the British sphere of influence. It will increasingly determine the relations between the empire and all those nations which it is endeavoring in every way to draw into its sphere of influence or to bring closer to itself. This change will increasingly determine the status of the "Arab question" in world politics.

8

Sidelights

(April 1922)

(Editor's prefatory note:)

In January 1922, Ramsay MacDonald (1866–1937), a leader of the British Labour Party who in 1924 was to serve as the prime minister of the first Labour cabinet, visited Palestine. Upon his return to England, he published and lectured widely on his visit. In the following article, published in *Der Jude* in April 1922, Buber responds to a report on one of MacDonald's speeches in which he told of having learned from the mandatory authorities in Palestine that the wartime government of Great Britain led by the Conservatives had entered into a number of secret and contradictory agreements in the Near East. This disclosure, Buber contends, is proof of Britain's imperialistic designs on Palestine. The Zionists, he continues, would deceive themselves if they believe a Labour government would view Britain's interests in Palestine differently. On the other hand, a Labour government would likely seek to hasten the policy of decentralization of the imperial realm, allowing a great measure of self-rule in its colonies and territories. Buber cites Colonel Josiah C. Wedgwood (1872–1943), a member of the executive of the Labour Party and an avid supporter of Zionism, as assuring that this would indeed be the direction of a Labour government's policy in Palestine. This prospect, and the implied need for the Jews and Arabs of Palestine to cooperate in the joint rule of the country, according to Buber, provide a renewed opportunity for Arab-Jewish rapprochement and political entente.

SIDELIGHTS

... Ramsay MacDonald, "a representative man" [English in original] in the English Labour Party, made a speech in his electoral district upon his return from Palestine. He said that in Palestine he learned that during the war the British government empowered the former High Commissioner to inform the Arabs that it would establish an Arab State if they supported Britain in the war.... At the same time it promised Palestine to the Jews as a national home and to facilitate Jewish immigration so that the Jews would ultimately form the majority in Palestine. At the same time, it made a third agreement with France according to which Syria, Palestine, and Mesopotamia would be divided between Britain and France. These three obligations, which are mutually contradictory, were nevertheless undertaken, and in such circumstances the present High Commissioner must make every effort to preserve British honor, respect, and authority.

The details mentioned by MacDonald (if his speech was accurately reported) lack a certain precision. ... The small imprecisions in his presentation do not, however, diminish the importance of his speech, which sheds light on the fact that we are dealing with steps taken in accordance with the politics of war, which proceeds recklessly, without regard to alternatives, thus necessarily resulting in a snarl of contradictions. These contradictions must be resolved by a peacetime policy, which with its traditional elasticity will be open to various alternatives. To be sure, this peacetime policy will not overcome the contradictions, it will simply act as if they did not exist.

The picture only becomes complete, however, if one considers that in addition to those who are charged with achieving a compromise among the various interests—a task rendered much more difficult by the governmental policy, but which they are willing to carry out— there are official and unofficial representatives of British power who are not enthusiastic about the honorable obligation of finding a compromise among the various elements of the population of Palestine, but who rather favor the cunning principle of rule: "Divide and conquer." Or perhaps their spirits are guided by the well-tried art of "turning anger against the Jews." MacDonald said in Palestine that he was afraid that certain circles are interested in stirring up hatred between the Arabs and the Jews.

What path do the men of the Labour Party advocate? They would consider giving up Palestine as little as any other serious English politician. (The proposal by a few anti-Zionists that Britain indeed relinquish the Mandate must be seen as pure tactics.) They recognize the strategic as well as the economic importance of the Land of Israel for the empire, and moreover its importance for transport, and they will attempt to maintain it. But it is evident that they intend to bring the decentralizing trend, which has gradually become dominant in the Commonwealth movement, to its fullest expression and to replace coercive imperialism fully by an imperialism of compromise and cooperation. If they come to power, they will allow India to follow Ireland and Egypt. . . . They will try, as Colonel Wedgwood said, "to put Palestine on a self-governing basis as soon as possible." "As soon as possible"—when will it be possible? We may assume that the opinion of the Labour Party is: as soon as an honorable, complete, and viable compromise between the interests of the Jewish and Arab nations has been reached. We have every reason to pave the way for such a compromise as soon as possible. It seems to me that now, after all the lost opportunities, a propitious moment has again come to make the attempt, honorably, and with some chance of success.

9

Responsa on Zionist Policy

(September 1922)

(Editor's prefatory note:)

After the débâcle of the Twelfth Zionist Congress, it became increasingly manifest to Buber that the dependence of the Zionist leadership on *Realpolitik* was a function of their Diaspora perspective. Zionism, he concluded, must detach itself from the problematics of the Diaspora, where the Jews are understandably beholden to the European powers, and view its political objectives exclusively in realistic terms of the Land of Israel. A Zionism rooted in the Land of Israel—nurturing its soil with love and devotion—will perforce confront the fulness of the Land's reality, a reality which includes an indigenous Arab population which like the Jews aspires to national dignity and independence. In contrast to the *political* Zionism of the Diaspora, Buber called a Zionism centered in the Land of Israel, and alert to its reality, *Wirklichkeitszionismus*, a realistic Zionism.[1] He first presented this call for a new orientation in Zionist policy in the form of Questions and Answers, published in *Der Jude* of September 1922—incidentally at the very time he was correcting the proofs of his masterpiece in religious philosophy, *I and Thou*, which appeared in December of that year.

Note

1. Hans Kohn, *Martin Buber: Sein Werk und seine Zeit*, 2nd ed. (Cologne: Joseph Melzer, 1966), p. 131.

Responsa on Zionist Policy

Q. You claim that we must not espouse the policies of the European states. But they determine our fate in the Land of Israel, whether we comply with it or not. You claim that we must form an alliance with the Orient and take an active part in its renaissance. But the Orient does not wish to enter into a convenant with us. What constructive policy can you recommend now?

A. A Land Policy [i.e., a policy centered in the *Land* of Israel].

Q. What do you mean by that?

A. To direct all of our efforts, to the limit of our powers, to the upbuilding of the Land of Israel, not simply to building our nation within the Land, nor only to the extent that is necessary for the success of our nation, but rather to building the Land truly for its own sake. If we succeed in this matter, then we will be immune to the policies of the European states. We will then appear before the Orient as irreplaceable pioneers in its renaissance, genuine pioneers, trustworthy, desirable. Of course it must be noted that we should not simply mask our *sacro egoismo* in a Land Policy—for no mask will deceive anyone today—but rather we must temper our egoism and subordinate it to a Land Policy. I say "Land Policy," but it would be more truthful to say "Love of the Land."

Q. And if despite everything, once we have accomplished our task of building up the Land, the Arabs are a majority, and they take away the fruits of our labor?

A. Oh, Man of Little Faith! God does not sign promissory notes. But blessed be the man who lends himself to God without any bill of exchange!

10

Brith Shalom

(1925)

(Editor's prefatory note:)

In the spring of 1925 a group of intellectuals gathered in Jerusalem to establish an association to promote what Buber called *Wirklichkeitszionismus*—a Zionism rooted in the complex reality of the Land of Israel. Initiated by Arthur Ruppin (1876–1943), the principal architect of Zionist settlement policy, the association was called *Brith Shalom*, literally the Covenant of Peace.[1] The founding members of Brith Shalom included veteran Jewish residents of Palestine, academics, members of Ha-Po'el Ha-Tza'ir, Mizrahi (the religious Zionist movement), and liberal Zionists. Gershom Scholem, a founding member who at the time was just establishing his renown as as a scholar of Jewish mysticism, has noted that what united this diverse group was a conviction "that the Land of Israel belongs to two peoples, and these peoples need to find a way to live together . . . and to work for a common future."[2] The Land of Israel was deemed by them to be *empirically* a land of two peoples—the indigenous Arab population and the Jews who were returning to their ancestral home. As Ruppin succinctly told the Fourteenth Zionist Congress which met in Vienna in August 1925. "Palestine will be a state of two nations [*ein*

Zweinationalitätenstaat]. Gentlemen, this is a fact, a fact which many of you have not yet sufficiently realized. It may also be that for some of you this is not a pleasant fact, but it nonetheless remains so."[3] The bi-national state Ruppin and his colleagues had in mind was a *modus vivendi* between Zionism and Palestinian Arab nationalism within the existing political framework of the Mandate which they tacitly assumed Britain, because of its imperialistic interests and might, would tenaciously maintain.[4] The Jewish National Home will somehow have to be realized within terms of the bi-national reality of Mandatory Palestine. Accordingly, Brith Shalom envisioned as the most reasonable solution to the problem of Palestine a constitutional arrangement whereby the Jews and Arabs would enjoy political and civil parity within the unitary framework of the Mandate. Brith Shalom, however, did not view itself as a political party, but merely as a study circle sponsoring informed and responsible discussion on the Arab question. Many of its most devoted members claimed to have drawn their inspiration from the teachings of Buber on the Arab question.[5] Buber himself became an active member in the German chapter of Brith Shalom.

Notes

1. The name of the association is apparently an allusion to Ezekiel 34, 25: "I will make with them a covenant of peace (*brith shalom*) . . ."

2. G. Scholem, Interview on Brith Shalom, May 1972. Department of Oral History. Institute for Contemporary Jewry, Hebrew University of Jerusalem. Transcript of tape no. 1960/1, p. 3.

3. *Protokoll der Verhandlungen des XIV. Zionistenkongresses* . . . (London, 1926), p. 438.

4. Robert Weltsch, Interview on Brith Shalom, May 1972. Department of Oral History. Institute for Contemporary Jewry, Hebrew University of Jerusalem. Transcript of tape no. 1959, p. 3.

5. This was especially true of S. H. Bergman, Hans Kohn, Ernst Simon, and Robert Weltsch; Ruppin and Scholem, however, did not consider themselves disciples of Buber.

BRITH   SHALOM

(THE PEACE ASSOCIATION)

STATUTES

§1. The name of the Association shall be "The Peace Association" (Brith Shalom).

§2. The seat of the Association shall be in Jerusalem. Branches may be established throughout Palestine and abroad.

§3. The object of the Association is to arrive at an understanding between Jews and Arabs as to the form of their mutual social relations in Palestine on the basis of absolute political equality of two culturally autonomous peoples, and to determine the lines of their co-operation for the development of the country.

§4. Towards this end the Association will promote:
  a)   The study of the problems arising out of the existence of the two peoples in Palestine, and out of the Mandate under the League of Nations;
  b)   The spreading of verbal and written information among Jews and Arabs on the history and culture of both peoples, and the encouragement of friendly relations between them;
  c)   The creation of a public opinion favorable to a mutual understanding;
  d)   The creation of institutions calculated to advance these ends;

§5. Any person in agreement with the object of the Association and elected by a majority decision of its Committee (§ 8) is eligible for membership.

§6. The membership fee shall be £1 a year. The Committee (§ 8) is empowered to reduce this fee for labourers and other persons of limited means.

§7. A General Meeting of the Association shall take place every year. Members shall be advised at least a fortnight in advance by an announcement in three Palestinian papers which appear regularly. The first General Meeting shall be convoked before December 31st, 1927.

§8. The Committee of the Association shall consist of between 7 and 15 members elected by the General Meeting. Branches of the Association in and outside of Palestine shall elect their local Committees on similar lines.

§9. Until the first General Meeting, the founders of the Association shall act as the Committee (§ 8) and shall have the right of co-optation.

BRITH SHALOM

"HAMADPIS" PRESS, JERUSALEM

بريت شالوم

برنامج

جمعية عهد السلام (بريت شالوم)

أولاً = ان الجمعية تدعى باسم: «جمعية عهد السلام»

ثانياً = ان الجمعية في القدس· ولها ان تنشئ الفروع في كل مكان سواء في فلسطين او في الخارج·

(غايات ومقاصد الجمعية)

ثالثاً = ان غاية الجمعية تمهيد السبيل بين اليهود والعرب، بإيجاد الطرق لحياة المشتركة في فلسطين، على قاعدة التعديل التام في حقوق الشعبين السياسية ذات السلطة الذاتية الواسعة، والبحث في كيفية اعمالها المشتركة في تقدم البلاد·

رابعاً = وللتوصل الى الغايات المتقدمة، تنفذ الإجراءات التالية: —

(١) — درس المسائل المتعلقة بحياة الشعبين المشتركة في فلسطين، وبانتداب عصبة الامم·

(٢) — تبيين ماهية وتمدن الشعبين شفاهاً ونشراً للعرب واليهود، وايجاد الملائق الودية بينها·

(٣) — إقناع الرأي العام بروح المحبة والسلام·

(٤) — انشاء المؤسسات التي من شأنها تعضيد الجمعية بالحصول على غاياتها·

خامساً = يقبل عضواً في الجمعية كل من يعترف ببرنامجها، بمقتضى اغلبية، آراء، اعضاء الهيئة الإدارية·

سادساً = ان رسم العضوية في الجمعية ليرة مصرية· على ان للادارة الحق في تخفيض هذا الرسم للعمال ولمديمي المقدرة المالية·

سابعاً = يعقد اجتماع عام للجمعية مرة في العام، حيث يدعى اليه الاعضاء بمقتضى دعوة تنشر في ثلاث جرائد فلسطينية على الاقل، تصدر بصورة دائمة· ويجب نشر هذه الدعوة قبل يوم الاجتماع بأسبوعين على الاقل· اما الاجتماع العام الاول، فيعقد قبل عام ١٩٢٧·

ثامناً = ان هيئة ادارة الجمعية تتألف من سبعة اعضاء، ينتخبون من خمسة عشر عضواً في الاجتماع العام· وكذلك على فروع الجمعية وسيختار الخارج انتخاب هيئات محلية لادارة شئونها·

تاسعاً = يعتبر الاعضاء، المؤسسون اعضاء للهيئة الادارية الى ان يعقد الاجتماع العام الاول· ولهم الحق بضم اعضاء آخرين اليهم·

אגודת ,ברית שלום'

תקנות

1. שם האגודה: ,ברית־שלום'.

2. מקום מושבה: ירושלים. סניפים לה יכולים להוסד בכל מקום, הן באיי והן בחו"ל.

3. תעודת האגודה: לסלול דרך חבנה בין עברים וערבים לצורות חיים משותפות בארץ־ישראל על יסוד שווי מהור בזכיותיהם הפוליטיות של שני לאומים בעלי אוטונומיה רחבה ולצורותיה של עבודתם המשותפת לטוב. התפתחותה של הארץ.

4. בתור אמצעים להשגת המטרה הזאת ישמשו:

א. חקירת הפרובלימות הכרוכות מתוך חייהם המשותפים של שני הלאומים באיי ומתוך המנדם של חבר הלאומים.

ב. הסברת ערכם ותרבותם של שני העמים בעל פה ובכתב לעברים וערבים ופתוח יחסי ידידות ביניהם.

ג. השפעה על דעת הקהל ברוח של הסכם שלום.

ד. יצירת מוסדות המסייעים להשגת מטרת האגודה.

5. חבר האגודה יכול להיות כל המודד בממטרת האגודה ומתקבל ע"י הועד ברוב דעות.

6. סכום דמי החבר הוא לירה מצרית אחת לשנה; והרשות בידי הועד להפחית את הסכום הזה בשביל פועלים ומחוסרי אמצעים.

7. בכל שנה נקראת אספת הכללית של האגדה. לאספה זו מוזמנים החברים ע"י הודעה לפחות בשלשה עתונים ארץ־ישראליים המופיעים בקביעות. ההודעה צריכה להתפרסם לכל הפחות שבועים לפני יום האספה. האספה הכללית הראשונה תקרא לפני קץ שנת תרפ"ז.

8. ועד האגודה מורכב משבעה עד חמשה עשר חברים. הועד נבחר ע"י האספה הכללית. סניפי האגודה באיי ובחו"ל בוחרים גם הם בועדים מקומיים.

9. עד האספה הכללית הראשונה נחשבים המיסדים בתור חברי הועד; והרשות בידם לצרף להם עוד חברים.

בדפוס ,המדפיס' ירושלם

11

Soul-Searching

(April 1926)

(Editor's prefatory note:)

Among the paramount concerns of Brith Shalom was to correct the regnant tendency of the Zionist leadership to view the Arab problem as preeminently demographic, that is, the view that the numerical superiority of the Arab population of Palestine (which in 1925 numbered 750,000 as compared to 75,000 Jews) must be neutralized by a rapid increase of the number of Jews in the country, eventually obtaining a majority status to ensure that the right of self-determination for Palestine would be accorded to the Jews. Brith Shalom held that this declared policy of creating a Jewish "majority" in Palestine was bound to exacerbate the Arabs' fear of Jewish domination, or, worse, this policy would lock the Jews and Arabs on a path of irreconcilable conflict. The only reasonable solution, Brith Shalom insisted, was a bi-national state in which both the Jews and Arabs would enjoy equal shares in the political and civil administration of the country, regardless of their proportion of the general population. Although such a solution involved mutual compromise and a new conception of national sovereignty, Brith Shalom held that it was the only solution that bore the promise of resolving the conflict with a minimal dimunition of the interests and dignity of the respective communities. As an immediate step to allay Arab fears, most members of Brith Shalom advocated a temporary limitation of Jewish immigration[1]—a proposal that rendered Brith Shalom perfidious in the eyes of many Zionists.

In the following essay Buber elaborates Brith Shalom's criticism of the policy of seeking a Jewish majority in Palestine. It was published in April 1926 in the *Jüdische Rundschau*, a prestigious Berlin Zionist bi-weekly, whose editor Robert Weltsch, a disciple of Buber, often lent eloquent and courageous support to Brith Shalom.

Note

1. Arthur Ruppin was a notable exception, and indeed he broke with Brith Shalom over this issue.

SOUL-SEARCHING

We desire to escape from the discomfiture of dependency, of the coercion that comes from without, and of our dispersion among many overlordships, in whose decisions we have no part at all, or no significant part. In Palestine we desire to build an autonomous community that, although quantitatively small, will have the power of becoming, from both a subjective and an objective point of view, an active factor in terminating our dependence. We do not undertake this endeavor merely as a people without a state, but also as a people whom no state will assist. (It is, of course, true that most of us refused to admit this fact for for a long time.) What rallying cry ought we adopt in this situation, and what rallying cry have we in fact adopted? The one we have adopted says: "The Creation of a [Jewish] majority in Palestine." A communal structure that would merely reverse our discomfiture, permitting us to do to others (even in kind and merciful ways) what others are doing to us here [in the Diaspora]—but can this approach deliver us from our discomfiture? The true rallying cry proclaims: Promoting the good of the other inhabitants of Palestine in the name of the society that will one day come into being there; a unification of their interests with ours, but also the advancement of their special interests in order to allow them to appreciate the desirability and feasability of a unity of interests—not, however, for that reason alone, but also for the sake of their welfare as our partners in the society that will come into being. For that purpose, we must have a sympathetic knowledge of our neighbors, which can only be acquired by the study of their language and traditions and, above all, by decisively discarding the invidious feeling of superiority. . . . When I say things like that to people who live in Palestine, they generally respond by describing the uncivilized character of the Arabs. It seems to me, however, that the values we have acquired by virtue of our tradition have become quite flawed in the meantime, and if one should say that we still maintain them, then let us give them expression in our personal and communal relationships. This is not a so-called "moral" claim, but rather a political argument. Only one question is considered here: How can we achieve our goal? Yes, our goal! Whosoever daily trades away a goal against the needs of the hour, whoever does not achieve a little of his goal every day, is destined in the end to betray it. One more thing:

Whether the goal sanctifies the means or not is a dialectical question which, it seems to me, has no practical significance. But everything depends on the means one uses, whether what one achieves by them has anything left in it of the initial goal or whether it is the total opposite, even though it bears the name of the goal—and this is a political fact.

12

No More Declarations

(August 1929)

(Editor's prefatory note:)

The struggle within Zionism to define a coherent policy toward the Mandatory government and Arab nationalism also gave rise to a rightwing Zionist movement, the Revisionists. Since its founding in 1925, the Revisionist movement led by Vladimir Ze'ev Jabotinsky (1880–1940), made rapid inroads into the Jewish community. The youth were especially receptive to Revisionism's militant nationalism, and, in the face of the exigencies of Jewish history, its refusal to compromise what were deemed Jewish rights, even for the sake of conciliation. The Socialist-Zionists were particularly alarmed by the sudden rise of the Revisionists, who also advocated free enterprise and anti-labor legislation for the Yishuv—the Jewish settlement in Palestine.

On the eve of the Sixteenth Zionist Congress in August 1929, Buber, who had been elected to head the Hitachdut's delegation to the Congress, was called upon to lead the fight against "Jabotinsky and his young fascists."[1] Joseph Sprinzak (1885–1959), a leader of *Ha-Po'el Ha-Tza'ir* in Palestine (and at the time head of the Aliyah or immigration department of the Zionist Executive), addressed an appeal to Buber, who was reluctant to come to the Congress because of his overextended scholarly and personal commitments, and urged him to accept the assignment: "Your appearance at the Congress is absolutely necessary."[2] Sprinzak argued that Buber's stature and spiritual vision would provide the answer that the Congress must give to Revisionism. He suggested that Buber not polemicize with the Revisionists, but appeal directly to the young reminding them of the primary spiritual and moral objectives of Zionism.

Buber heeded the call, and addressed the Congress. In his relatively brief speech, he reminded Jewish youth that Zionism does not seek a "clumsy imitation" of the prevailing type of nationalism in Europe, guided by *sacro egoismo*. Adopting such a nationalism would be tantamount to "national assimilation." Zionism, on the other hand, wishes to further Judaism by placing it in the matrix of concrete national existence within a complex social and political reality, thereby to confront Judaism with the awesome challenge to give life to its teachings. From this perspective, the Arab question is a decisive test for Judaism.

Notes

1. Buber, *Briefwechsel*, vol. 2, pp. 336f.(letter of 11 July 1929).
2. *Ibid.*, vol. 2, p. 337 (letter of 17 July 1929). Sprinzak's request was conveyed in a letter by Robert Weltsch.

NO MORE DECLARATIONS

In discussing the Arab question one must focus on the facts—the facts with all their grave and cruel complexity—with utter earnestness and clarity. I fear that in this matter as well, the assimilation of our nation has affected us. Let us bear in mind—and actually there is no need for me to remind you, for our whole life is permeated by it—that other nations regarded us, and in some places still do so, as alien and inferior. Let us beware of considering and behaving toward anyone who is foreign and as yet insufficiently known to us as if he were inferior! Let us beware of doing ourselves what has been done to us! Certainly, and again I emphasize this point, the maintenance of our existence is undoubtedly an essential prior condition of all our actions. But this is not enough. We also need imagination. Another thing we need is the ability to put ourselves in the place of the other individual, the stranger, and to make his soul ours. I must confess that I am horrified at how little we know the Arabs. I do not delude myself into believing that at this time there is peace between what is good for us and what is good for the Arabs, or that it is easy to attain a peace of this sort. And yet, despite the great division between one and the other, and despite the fact that this division is not the result of a mere illusion or of politics, there is room for a joint national policy, because both they and we love this country and seek its future welfare; as we love the country and together seek its welfare, it is possible for us to work together for it. . . .

Many of us say: We do not wish to be ruled as a minority by a majority, and I too say that together with them. I should not like, however, our unwillingness to be subject to a majority to be interpreted as a desire to submit others to our rule. Our rallying cry must be: We do not wish to submit to the majority as a minority, and nor do we wish to become a majority and make the minority submit to us.

Do not ask for a prescription from me in a matter demanding personal responsibility in a thousand small decisions. Let us make no more declarations. Let us make no more general resolutions. Rather, at every moment, let everyday reality show [the Arabs] what our true intentions are. We must demonstrate them in practice: in our policies, in our cultural activity, in our social affairs, in our interpersonal relations.

I should like to recommend that as a sign of our good intentions there be established in Palestine a standing commission which will serve the Zionist Executive as an advisory body on all matters pertaining to the Arab question. (Interlocutor: "Brith Shalom!") Many find this group offensive. For me and all those like myself who regard our present historical situation with such deep concern that we no longer [find it adequate] to respond with mere phrases—for us the situation calls for the beginning of a new era not of declarations but of deeds. There are no formulas: for truly responsible conduct there is only an orientation, but no formulas.

13

The National Home and National Policy in Palestine

(October 1929)

(Editor's prefatory note:)

In marked contrast to Brith Shalom, the Zionist leadership assumed the pessimistic view that Arab opposition could not be appeased by a peace initiative, gestures of brotherhood, and a reduction in the objectives of the Zionist movement. Rather it was deemed necessary to strengthen the Zionist position in Palestine. To this end, the Sixteenth Zionist Congress, meeting in Zurich from 28 July to 10 August 1929, moved to expand the Jewish Agency—the governing body of Zionist endeavors in Palestine—to include non-Zionists so as to rally world Jewry to support the upbuilding of the Jewish National Home. To the Arabs of Palestine the expansion of the Jewish Agency evoked the specter of a worldwide Jewish plot to deny them their country. On 28 August 1929, in direct response the Arab leadership staged a massive demonstration in Jerusalem. The atmosphere was already charged with a mounting tension over disputed rights to the Western Wall,[1] and the demonstration quickly erupted into a violent rampage against the Jews which spread throughout the country. The most vicious attacks were against the ancient centers of Jewish piety in Hebron (24 August) and Safed (28 August). In all 133 Jews were killed and 440 wounded.[2]

Speaking to a Berlin chapter of Brith Shalom two months after the Arab riots,[3] Buber called upon his fellow Zionists to restrain their emotions and justifiable outrage, and to regain a sober political perspective on the horrible events from the broad context of the Arab-Jewish conflict in Palestine. In the ensuing discourse he develops one of his most systematic treatments of the problem.

Notes

1. See the introduction to the next selection, "The Wailing Wall."
2. Although there were incidents of Jewish reprisals, most of the Arab casualties—116 killed and 232 wounded—were inflicted by British troops and police.

3. On the activities of Brith Shalom in Berlin, see Jehuda Reinharz, ed., *Dokumente zur Geschichte des deutschen Zionismus: 1882–1933* (Tübingen: J. C. B. Mohr, 1981), pp. 426–30.

THE NATIONAL HOME AND NATIONAL POLICY IN PALESTINE

It gives me much pleasure to speak to you here at the invitation of Brith Shalom, mainly because I regard Brith Shalom—significantly calling itself "Covenant for Peace"—as a manifestation, irrespective of the size of its membership, of the fact that Judaism intends to take its ideal of peace seriously, for the first time presenting Judaism as a community which has an opportunity to put this ideal into practice in the reality of politics. Beyond all official declarations, beyond all Messianism, beyond all proclamations of peace on earth, there exists a here and now where Judaism can translate its great idea of peace, first proclaimed by its prophets, into the reality of its life and deeds. That is how I understand "Brith Shalom," and this is why I gladly accepted its invitation [to address you]. I wish to add, though, that I am speaking entirely for myself. This group has no firm program. It indicates a direction, not a theoretical one, but a roadsign for common action in which each individual thinks for himself.

Let me say a word about this present moment at which I am speaking. In recent weeks, whenever I somehow mentioned to others what I want to say to you, I often heard the objection that at this hour, this difficult hour for the Jewish people, we have every right to react emotionally: that it is inadmissible to talk of convenants while we are mourning. And I am being asked whether it is not callous opportunism to speak, above and beyond emotional reaction, beyond the essential duty of this moment, about the need for a convenant [with the Arabs]. Well, nobody can deny us the right to an emotional response, and I dare say that we who are speaking to you here so earnestly did not experience less intensely than any of our critics [the pogroms at] Hebron and Safed with our whole being, and that it is not a matter of sensitivity or lack of it, but whether we—having gone through what had to be experienced—are now aware that this is an hour of decision.

And that this decision must be considered unemotionally, not due to a lack of feeling, but because it is necessary to exercise restraint over one's soul. My personal views on the subject of my talk here have not been influenced by that hour. I have changed in many respect over the past decade; but my opinion on this matter, on our relations with the Arab people, has not changed. This is not a consistency which gives me joy, rather it causes me great anguish. Therefore I feel compelled to refute the charge of opportunism, although there exists a kind of opportunism to which I subscribe, that which consists in simultaneously keeping in view both the ideal and the temporary situation, in not allowing one's view of the ideal to be dimmed by the situation, nor one's view of the situation by the ideal: one's view of the ideal should not be debased as dogmatism, nor should one's view of the temporary situation be perverted by the dictates of mere expedience. If you wish to call this "double view" of reality opportunism, then I plead guilty of it.

It is necessary to consider first of all what Judaism has to do with Palestine. First, the problem of the relations between the Jews and the Arabs in Palestine can be understood only if it is considered against the background of the close connection between the Jewish nation and Palestine. We who have been considered by others to have betrayed the national ideal feel more than other sections of the Zionist movement that this connection between the Land of Israel and the people of Israel is a historical fact and even more, and that the connection is of supreme importance. And we maintain that this cannot be expressed by a national-economic formula. It is unjust to speak in the same terms about this nation and this land and the interrelations between them that are used for ordinary nationalism, for this is an exceptional case, where the accepted ideas are irrelevant. Our position rests on this uniqueness. The Jewish nation remained in existence in opposition to the laws of history because it was the organic bearer of a mission, which it bore not consciously or willingly, but by its very existence; it is the mission for which it was created and by which it lives. The view that a belief in a mission is not the empty consolation of the masses, comforting them for the fact of our dispersion, but something on which our very existence depends, is the underlying motif of what we call Zionism. One thing can be said about this undefinable task: it cannot be maintained by a spiritual undertaking but only through the life we live, and not by the individual's life but through the life of the community. The fulfillment of this task includes, therefore, the creation of a society which establishes a way of life for itself in the country where this task is closely and organically connected with the nation, just as it has been since this nation came into existence as a result of this task.

Not so long ago the yearning for Zion was expressed in the defined and delimited form of the labor of re-settling Palestine. This labor had a double implication: the revival of national life and, at the same time, the inception of the fulfillment of a task, which was indissolubly connected with national revival. Anyone who regards our undertaking as one of [pioneering] settlement in Palestine simply in order to maintain our existence ignores the uniqueness of our activities. This misconception of our task may have grave repercussions.

Zionism affirms the right of the Jewish nation to return to its country and put down roots there. This requires explanation, and we are obliged to delineate our threefold right [to the Land of Israel].

The first right rests on the ancient link between us and the Land. This right differs from what is customarily called our "historic right." A historic right in this overall sense does not exist at all: every chapter in world history which is used as an authority for justifying a given right was preceded by another chapter, which in turn can support a different right. Consequently, it is impossible to claim a right in terms of time. Would not the remnants of those ancient peoples which were dispossessed by the Israelites have the right to question our "historic right?" The ancient link to which I refer is something totally different. What I mean is something evolved from that link, not that complex which we call "culture"—even if it is of an extremely high level, "culture" is no more than one of the various objects which have been the property of nations since the world began. What I am referring to is and will always be a perpetual good for all of humankind; and anyone who recognizes this will also acknowledge our right.

Our second right rests on a proven fact: after thousands of years in which the country was a wasteland, we have transformed it into a settled country, where it was open to us to do so, by years of labor. The right deriving from creation and fertilization is in fact the right of settlers. The historical approach which rules in these times regards historical events such as the distribution of forces and their influence, the clash of ordered armies, as indisputable proof. This perspective, however, is by no means adequate. Obviously, it is impossible to do anything of historical importance without "power," that is, without the ability to do whatever it is you want to do. However, this is vastly different from that superior power which has been held in such high esteem by contemporary political historians. The vital aspect of the great situations in history has not been which side has "more" power when forces clash with one another, but who has a certain ability to conquer the confusion of the situation and the period after it, who can fulfill the hidden requirements. There are victories which are the outcome of physical superiority alone, but these invariably end in chaos. The right of settlement in Palestine belongs to those who are able to cope with a specific settlement situation. And let us state quite openly that the situation of our settlement includes the lives of the Arab inhabitants of the country, whom we do not intend to expel, and that therefore we must include them in our undertaking if we really wish to conquer the specific confusion which exists here.

The third right applies to the future. The activities which we have begun in Palestine are not directed toward creating just another small nation in the family of nations, another tiny people in the world of peoples, another creature to jump and intervene in world disputes. No, our aim is to start something new, to begin the fulfillment of a task. Within the small groups which exist in our Palestine something is being quietly created which hints at the establishment of a new type of individuals, people who will bear the burden of fulfilling an ancient purpose, leading to the revival to which the Jews have borne witness and which they have bestowed on all nations. It is an error to regard these attempts at communal living merely as an experiment; for these attempts, which will probably give rise to a new kind of society, are, in my opinion, more important than the vast Russian experiment, which must inevitably end in political centralization. Even those who regard these communities as romantically utopian have themselves been blinded by contemporary doctrines, since more than anywhere else in the world, in these Palestine *kibbutzim* there is a healthy realism. And let us not be blinded or struck dumb by the abstract concept of realism which derides all spiritual romanticism and adheres to concrete facts only. More than anywhere else in the world there is here a topos—a place where there is a concrete social transformation, not of institutions and organizations, but of interpersonal relations. At the same time, roots are being struck in the land of the ancient, chosen homeland. The social revolution, however, is an indispensable precondition for this striking of roots.

Something is being created here which is of unprecedented importance, an example for all mankind marking out the path for it, by trial and error, and even by missing the way from time to time. We thereby demand justice, in the fullest sense of the word, from humanity, provided it is aware of its real troubles and its genuine needs.

We are now faced, however, with the added responsibility for that nation which has become our neighbour in Palestine and which in so many respects shares a common fate with us. No contradiction could be greater, if we continue to preserve the idea of our internal mission, than for us to build a true communal life within our own community, while at the same time excluding the other inhabitants of the country from participation, even though their lives and hopes, like ours, are dependent upon the future of the country.

. . . It is said that when the Zionist leader Max Nordau first heard that there were Arabs in Palestine, he rushed excitedly to Herzl proclaiming: "I didn't know that! If that is the case, then we are doing an injustice." In recent years it has sometimes happened that I heard people who generally support Nordau's ideas maintain: "Life cannot exist without injustice; anyone who is not prepared to commit injustice is forced to deny his own existence. As regards a nation—it is inconceivable that a nation should behave in such a manner!"

It is indeed true that there can be no life without injustice. The fact that there is no living creature which can live and thrive without destroying another existing organism has a symbolic significance as regards our human life. But the *human* aspect of life begins the moment we say to ourselves: we will do not more injustice to others than we are forced to do in order to exist. Only by saying that do we begin to be responsible for life. This responsibility is not a matter of principle and is never fixed; the extent of the injustice that cannot be determined beforehand but must be reassessed each time, must be recognized anew in the inner recesses of the mind, whence the lightning of recognition flashes forth. Only he who acknowledges it, as the result of serious examination which leaves no room for pricks of conscience, only he can live a human life; and a nation that does so—its life is that of a humanitarian nation. The group's responsibility for life is not qualitatively different from that of the individual; for if this were not the case the members of the group would truly fulfill their responsibility only as individuals. The collective element within them would necessarily oppose the individual aspect within them, and would undermine and even destroy it; anyone who is [morally] severe with himself as an individual and lenient with himself as a member of a group will eventually, whether consciously or not, falter when he has to fulfill personal responsibility.

Every responsible relationship between an individual and his fellow begins through the power of a genuine imagination, as if we were the residents of Palestine and the others were the immigrants who were coming into the country in increasing numbers, year by year, taking it away from us. How would we react to events? Only if we know this will it be possible to minimize the injustice we must do in order to survive and to live the life which we are not only entitled but obliged to live, since we live for the eternal mission, which has been imbedded within us since our creation.

. . . Our relations with the Arabs ought to be developed positively in every respect. Economically, by developing a practical community of interests and not, as we have done all the time, by giving assurances of an existing solidarity of interests. Everywhere and at all times when economic decisions have to be taken, the interest of the Arab people should be taken into account. This has not been done often enough. Everybody who knows the situation is aware of the many opportunities that have been missed.

As regards internal policy: it was a matter of establishing a combination between national independence and possible coexistence—what is called a bi-national state. The question of the political representation of the [two] peoples would mean the first stage in the institution of the idea. It is a terribly difficult decision that has confronted us these many years, but we have evaded it. You will ask whether we are sufficiently mature to make this decision. I believe so. If we were to assure the Arab people that we are demanding popular representation together with them, our right to exist would of necessity be safeguarded. This means that a parliament can only be established with the consent of both peoples on the basis of a Magna Carta, of a primary constitution guaranteed by the competent authorities of the world, securing our as well as the Arabs' basic rights, i.e., above all the right to immigrate [to Palestine]. There may be many who think otherwise. To me it is a question of a parliament, and that this matter of life or death cannot simply be decided by a majority.

As regards external policy: I remember having raised—in 1921 in the Political Commission of the Twelfth Congress—the question whether we should not take into consideration the beginnings of a development toward an alliance between us and the Arab states; whether we should not include in our perspective also this possibility. At the time, I was told by a competent source that this was not an actual possibility. I do not want to investigate how actual it has become now, but it seems beyond doubt that in our policy and calculations, as well as in our discussions and negotiations, we must declare unambiguously that we would not stand in the way of such a development, that we would not be the forerunners of any power that would wish to prevent it.

As to the question of religion: Islam is a much greater reality than we would wish to admit. It is our duty to get to know this reality. I must confess to you that the present religious reality of Judaism is less evident to me. I mean to say that the Arab population is much more strongly conditioned by Islam than the Jews in general are by Judaism. Religion for the Arabs is also a matter of culture; hence we have been remiss in not acquainting ourselves with Islam and in establishing contacts with its religious authorities. In Palestine I have often observed that Jews who are conversant with Islam are beloved and honored by the Arabs. But there are only a handful of such Jews. The prime necessity for personal contact is a knowledge of the Arabic language. Mutual understanding is only possible through language. As far as socializing is concerned, surely there are social contacts between Jewish and Arab villages, which even take very beautiful, genuine oriental forms. But in the towns there exists much less genuine social intercourse between the two peoples. The situation is better in proletarian circles; but real socializing between Arabs and Jews is still the exception. In this context the cultural question is relevant. Nationally there can be no merging of cultures, but there could be a cultural accommodation with Arabism as a whole, cultural exchange in educational institutions, exchange of cultural values and achievements, real cooperation.

. . . It especially disgusts me when people speak against the politics of mutual understanding in the name of "National Pride." True national pride would logically bring us closer to the Arabs, for it is only on the basis of agreement with them that we can expand and assure our enterprise—building up the land—whose guarantee is our national honor. What distances us from the Arabs is our national arrogance.

A few years ago I spoke about the Arab question with the director of a great cultural institution of the Yishuv. The man spoke to approximately this effect: "You know me, and you know that I am no chauvanist, but—they are an inferior race." We are spoken of in similar terms in several parts of Europe. Who is right? As long as we have not imagined to ourselves the inner reality of a nation whose life is motivated by other factors and whose principles are different in nature from our own, as long as we do not come to know and understand what goes on in that nation's heart of hearts, and what is expressed by those factors and principles, we shall always consider what is different as inferior. The inner reality of every nation has its own value, and any external criterion by which you come to judge it can only be erroneous.

. . . The Closed-minded attitudes inform the dominant type of nationalism, which has gained so many adherents among us—the most worthless assimilation—it teaches that everyone must consider his own nation as an absolute and all other nations as something relative; that one must evaluate one's own nation on the basis of its greatest era, and all other nations on the basis of their lowest points. If this idea continues to gain acceptance it will lead to a worldwide disaster.

The open-minded attitude of humanitarian nationalism, which claims supporters from our midst who have been "fighting for the Arabs" as long as Zionism has been a political doctrine, demands of us that we judge other nations as we would wish to be judged ourselves, not by our own basest deeds, nor by our greatest acts, but by those which are characteristic of us, which reflect our character. Only a system of this nature can educate mankind, guaranteeing its stand in face of the dangers which are likely to assail it in the generation to come, and which no words can express.

Assuredly there are many aspects of the Palestinian Arabs which are annoying to us (just as there are things in us which, in certain respects, are displeasing to me); but we must not ignore the fact that among them the connection with the land—something which will take us a long time still to accomplish—has taken a positive, even organic, form; it is an accepted fact which is no longer even considered. They, not we, have something which can be called a Palestinian style; the huts of the village *fellahin* have grown out of this earth, while the houses of Tel Aviv were built on its back. The prostration of Abraham the Patriarch when he invited the passers-by into his house can be seen still today, but not amongst us. . . .

There is another attitude which should be given greater attention by us than "national pride," and this is the essential point to which many of our workers faithfully hold.

This attitude is based upon the conception of Palestinian society as being divided into classes. It is claimed that the masters, the *effendis*, incite the proletarians, the *fellahin*, against us in order to divert their attention from the class-consciousness awakening among them, from their revolt against social suppression; the Arab nationalist movement is, therefore, an artificial creation, and should be evaluated as such. It is unjust on our part to negotiate with the *effendis*, who cannot be considered to be representatives of the nation; it is our duty, however, to pierce the unnatural front which they have established together with the proletariat, and we will achieve this by making the proletariat aware of their class and uniting them in a socialist front which includes members of both nations. Then they will no longer be led astray by nationalist slogans.

It cannot be disputed that this second attitude does embody an important element of the truth, and that those things which it upholds are of the utmost importance, both now and in the future: cooperation between the two bodies of workers, the enhancement of the organizations and institutions of the Arab proletariat, and the influence of socialist education. But this view also embodies an oversimplification without an adequate basis in fact.

First of all, we must make it clear to ourselves that the nature of things is such that the class-consciousness of the Arab masses will develop very slowly and that it will need far more time to develop than has their national awareness, part of which is nothing but old religious fanaticism in a new guise. The socialist process is indeed preferable from the standpoint of feasibility, but the political process is preferable as regards the pace, and in the prevailing circumstances this is of supreme importance for us.

Moreover, the idea that the Arab nationalist movement in Palestine is artificial is basically unsound. In discussing this from a historical point of view, beginning with the development of the concept of Arab independence, which takes on different forms according to the political conditions in each country and conducts each battle differently, one reaches the conclusion that the internal revolution which has taken place in Palestine [among the Arab population] is only one expression of this general movement. We have our *effendis,* not only since the establishment of the expanded Jewish Agency, but since the rise of Zionism, which rests on the alliance between the Jewish bourgeoisie and proletariat. We know that despite this alliance we have a genuine national unity and real nationalist movement; why should we assume that these do not exist among the Arabs? It is true that in general our *effendis* in Palestine do not evince the tendency of their Arab counterparts to undermine society through class-warfare; but are not their feelings of social egoism accompanied by a measure of national enthusiasm? Have we not seen, alongside those shadow figures, honest national politicians who will eventually weaken the position of the former?

I do not know of any political activity more harmful than regarding one's ally or opponent as if he were cast in one fixed mold. When we consider him as "like that," we fall victim to the irrationality of his existence; only when we pay attention to the fact that human nature is much the same all over the world will be be able to come to grips with reality.

We have not settled Palestine together with the Arabs but alongside them. Settlement "alongside" [*neben*], when two nations inhabit the same country, which fails to become settlement "together with" [*mit*] must necessarily become a state of "against." This is bound to happen here—and there will be no return to a mere "alongside." But despite all the obstacles in our path, the way is still open for reaching a settlement "together with." And I do not know how much time is left to us. What I do know is that if we do not attain [such a relationship with the Arabs of Palestine], we will never realize the aims of Zionism. We are being put to the test for the third time in this country.

14

The Wailing Wall

(October 1929)

(Editor's prefatory note:)

From the start, the Arab-Jewish conflict in Palestine was exacerbated by an intermingling of national and religious sentiments. The focus of these sentiments was Jerusalem, in particular the Wailing Wall. Abutting the Temple Mount, the site of the Biblical Temples of the Lord, the Wailing Wall (or Western Wall) is the last remaining vestige of Israel's ancient glory. Since the destruction of the Temple in 70 C. E., Jews the world over have made pilgrimage to the Wall—Judaism's most sacred site—to bewail the fate of Israel and to offer prayers. The Wailing Wall area is also revered by Islam, for on the ruins of the Temple, the Muslims built two of their most sacred shrines, the Dome of the Rock and the al-Aqsa mosque.

With the British conquest of Palestine, Jews, not necessarily Zionists, sought to enhance their rights of worship at the Wailing Wall—rights considerably curtailed in the previous century by the Ottoman rulers. These attempts to reassert the Jewish presence at the Wailing Wall corroborated Muslim fears that Zionism was not only intent on changing the demographic and national status of the country, but was plotting to remove the Muslims from the Temple Mount and to rebuild Solomon's edifice to God. From September 1928, the Supreme Muslim Council of Palestine conducted an energetic and systematic campaign to alert the Islamic world to the alleged Zionist threat to the Muslim holy places. The issue of the Wall thus gave the struggle against Zionism a religious dimension, which faciliated the enlistment of the urban and rural masses which had hitherto been little affected by the secular slogans of the Arab intelligentsia.[1] In order to underscore the volatile nature of the situation and force the Mandatory government to restrict the Jewish presence at the Wall, the Supreme Muslim Council initiated in May 1929 a variety of steps to disturb the Jewish prayer service at the Wall. The Betar Zionist youth movement, which was associated with the Revisionists, responded to the provocation. On 16 August 1929, *Tisha b'Av*, the day of mourning which commemorates the destruction of the Temple, Betar staged a demonstration at the Wall which concluded with the singing of *Ha-Tikvah*, the Zionist anthem. The following day the Muslims held a huge counter-demonstration at the Wall.

At the time it was the common perception that the Betar demonstration and the Muslim counter-demonstration led to the Arab riots against the Jews which broke out on August 28th.[2] This perception is shared by Buber in the following article, which was actually an excursus to the speech he delivered at the Berlin chapter of Brith Shalom in October 1929. (See the previous selection.) Statements like Buber's and similar ones by other members of Brith Shalom emphasizing Jewish blame were regarded by most Zionists as politically imprudent and, moreover, offensive to Jewish sensibilities.[3]

Notes

1. Y. Porath, *The Emergence of the Palestinian-Arab National Movement, 1918–1919* (London: Frank Cass, 1974), p. 266.

2. Contemporary scholarship tends to discount any connection between the Betar demonstration and the subsequent Arab riots, noting that "the bloody outbreaks occurred a week [after the Betar demonstration] and not necessarily in response to [it]." *Ibid.*, p. 269.

3. While not denying the validity of their charges of Jewish blame, Buber and the others acknowledged the poor timing of these statements which deepened their isolation within the Zionist movement, and in effect led to the demise of Brith Shalom. Cf. A. Kedar, "The World Views of Brith Shalom," in Ben-Zion Yehoshua and A. Kedar, eds., *Zionist Ideology and Policy* (Jerusalem: Zalman Shazar Centre, 1978), pp. 107 ff. (Hebrew).

THE WAILING WALL

. . . Alas, it has transpired that in any fundamental sense, we have not lived nor do we now live "together *with*" the Arabs, but merely "alongside" them. And the consequence of this situation is that this "alongside" [*neben*] had been rendered an "against" [*gegen*]. Had we been prepared to live in genuine togetherness [*Miteinanderleben*] with the Arabs, the latest events would not have been possible.

We must now examine the issue which provided the immediate occasion for these events [the Arab riots of August 1929], namely the question of the Wailing Wall. The "alongside" has been rendered an "against," and we are not free from blame for the fact that this "against" found expression in the form of religious fanaticism. I trust you know that the Wailing Wall means a great deal to me, and I may assume you know that I appreciate the significance of the Wailing Wall [to Judaism]. Yet during the past months I have witnessed the desecration of the Wailing Wall not only by an Arab mob, but also its desecration by a misguided part of our youth who made it an object of nationalist propaganda and demonstrations. And for such the Wailing Wall is, to say the least, most inappropriate. The Wailing Wall is the concern of those who revere the memory of the Temple and who pray for its restoration. When a nationalist front is formed around the Wailing Wall, it is a false front desecrating it. While on the Arab side it appeared that the front was formed by genuine believers in [what they held to be] a holy cause, the front on our side seemed to consist of both believers and non-believers. It has rightly been said that we fell into a trap, that we let ourselves be exploited to the misuse of a holy shrine. And perhaps we ourselves provided the motive for the religious fanaticism of the [Arab] masses. This is not said to exonerate the British government. There can be no differences of opinion about the ineptitude, the injustice, and the irresponsibility of the British government and its representatives.

I need not describe the situation in Palestine to you. It is as it is. In the face of this situation we are asking ourselves: what is to be done? I have no panacea to offer. Nobody, I dare say, has one. Let's face the bitter truth: we got ourselves into a quagmire. But something can still be done. At this moment perhaps nothing but the first steps toward the great effort needed to extricate ourselves. Please don't exclaim that this is too little. It's the "little things" that must be done. Permit me to mention two. First, the most urgent one: the death sentences [against the Arabs convicted of murder in the recent riots] must be commuted, and we Zionists, we Jews, must intervene. We have no jurisdiction in this matter, but we must demonstrate, we must tell the world that we demand that the death sentences pronounced for our sake, for the crimes committed against us, must not be carried out. Not just a part of the Jewish people but their leaders must intervene. Second, the question of the Wailing Wall must become the subject of negotiations between both camps. Hitherto this has not occurred. By "both camps" I do not mean the population of Palestine and ourselves, but Islam and Judaism. Those are the parties who should talk with one another. For the matter at stake is a place which is sacred to both religions, it is

matter of finding a solution for this difficult question by trying first of
all to discuss it while sitting at one table. This is not up to the English,
it is up to us. It is up to us to appoint representatives. This is an
endeavor that must be initiated by us. And should we succeed in reaching an agreement on the Wailing Wall, then we would have made a
first and significant step. To be sure, it will not be a Locarno Pact,[1] but
nonetheless a step on the road toward a comprehensive solution [of the
conflict between Zionism and the Arab National movement].

Note

1. The Locarno Pact (1925) concluded a conference held at Locarno, Switzerland,
by the representatives of England, Germany, Italy, Belgium, Czechoslovakia, France,
and Poland. It comprised a series of separate treaties of mutual guarantees and arbi-
tration of the outstanding issues that still divided these nations after the First World
War. The "spirit of Locarno" symbolized hopes for an era of international peace and
good will.

15

Hans Kohn:
"Zionism Is Not Judaism."

(November 1929)

(Editor's prefatory note:)

The ferocity and extent of the Arab riots of August 1929 led many Zionists
to the realization that the conflict with the Arabs would be increasingly, perhaps unavoidably, violent. The relatively peaceful atmosphere that prevailed
in the 1920s in Palestine was now seen as the quiet before the storm. A mood
of pessimism gripped the Zionist movement. For some the realization that
the Zionist endeavor would be accompanied by violence was traumatic.

For Hans Kohn (1891–1971), one of Buber's closest disciples and friends, the riots of 1929 brought to a head his years of moral torment over the direction that Zionism was taking. Kohn had been a devoted Zionist since 1909, when he joined the Bar Kochba students' circle in Prague (together with *inter alios* S.H. Bergman, Robert Weltsch, and Franz Kafka). In 1925 he settled in Palestine to become one of the directors of *Keren Hayesod* (the Palestine Foundation Fund), the financial arm of the World Zionist Organization. A founding member of Brith Shalom, he was a prolific publicist, particularly engaged in the problems of nationalism and the Arab question. His first important theoretical statement on nationalism, published in *Der Jude* in 1922, was dedicated to Martin Buber. In this essay, entitled "Nationalism,"[1] Kohn avers that in the nineteenth century nationalism had become the handmaiden of state politics, and thus virtually identical with "the attachment of a sovereign people to a specific territory that is owned and possessed." Gradually, but especially since the purgatory of the First World War, nationalism was being freed from its enslavement to the idea of the nation state, and we were then capable of distinguishing between state-nationalism and nationalism as a cultural and moral sensibility. Among the Jews, Kohn observes, "Martin Buber gave form and expression to this movement. With the deep awareness and the painful isolation of the Jew, this movement found a clearer and more powerful utterance. Jewish fervor and Messianic responsibility imbued the concept of nationalism. . . . Jewish nationalism was brought before the tribunal of moral words, of eternity; it found its justification as a link in world redemption. It was not a camouflage for state needs and collective power aspirations; spiritual necessity alone drove it. . . . [The] ethical stature of a nation is independent of the play of interest conflicts, of the vain delusion of political independence. Nationalism reaches for the stars here [in the thought of Buber]."

Clearly the prospect of ceaseless conflict with the Arabs, and especially that of armed Jewish resistance and even punitive retaliation against the Arabs (as occurred during the riots of 1929), radically compromised Kohn's vision of Zionism as an ethical and meta-political force. Hence, Kohn resolved to leave the Zionist movement. In a series of letters to Buber he outlined his reasons: "The events in Palestine are very distressing. We all are guilty, for we should never have let it come to that."[2] "You are so lucky not to see the details of Palestinian and Zionist reality, but Zionism *as it is today* . . . is unacceptable. . . . I am not concerned about Ishmael, only about Isaac, that is, our aims, our life, our actions. I am afraid what we support we cannot vouch for. And because of false solidarity we shall sink deeper into the quagmire. Either Zionism will be pacific or else it will be without me. *Zionism* is not *Judaism*."[3] His most elaborate explanation for his resignation was addressed to Berthold Feiwel (1875–1937), a mutual friend of his and Buber's and one of the directors of *Keren Hayesod*. Kohn sent a copy of the letter, reproduced here, to Buber.[4]

Notes

1. H. Kohn, "Nationalismus," *Der Jude*, vol. 6 (1921–1922), pp. 674–86; trans. in Arthur A. Cohen, ed., *The Jew: Essays from Martin Buber's Journal "Der Jude," 1916–1928* (University, Alabama: The University of Alabama Press, 1980), pp. 20–30.

2. Buber, *Briefwechsel*, vol. 2, p. 345 (letter dated 26 August 1929).

3. *Ibid.*, vol. 2, p. 351 (letter dated 25 September 1929).

4. For a complete translation of this letter, see Aharon Kedar, "Brith Shalom," *The Jerusalem Quarterly* 18 (Winter 1981), 78–82.

HANS KOHN: "ZIONISM IS NOT JUDAISM."

Jerusalem
21 November 1929

Dear Dr. Feiwel:

. . . Lately I have become increasingly aware that the official policy of the Zionist Organization and the opinion of the vast majority of Zionists are quite incompatible with my own convictions. I, therefore, feel that I can no longer remain a leading official within the Zionist Organization. The Zionism championed by me since 1909 was at no time political. I and a group of my friends regarded Zionism as a moral-*cum*-spiritual movement within which we could realize our most fundamental humane convictions: our pacifism, liberalism, and humanism. It has often been argued that we [Jews] could not unreservedly sponsor pacifism or ethical politics among the European peoples, since this would result in our being regarded as aliens and traitors. Zion was to be the place where we would be able to realize our humanitarian aspirations.

The reality of the Zionist movement and of Jewish settlement in Palestine is far from all this. You know that for years I have been fighting the battle for those ideas which to me had been the very meaning of Zionism. Eventually these ideas gained focus in the so-called Arab question. For me this question became the [moral] touchstone of Zionism. This conclusion was, however, not prompted by any particular sympathy for the Arabs. . . . I was not concerned with the Arabs but with the Jews, their Jewishness, and the confirmation of their humane [values]. It has, alas, become increasingly clear to me that in this respect the Zionist Organization has failed utterly. The decisive experience was the Arab national uprising of August 1929. Such events are eye-openers and call for decisions, the urgency of which we fail to appreciate in "normal times," although they are just as vital even then. In the midst of this crisis, it was still possible to turn over a new leaf and to adopt a fresh attitude after the [initial] shock: to reappraise the moral and spiritual foundations of Zionism and to attempt a new solution [to the Arab question]. This opportunity has been missed. The overwhelming majority of Zionists feel justified in pursuing a course which I cannot follow. For the few who think like me, the need for an honest and clear decision has arrived.

As a Jew and a human being, as a Jewish human being—two qualities which in me are inseparable and parallel—I am a pacifist, an anti-imperialist, and what in America is called a radical. I am emphasizing these three points only because they are called into question by the official Zionist policy. I cannot concur with this policy when the Arab national movement is being portrayed as the wanton agitation of a few big landowners. I know all too well that frequently the most reactionary imperialist press in England and France portrays the national movements in India, Egypt, and China in a similar fashion—in short, wherever the national movements of oppressed peoples threaten the interests of the colonial power. I know how false and hypocritical this portrayal is. I can even less be a party to this approach when such is the attitude of a people which consciously regards itself as a chosen people, and when the future of a movement, the Zionist movement, which I can only envisage if it is built on ethical foundations, is at stake. The means determine the goal. If lies and violence are the means, the results cannot be good.

We pretend to be innocent victims. Of course the Arabs attacked us in August. Since they have no armies, they could not obey the rules of war. They perpetrated all the barbaric acts that are characteristic of a colonial revolt. But we are obliged to look into the deeper cause of this revolt. We have been in Palestine for twelve years [i.e., since the establishment of the British Mandate and Jewish National Home in

Palestine] without having even once made a serious attempt at seeking through negotiations the consent of the indigenous people. We have been relying exclusively upon Great Britain's military might. We have set ourselves goals which by their very nature had to lead to conflict with the Arabs. We ought to have recognized that these goals would be the cause, the just cause, of a national uprising against us. . . . Having come to this country [as immigrants], we were duty bound to come up with constitutional proposals which, without doing serious harm to Arab rights and liberty, would have also allowed for our free cultural and social development. But for twelve years we pretended that the Arabs did not exist and were glad when we were not reminded of their existence.

. . . The Arab riots, which were suppressed by the British, should have been met as quickly as possible by peace proposals instead of evasive manoeuvres. That was our duty! But just like the the powers in the [First] World War, we have declared that we would gladly make peace if only we were strong enough. That means that we are seeking a victorious peace just as they were—a peace whereby the opponent does what we want. Naturally each party wants peace on the condition that he can obtain what he considers essential, not, however, a higher forum and not a more lofty conscience. . . . It was against this attitude taken by the powers in the [First] World War and against this point of view that the true pacifists rebelled. I would be glad if we also had a few such pacifists among our ranks. If only the Jews could show such courage in their own affairs as was demonstrated, for example, by the English pacifists in the World War.

Each delay in the signing of a peace treaty renders peace more difficult by widening the gap between the two peoples. The Arab national movement is growing and will continue to grow. In a short time it will be much more difficult for us to reach an agreement than it is today. Increasing our numbers by tens of thousands will not make it any easier. I believe that it will be possible for us to hold Palestine and continue to grow for a long time. This will be done first with British aid and then later with the help of our own bayonets—shamefully called *Haganah* [i.e., defense]—clearly because we have no faith in our own policy. But by that time we will not be able to do without the bayonets. The means will have determined the goal. Jewish Palestine will no longer have anything of that Zion for which I once put myself on the line.

... This letter is only meant for you. It requires no answer. It deals with questions which each individual must ultimately answer for himself. My resignation from *Keren Ha-Yesod* closes an era of my life. Twenty years spent exclusively in Zionist activity, ten of them in *Keren Ha-Yesod*, is no small part of a human life. One is accountable both to himself and to his friends for such a period. I have written to you about the road which I have now placed behind me. I still know very little about the road ahead of me. The old beaten paths of national policy as they were followed by the European peoples in the nineteenth century, the Eastern peoples in the twentieth century, and now by the Jewish people, are for me no longer valid. We must search for completely new and different paths. Sometimes I still retain a proud hope that the Jews—nationally conscious Jews—might forge these new paths. ...

With most cordial wishes and greetings,

Faithfully yours,

Hans Kohn

16

And If Not Now, When?

(July 1932)

(Editor's prefactory note:)

Kohn's resignation from the Zionist movement posed a profound challenge to Buber's own Zionism. He regarded Kohn as one of his most talented and devoted disciples within the movement. Indeed, on the eve of his resignation, Kohn was completing a monumental biography of Buber: *Martin Buber: Sein Werk und seine Zeit* (1930).[1] In this nuanced and still unsurpassed study, which traces Buber's intellectual development through the first three decades of the twentieth century, Kohn presented Buber's struggle to shape Zionist policy as the practical reflex of his philosophical and religious teachings. In his letters to Buber and Feiwel justifying his decision to leave Zionism, Kohn by implication suggested that this struggle was in vain, and that his critique of the Zionist reality was consonant with, indeed, demanded by Buber's own teachings.

Buber's response to Kohn is unfortunately not accessible.[2] We may, however, view the following article—an address to a convention of Jewish youth in Antwerp in July 1932—as containing Buber's answer to what in a letter to his wife he elliptically referred to as Kohn's moral "doctrinarism."[3] In this essay Buber cites the French critic Julien Benda's treatise, *The Betrayal of the Intellectuals*, in which it was argued that Western society had lost its moral clarity because intellectuals have become increasingly involved in the compromising realm of politics. As the custodians of moral and spiritual truths, Benda held, the intellectuals *(clercs)* should withdraw from the mundane world of politics and return to the cloisters of pure spirit, therein to pursue truth.[4] Buber argues that such an approach is tantamount to abandoning the mundane to the rule of the amoral and cynical—and *this* would be the ultimate betrayal of the intellectuals. For "he who hears the voice [of God] and sets a limit to the area beyond which its rule shall not extend is not merely moving away from God, like the person who refuses to listen; he is standing up directly against him." To be sure, the mundane order resists spiritual and moral truth, but the intellectual *(der Geistige)*—the spokesman of these truths—does not wait for the messianic hour when the world would be fully amenable to "the truth of God." The intellectual accepts the given historical reality, befuddled as it is by politics, violence, and mistrust, and cognizant that he is destined to repeated disappointment and defeat, persistently seeks to embody the truth of God in the real world—"And if not now, when?"[5]

Notes

1. A second edition, with an epilogue by Rober Weltsch covering the period 1930–60, was published in 1961 by Joseph Melzer Verlag, Colonge.

2. Kohn's archives, which are located in the Leo Baeck Institute in New York, are by order of his will closed until 1990.

3. Buber, *Briefwechsel*, vol. 2, p. 353. In this letter, dated 3 October 1929, Buber mildly criticizes Kohn for being given more to "declarations than to the actual blazing of trails through the thicket of reality."

4. *The Betrayal of the Intellectuals (La trahison des clercs*, Paris, 1927) trans. R. Aldington (Boston: Beacon Press, 1955).

5. Ethics of the Fathers, 1:14.

AND IF NOT NOW, WHEN?

We are living in an age of the depreciation of words. The intellect with its gift for language has been all too willing to put itself at the disposal of whatever trends prevail at the time. Instead of letting the word grow out of the thought in responsible silence, the intellect has manufactured words for every demand with almost mechanical skill. It is not only the intellectuals, who are now finding a suspicious reception for their disquisitions, who must suffer for this "betrayal."[1] What is worse is that their audience, above all the entire younger generation of our time, is deprived of the noblest happiness of youth: the happiness of believing in the spirit. It is easily understood that many of them now see nothing but "ideologies" in intellectual patterns, nothing but pompous robes for very obvious group interests; that they are no longer willing to believe there is a truth over and above parties, above those who wield and are greedy for power. They tell us, tell one another, and tell themselves, that they are tired of being fed on lofty illusions, that they want to go back to a "natural" foundation, to unconcealed instincts, that the life of the individual as well as that of every people must be built up on simple self-assertion.

No matter what others may do, we, my friends, should not choose this way. If we really are Jews, meaning the bearers of a tradition and a task, we know what has been transmitted to us. We know that there is a truth which is the seal of God, and we know that the task we have been entrusted with is to let this one truth set its stamp on all the various facets of our life. We cannot own this truth, for it belongs to God. We ourselves cannot use the seal, but we can be the divers wax which takes the seal. Every individual is wax of a different form and color, but all are potentially receptive to the stamp of truth, for all of us, created "in the image of God," are potentially able to become images of the divine. We do not own the truth. But this does not mean that we must depend either on vain ideologies or on mere instincts, for every one of us has the possibility of entering into a real relationship to truth. Such a relationship, however, cannot grow out of thinking alone, for the ability to think is only one part of us; but neither is feeling enough. We can attain to such a relationship only through the undivided whole of our life as we live it. The intellect can be redeemed from its last lapse into sin, from the desecration of the word, only if the word is backed and vouched for with the whole of one's life. The betrayal of the intellectuals cannot be atoned for by the intellect's retreating into itself, but only by its proffering to reality true service in place of false. It must not serve the powers of the moment and what they call reality—not the short-lived semblance of truth. The intellect should serve the true great reality, whose function it is to embody the truth of God; it must serve. No matter how brilliant it may be, the human intellect which wishes to keep to a plane above the events of the day is not really alive. It can become frutiful, beget life, and live only when it enters into the events of the day without denying, but rather proving, its superior origin. Be true to the spirit, my friends, but be true to it on the plane of reality. Our first question must be: What is the truth? What has God commanded us to do? But our next must be: How can we accomplish it from where we are?

We shall accomplish nothing at all if we divide our world and our life into two domains: one in which God's command is paramount, the other governed exclusively by the laws of economics, politics, and the "simple self-assertion" of the group. Such dualism is far more ominous than the naturalism I spoke of before. Stopping one's ears so as not to hear the voice from above is breaking the connection between existence and the meaning of existence. But he who hears the voice and sets a limit to the area beyond which its rule shall not extend is not merely moving away from God, like the person who refuses to listen; he is standing up directly against him. The atheist does not know God, but the adherent of a form of ethics which ends where politics begin has the temerity to prescribe to God, whom he professes to know, how far his power may extend. The polytheists distribute life and the world among many powers. As far as they are concerned, Germany has one god and France another; there is a god of business, and a god of the state. Each of these domains has its own particular code of laws and is subject to no superior court. Western civilization professes one God and lives in polytheism. We Jews are connected to this civilization by thousands of strands, but if we share in its dualism of life and profession of faith, we shall forfeit our justification for living. if we were only one nation among others, we should long ago have perished from the earth. Paradoxically we exist only because we dared to be serious about the unity of God and his undivided, absolute sovereignty. If we give up God, he will give us up. And we do give him up when we profess him in synagogue and deny him when we come together for discussion, when we do his commands in our personal life, and set up other norms for the life of the group we belong to. What is wrong for the individual cannot be right for the community; for if it were, then God, the God of Sinai, would no longer be the Lord of peoples, but only of individuals. If we really are Jews, we believe that God gives his commands to men to observe throughout their whole life, and that whether or not life has a meaning depends on the fulfillment of those commands. And if we consult our deep inner knowledge about God's command to mankind, we shall not hesitate an instant to say that it is peace. There are many among us who think this command is intended for some more propitious future; for the present, we must participate in the universal war, in order to escape destruction. But it is only if we do participate in this war that we shall be destroyed; for as far as we are concerned, there is only one possible kind of destruction: God letting us slip out of his hand.

I frequently hear some among us saying: "We too want the spirit of Judaism to be fulfilled; we too want the Torah to issue forth from Zion, and we know that to realize this purpose the Torah must not be mere words, but actual life; we want God's word on Zion to become a reality. But this cannot happen until the world again has a Zion, and so first of all we want to build up Zion, and to build it—with every possible means." It may however be characteristic of Zion that it *cannot* be built with "every possible means," but only *bemishpat* (Isa. 1:27), only "with justice." It may be that God will refuse to receive his sanctuary from the hands of the devil. Suppose a man decided to steal and rob for six years, and, in the seventh, to build a temple with the fortune thus amassed; suppose he succeeded—would he really be rearing temple walls? Would he not rather be setting up a den of robbers (Jer. 7:11), or a robber's palace, on whose portals he dares to engrave the name of God? It is true that God does not build his own house. He wants us to build it with our human hands and our human strength, for "house" in this connection can mean only that at long last we may begin to live God's word on earth! But after we have laid the foundations of this house by his means, *bemishpat*, do you really imagine that God is not strong enough to let it be finished by those same means? If you do imagine that, stop talking about Judaism, Jewish spirit, and Jewish teachings! For Judaism is the teaching that there is really only One Power which, while at times it may permit the sham powers of the world to accomplish something in opposition to it, never permits such accomplishment to stand. But whatever is done in the service of that power, and done in such a way that not only the goal but the means to that goal are in accord with the spirit of justice, will survive, even though it may have to struggle for a time, and may seem in great peril, and weak compared to the effective sham powers.

I should like to bring a concept of the utmost importance home even to those who cannot or will not understand the language of religion, and, therefore, believe that I am discussing theology. I am speaking of the *reality of history.* In historical reality we do not set ourselves a righteous goal, choose whatever way to it an auspicious hour offers, and, following that way, reach the set goal. If the goal to be reached is like the goal which was set, then the nature of the way must be like the goal. A wrong way, i.e., a way in contradiction to the goal, must lead to a wrong goal. What is accomplished through lies can assume the mask of truth; what is accomplished through violence, can go in the guise of justice, and for a while the hoax may be successful. But soon people will realize that lies are lies at bottom, that in the final analysis, violence is violence, and both lies and violence will suffer the destiny history has in store for all that is false. I sometimes hear it said that a generation must sacrifice itself, "take the sin upon itself," so that coming generations may be free to live righteously. But it is self-delusion and folly to think that one can lead a dissolute life and raise one's children to be good and happy; they will usually turn out to be hypocrites or tormented.

History has much to teach us, but we must know how to receive her teaching. These temporary triumphs which are apt to catch our attention are nothing but the stage-setting for universal history. If we keep our eyes fixed on the foreground, the true victories, won in secret, sometimes look like defeats. True victories happen slowly and imperceptibly, but they have far-reaching effects. In the limelight, our faith that God is the Lord of history may sometimes appear ludicrous; but there is something secret in history which confirms our faith.

He who makes peace, our sages taught, is God's fellow worker. But addressing conciliatory words to others and occupying oneself with humane projects is not the way to make peace. We make peace, we help bring about world peace, if we make peace wherever we are destined and summoned to do so: in the active life of our own community and in that aspect of it which can actively help determine its relationship to another community. The prophecy of peace addressed to Israel is not valid only for the days of the coming of the Messiah. It holds for the day when the people will again be summoned to take part in shaping the destiny of its earliest home; it holds for today. "And if not now, when?" (Ethics of the Fathers, 1:14). Fulfillment in a Then is inextricably bound up with fulfillment in the Now.

Note

1. Cf. Julien Benda, *The Betrayal of the Intellectuals.*

17

Mohandas K. Gandhi: The Jews

(November 1938)

With the ascendancy of the Nazis Buber directed his attention to the affairs of his fellow German Jews. Upon the exclusion of the Jews from German universities and cultural life in 1933, Buber was instrumental in the establishment of an elaborate network of educational institutions and cultural activities[1] to provide German Jewry with a "spiritual homeland" in the midst of the nation that rejected them.[2] Until he was forbidden to do so by the S.S., Buber also travelled tirelessly throughout Germany lecturing, teaching, and encouraging Jews to affirm culture and human dignity and thereby maintain a "spiritual resistance" to Hitler. He thus became one of the "faithful shepherds of German Jewry in its direst hour which was also its greatest."[3]

It was then perhaps ironic that one of Buber's first tasks upon his immigration to Palestine in March 1938 was to address a response to the following statement by M. K. Gandhi (1869–1948), which was published on 26 November 1938 in *Harijan*, the Mahatma's prestigious weekly. The great leader of India's non-violent resistance to British imperial rule had been implored by several Jewish associates to lend his commanding moral voice in support of Zionism, especially in light of its effort to provide a National Home for the Jews fleeing Hitler's fury.[4] When Gandhi finally consented to issue a statement on the question of Palestine, it was to the profound chagrin of his Jewish friends decidely unsympathetic to Zionism. Palestine, he categorically declared, "belongs to the Arabs." With regard to the Jews scurrying to flee Hitler, Gandhi recommended that they remain in Germany and pursue *satyagraha* (holding onto truth)—passive non-violent resistance even unto death.

Notes

1. This organization which Buber directed was called *Mittelstelle für jüdische Erwachsenenbildung* (Central Office for Jewish Adult Education). Ernst Simon has devoted a monographic study to the *Mittelstelle* and Buber's efforts on its behalf: *Aufbau im Untergang: Jüdische Erwachsenenbildung im nationalsozialistischen Deutschland als geistiger Widerstand* (Tübingen: J. C. Mohr, 1959). Also see E. Simon, "Jewish Education in Nazi Germany: A Spiritual Resistance;" *Leo Baeck Institute Year Book*, I (1959), pp. 68–104.

2. Grete Schaeder, "Einleitung: Martin Buber. Ein biographischer Abriss;" *Martin Buber: Briefwechsel*, I, p. 106.

3. E. Simon, "Martin Buber and German Jewry," *Leo Baeck Institute Year Book*, III (1958), p. 39.

4. Foremost among the Jews appealing for Gandhi's approbation of Zionism was Hermann Kallenbach (1871–1945), who worked closely with Gandhi during his struggle to end discrimination against Indians in South Africa. On Gandhi's Jewish associates and their attempt to solicit a pro-Zionist statement from him, see Gideon Shimoni, *Gandhi. Satyagraha and the Jews: A Formative Factor in India's Policy towards Israel* (Jerusalem: The Leonard Davis Institute for International Relations, 1977), pp. 22–55.

Mohandas K. Gandhi: The Jews

Several letters have been received by me asking me to declare my views about the Arab-Jew question in Palestine and the persecution of the Jews in Germany. It is not without hesitation that I venture to offer my views on this very difficult question.

My sympathies are all with the Jews. I have known them intimately in South Africa. Some of them became life-long companions. Through these friends I came to learn much of their age-long persecution. They have been the untouchables of Christianity. The parallel between their treatment by Christians and the treatment of untouchables by Hindus is very close. Religious sanction has been invoked in both cases for the justification of the inhuman treatment meted out to them. Apart from the friendships, therefore, there is the more common universal reason for my sympathy for the Jews.

But my sympathy does not blind me to the requirements of justice. The cry for the national home for the Jews does not make much appeal to me. The sanction for it is sought in the Bible and the tenacity with which the Jews have hankered after return to Palestine. Why should they not, like other peoples of the earth, make that country their home where they are born and where they earn their livelihood?

Palestine belongs to the Arabs in the same sense that England belongs to the English or France to the French. It is wrong and inhuman to impose the Jews on the Arabs. What is going on in Palestine today cannot be justified by any moral code of conduct. The mandates have no sanction but that of the last war. Surely it would be a crime against humanity to reduce the proud Arabs so that Palestine can be restored to the Jews partly or wholly as their national home.

The nobler course would be to insist on a just treatment of the Jews wherever they are born and bred. The Jews born in France are French in precisely the same sense that Christians born in France are French. If the Jews have no home but Palestine, will they relish the idea of being forced to leave the other parts of the world in which they are settled? Or do they want a double home where they can remain at will? This cry for the national home affords a colorable justification for the German expulsion of the Jews.

But the German persecution of the Jews seems to have no parallel in history. The tyrants of old never went so mad as Hitler seems to have gone. And he is doing it with religious zeal. For he is propounding a new religion of exclusive and militant nationalism in the name of which any inhumanity becomes an act of humanity to be rewarded here and hereafter. The crime of an obviously mad but intrepid youth is being visited upon his whole race with unbelievable ferocity. If there ever could be a justifiable war in the name of and for humanity, a war against Germany, to prevent the wanton persecution of a whole race, would be completely justified. But I do not believe in any war. A discussion of the pros and cons of such a war is therefore outside my horizon or province.

But if there can be no war against Germany, even for such a crime as is being committed against the Jews, surely there can be no alliance with Germany. How can there be alliance between a nation which claims to stand for justice and democracy .and one which is the declared enemy of both? Or is England drifting towards armed dictatorship and all it means?

Germany is showing to the world how efficiently violence can be worked when it is not hampered by any hypocrisy or weakness masquerading as humanitarianism. It is also showing how hideous, terrible, and terrifying it looks in its nakedness.

Can the Jews resist this organized and shameless persecution? Is there a way to preserve their self-respect, and not to feel helpless, neglected, and forlorn? I submit there is. No person who has faith in a living God need feel helpless or forlorn. Jehovah of the Jews is a God more personal than the God of the Christians, the Musulmans or the Hindus, though, as a matter of fact in essence, He is common to all and one without a second and beyond description. But as the Jews attribute personality to God and believe that He rules every action of theirs, they ought not to feel helpless. If I were a Jew and were born in Germany and earned my livelihood there, I would claim Germany as my home even as the tallest gentile German may, and challenge him to shoot me or cast me in the dungeon; I would refuse to be expelled or to submit to discriminating treatment. And for doing this, I should not wait for fellow Jews to join me in civil resistance but would have confidence that in the end the rest are bound to follow my example. If one Jew or all the Jews were to accept the prescription here offered, he or they cannot be worse off than now. And suffering voluntarily undergone will bring them an inner strength and joy which no number of resolutions of sympathy passed in the world outside Germany can. Indeed even if Britain, France, and America were to declare hostilities against Germany, they can bring no inner joy, no inner strength. The calculated violence of Hitler may even result in a general massacre of the Jews by way of his first answer to the declaration of such hostilities. But if the Jewish mind could be prepared for voluntary suffering, even the massacre I have imagined could be turned into a day of thanksgiving and joy that Jehovah had wrought deliverance of the race even at the hands of the tyrant. For to the God-fearing, death has no terror. It is a joyful sleep to be followed by a waking that would be all the more refreshing for the long sleep.

It is hardly necessary for me to point out that it is easier for the Jews than for the Czechs to follow my prescription. And they have in the Indian Satyagraha campaign in South Africa an exact parallel. There the Indians occupied precisely the same place that the Jews occupy in Germany. The persecution had also a religious tinge. President Kruger used to say that the white Christians were the chosen of God and Indians were inferior beings created to serve the whites. A fundamental clause in the Transvaal constitution was that there should be no equality between the whites and colored races including Asiatics. There too the Indians were consigned to ghettos described as locations. The other disabilities were almost of the same type as those of the Jews in Germany. The Indians, a mere handful, resorted to Satyagraha without any backing from the world outside or the Indian Government. Indeed the British officials tried to dissuade the Satyagrahis from their contemplated step. World opinion and the Indian Government came to their aid after eight years of fighting. And that too was by way of diplomatic pressure not of a threat of war.

But the Jews of Germany can offer Satyagraha under infinitely better auspices than the Indians of South Africa. The Jews are a compact, homogenous community in Germany. They are far more gifted than the Indians of South Africa. And they have organized world opinion behind them. I am convinced that if someone with courage and vision can arise among them to lead them in non-violent action, the winter of their despair can in the twinkling of an eye be turned into the summer of hope. And what has today become a degrading man-hunt can be turned into a calm and determined stand offered by unarmed men and women possessing the strength of suffering given to them by Jehovah. It will be then a truly religious resistance offered against the godless fury of dehumanized man. The German Jews will score a lasting victory over the German Gentiles in the sense that they will have converted the latter to an appreciation of human dignity. They will have rendered service to fellow-Germans and proved their title to be the real Germans as against those who are today dragging, however unknowingly, the German name into the mire.

And now a word to the Jews in Palestine. I have no doubt that they are going about things the wrong way. The Palestine of the Biblical conception is not a geographical tract. It is in their hearts. But if they must look to the Palestine of geography as their national home, it is wrong to enter it under the shadow of the British gun. A religious act cannot be performed with the aid of the bayonet or the bomb. They can settle in Palestine only by the goodwill of the Arabs. They should seek to convert the Arab heart. The same God rules the Arab heart who rules the Jewish heart. They can offer Satyagraha in front of the

Arabs and offer themselves to be shot or thrown into the Dead Sea without raising a little finger against them. They will find the world opinion in their favor in their religious aspiration. There are hundreds of ways of reasoning with the Arabs, if they will only discard the help of the British bayonet. As it is, they are co-sharers with the British in despoiling a people who have done no wrong to them.

I am not defending the Arab excesses. I wish they had chosen the way of non-violence in resisting what they rightly regarded as an unwarrantable encroachment upon their country. But according to the accepted canons of right and wrong, nothing can be said against the Arab resistance in the face of overwhelming odds.

Let the Jews who claim to be the chosen race prove their title by choosing the way of non-violence for vindicating their position on earth. Every country is their home including Palestine not by aggression but by loving service. A Jewish friend has sent me a book called *The Jewish Contribution to Civilisation* by Cecil Roth. It gives a record of what the Jews have done to enrich the world's literature, art, music, drama, science, medicine, agriculture, etc. Given the will, the Jew can refuse to be treated as the outcaste of the West, to be despised or patronized. He can command the attention and respect of the world by being man, the chosen creation of God, instead of being man who is fast sinking to the brute and forsaken by God. They can add to their many contributions the surpassing contribution of non-violent action.

18

A Letter to Gandhi

(February 1939)

(Editor's prefatory note:)

Buber's response to Gandhi was written at the behest of his friends in the small circle of Zionist intellectuals in Jerusalem called *Ha'ol*—the Yoke: the yoke of the Kingdom of God. The binding principle of this circle was formulated in a rhetorical question:

Are we Jews merely a persecuted people asking for mercy, or have we a message which we want both to proclaim and to carry out? Are we conscious of the Yoke which our Father has placed upon us?[1]

The members of *Ha'ol* were all passionate advocates of Arab-Jewish reconciliation, many of whom had viewed Gandhi's peaceful, spiritual mode of political action as a model for achieving Arab-Jewish amity.

On 24 February 1939, Buber completed his letter to Gandhi, composed over several weeks with great care and delibaration. "Day and night I took myself to task, searching . . . whether I had not fallen into the grievous error of collective egoism." He had greatly admired Gandhi, and indeed he had previously written an essay in which he affectionately extolled the Mahatma's "great work in India," celebrating it as illuminating for the West a way of overcoming the fateful "duality of politics and religion."[2] In his letter to Gandhi, Buber presents himself as a sufferer who listens imploringly to "a voice that he has long known and honored." But, alas, "what he hears, containing though it does elements of a noble and praiseworthy conception . . . is yet barren of all application to his [the sufferer's] circumstances." Together with a similar letter by another member of *Ha'ol*, Judah L. Magnes (1877–1948), President of the Hebrew University of Jerusalem, Buber's letter was mailed to Gandhi's ashram at Segaon on 9 March 1939.[3] Gandhi did not reply.[4]

Notes

1. Cited on the inside cover of a pamphlet containing Buber's letter to Gandhi, published in English and Hebrew by *Ha'ol*. The front cover of this pamphlet carries the motto from the rabbinic Midrash: "Take upon yourselves the Yoke of the Kindgom of Heaven, and judge one another in the fear of God, and act toward one another in loving kindness." (Sifre Deuteronomy 32:29) Concretely, what this group had in mind was "religious socialism": "We are united in the feeling of responsibility toward society in general, and the life of Israel in its land and in the Dispersion in particular. This sense of responsibility stems from a faith in eternal values whose source is God. We believe in a life of faith which carries a commitment to social action and practical political work, and we reject any attempt to separate the dominions, which are one in theory and practice." (In Hebrew.) Judah L. Magnes Archives, Hebrew University of Jerusalem, file *Ha'ol*. (I wish to thank Professor Aryeh Goren for bringing this document to my attention.) The society was short-lived, its activities being superseded by those of the League for Jewish-Arab Rapprochement founded in the autumn of 1939, and especially by the Ichud, established in 1942.

2. "Gandhi, Politics, and Us" (1930), in *Pointing the Way: Collected Essays by Martin Buber*, ed. and trans. by M. Friedman (New York: Schocken, 1974), pp. 126–38.

3. Buber's and Magnes's letters were later published in a pamphlet sponsored by

Ha'ol, which called itself in English "The Bond"; *Two Letters to Gandhi* (Jerusalem: Rubin Mass, 1939), pamphlet no. 1 of "The Bond."

4. G. Shimoni notes that there is evidence that Gandhi did not receive the letters. For one thing, he was not at Segaon when the letters arrived, and thus they had to be forwarded to him, likely going astray. Gandhi generally answered such letters. In fact, he replied to a similar letter from Hayim Greenberg, a leader of the Socialist Zionists in America. Gideon Shimoni, *Gandhi, Satyagraha and the Jews* (Jerusalem: The Lady Davis Institute, 1977), pp. 47f.

A LETTER TO GANDHI

Jerusalem
24 February 1939

My dear Mahatma Gandhi,

He who is unhappy lends a deaf ear when idle tongues discuss his fate among themselves. But when a voice that he has long known and honored, a great voice and an earnest one, pierces the vain clamor and calls him by his name, he is all attentinon. Here is a voice, he thinks, which can but give good counsel and genuine comfort, for he who speaks knows what suffering is: he knows that the sufferer is more in need of comfort than of counsel; and he has both the wisdom to counsel rightly and that simple union of faith and love which alone is the open-sesame to true comforting. But what he hears—containing though it does elements of a noble and most praiseworthy conception such as he expects from this speaker—is yet barren of all application to his peculiar circumstances. These words are in truth not applicable to him at all. They are inspired by most praiseworthy general principles; but the listener is aware that he, the speaker, has cast not a single glance at the situation of him whom he is addressing, that he sees him not nor does he know him and the straits under which he labors. Moreover, intermingled with the counsel and the comfort, a third voice makes itself heard drowning both the others, the voice of reproach. It is not that the sufferer disdains to accept reproach in this hour from the man he honors: on the contrary, if only there were mingled with the good

counsel and the true comfort a word of just reproach giving to the
former a meaning and a reason, he would recognize in the speaker the
bearer of a message. But the accusation voiced is another altogether
from that which he hears in the storm of events and in the hard beating
of his own heart: it is almost the opposite of this. He weighs it and
examines it—no, it is not a just one! and the armor of his silence is
pierced. The friendly appeal achieves what the enemy's storming has
failed to do: he must answer. He exclaims: Let the lords of the ice-
inferno affix my name to a cunningly constructed scarecrow; this is the
logical outcome of their own nature and the nature of their relations
to me. But you, the man of good will, do you not know that you must
see him whom you address, in his place and circumstance, in the throes
of his destiny?

Jews are being persecuted, robbed, maltreated, tortured, murdered.
And you, Mahatma Gandhi, say that their position in the country
where they suffer all this is an exact parallel to the position of Indians
in South Africa at the time when you inaugurated your famous "Force
of Truth" or "Strength of the Soul" (Satyagraha) campaign. There the
Indians occupied precisely the same place, and the persecution there
also had a religious tinge. There also the constitution denied equality
of rights to the white and the black race including the Asiatics; there
also the Indians were assigned to ghettos and the other disqualifications
were, at all events, almost of the same type as those of the Jews in
Germany. I read and reread these sentences in your article without
being able to understand. Although I know them well, I reread your
South African speeches and writings and called to mind, with all the
attention and imagination at my command, every complaint which
you made therein; and I did likewise with the accounts of your friends
and pupils at that time; but all this did not help me to understand what
you say about us. In the first of your speeches with which I am
acquainted, that of 1896, you quoted two particular incidents to the
accompaniment of the hisses of your audience: first, that a band of
Europeans had set fire to an Indian village shop causing some damage;
and, second, that another band had thrown burning rockets into an
urban shop. If I oppose to this the thousands on thousands of Jewish
shops, destroyed and burnt-out, you will perhaps answer that the difference is only one of quantity and that the proceedings were almost
of the same type. But, Mahatma, are you not aware of the burning of
Synagogues and scrolls of the Law? Do you know nothing of all the

sacred property of the community—in part of great antiquity—that has been destroyed in the flames? I am not aware that Boers and Englishmen in South Africa ever injured anything sacred to the Indians. I find further only one other concrete complaint quoted in that speech, namely, that three Indian school-teachers, who were found walking in the streets after 9 P.M. contrary to orders, were arrested and only acquitted later on. That is the only incident of the kind you bring forward. Now do you know or do you not know, Mahatma, what a concentration camp is like and what goes on there? Do you know of the torments in the concentration camp, of its methods of slow and quick slaughter? I cannot assume that you know of this; for then this tragi-comic utterance "almost of the same type" could scarcely have crossed your lips. Indians were despised and despicably treated in South Africa; but they were not deprived of rights, they were not outlawed, they were not hostages for the coveted attitude of foreign powers. And do you think perhaps that a Jew in Germany could pronounce in public one single sentence of a speech such as yours without being knocked down? Of what significance is it to point to a certain something in common when such differences are overlooked?

It does not seem to me convincing when you base your advice to us to observe Satyagraha in Germany on these similarities of circumstance. In the five years which I myself spent under the present régime, I observed many instances of genuine Satyagraha among the Jews, instances showing a strength of spirit wherein there was no question of bartering their rights or of being bowed down, and where neither force nor cunning was used to escape the consequences of their behaviour. Such actions, however, exerted apparently not the slightest influence on their opponents. All honor indeed to those who displayed such strength of soul! But I cannot recognize herein a parole for the general behavior of German Jews which might seem suited to exert an influence on the oppressed or on the world. An effective stand may be taken in the form of non-violence against unfeeling human beings in the hope of gradually bringing them thereby to their senses; but a diabolic universal steam-roller cannot thus be withstood. There is a certain situation in which from the "Satyagraha" of the strength of the spirit no "Satyagraha" of the power of truth can result. The world "Satyagraha" signifies testimony. Testimony without acknowledgment, ineffective, unobserved martyrdom, a martyrdom cast to the winds—that is the fate of innumerable Jews in Germany. God alone accepts their testimony, God "seals" it, as is said in our prayers. But no maxim for suitable behavior can be deduced therefrom. Such martyrdom is a deed—but who would venture to demand it?

But your comparing of the position of the Jews in Germany with that of the Indians in South Africa, compels me to draw your attention to a yet more essential difference. True, I can well believe that you were aware of this difference, great as it is, when you drew the exact parallel. It is obvious that when you think back to your time in South Africa it is a matter of course for you that then as now you always had this great Mother India. That fact was and still is so taken for granted that apparently you are entirely unaware of the fundamental differences existing between nations having such a mother (it need not necessarily be such a great Mother, it may be a tiny motherkin, but yet a mother, a mother's bosom and a mother's heart) and a nation that is orphaned, or to whom one says in speaking of his country: "This is no more your mother"!

When you were in South Africa, Mahatma, there were living there 150,000 Indians. But in India there were far more than 200 million! And this fact nourished the souls of the 150,000, whether they were conscious of it or not: they drew from this source their strength to live and their courage to live. Did you ask then as you ask the Jews now, whether they want a double home where they can remain at will? You say to the Jews: if Palestine is their home, they must accustom themselves to the idea of being forced to leave the other parts of the world in which they are settled. Did you also say to the Indians in South Africa that if India is their home, they must accustom themselves to the idea of being compelled to return to India? Or did you tell them that India was not their home? And if—though indeed it is inconceivable that such a thing could come to pass—the hundreds of millions of Indians were to be scattered tomorrow over the face of the earth; and if the day after tomorrow another nation were to establish itself in India and the Jews were to declare that there was yet room for the establishment of a national home for the Indians, thus giving to their diaspora a strong organic concentration and a living center; should then a Jewish Gandhi—assuming there could be such—answer them, as you answered the Jews, that this cry for the national home affords a colorable justification for your expulsion? Or should he teach them, as you teach the Jews, that the India of the Vedic conception is not a geographical tract, but that it is in your hearts? A land about which a sacred book speaks to the sons of the land is never merely in their hearts; a land can never become a mere symbol. It is in the hearts because it is the prophetic image of a promise to mankind; but it would be a vain metaphor if Mount Zion did not actually exist. This land is called "Holy"; but this is not the holiness of an idea, it is the holiness of a piece of earth. That which is merely an idea and nothing more cannot become holy; but a piece of earth can become holy just as a mother's womb can become holy.

Dispersion is bearable; it can even be purposeful if somewhere there is ingathering, a growing home center, a piece of earth wherein one is in the midst of an ingathering and not in dispersion and from whence the spirit of ingathering may work its way out to all the places of the dispersion. When there is this, there is also a striving, common life, the life of a community which dares to live today because it hopes to live tomorrow. But when this growing center, this increasing process of ingathering is lacking, dispersion becomes dismemberment. On this criterion the question of our Jewish destiny is indissolubly bound up with the possibility of ingathering and this in Palestine.

You ask: "Why should they not, like other nations of the earth, make that country their home where they are born and where they earn their livelihood?" Because their destiny is different from that of all other nations of the earth: it is a destiny which in truth and justice should not be imposed on any nation on earth. For their destiny is dispersion, not the dispersion of a fraction and the preservation of the main substance as in the case of other nations; it is dispersion without the living heart and center; and every nation has a right to demand the possession of a living heart. It is different, because a hundred adopted homes without one original and natural one render a nation sick and miserable. It is different, because, although the well-being and the achievement of the individual may flourish on stepmother soil, the nation as such must languish. And just as you, Mahatma, wish that not only should all Indians be able to live and work, but that also Indian substance, Indian wisdom, and Indian truth should prosper and be fruitful, so do we wish this for the Jews. For you there is no need to be aware that the Indian substance could not prosper without the Indian's attachment to the mother-soil and without his ingathering therein. But we know what is the essential; we know it because it is just this that is denied us or was, at least, up to the generation which has just begun to work at the redemption of the mother-soil.

But this is not all: because for us, for the Jews who think as I do, painfully urgent as it is, it is indeed not the decisive factor. You say, Mahatma Gandhi, that to support the cry for a national home which "does not make much appeal to you," a sanction is "sought in the Bible." No—this is not so. We do not open the Bible and seek therein sanction. The opposite is true: the promises of return, of re-establishment, which have nourished the yearning hope of hundreds of generations, give those of today an elementary stimulus, recognized by few in its full meaning but effective also in the lives of many who do not believe in the message of the Bible. Still this too is not the determining factor for us who, although we do not see divine revelation in every sentence of Holy Scriptures, yet trust in the spirit which inspired their speakers. Decisive for us is not the promise of the Land—but the command, the fulfillment of which is bound up with the land, with the existence of a free Jewish community in this country. For the Bible tells us and our inmost knowledge testifies to it, that once, more that 3000 years ago, our entry into this land was in the consciousness of a mission from above to set up a just way of life through the generations of our people, such a way of life as can be realized not by individuals in the sphere of their private existence but only by a nation in the establishment of its society: communal ownership of the land,[1] regularly recurrent leveling of social distinctions,[2] guarantee of the independence of each individual,[3] mutual help,[4] a common Sabbath embracing serf and beast as beings with equal claim,[5] a Sabbatical year whereby, letting the soil rest, everybody is admitted to the free enjoyment of its fruits.[6] These are not practical laws thought out by wise men; they are measures which the leaders of the nation, apparently themselves taken by surprise and overpowered, have found to be the set task and condition for taking possession of the land. No other nation has ever been faced at the beginning of its career with such a mission. Here is something which allows of no forgetting, and from which there is no release. At that time we did not carry out what was imposed upon us. We went into exile with our task unperformed; but the command remained with us and it has become more urgent than ever. We need our own soil in order to fulfil it. We need the freedom of ordering our own life. No attempt can be made on foreign soil and under foreign statute. It may not be that the soil and the freedom for fulfillment be denied us. We are not covetous, Mahatma: our one desire is that at last we may obey.

Now you may well ask whether I speak for the Jewish people when I say "we." I speak only for those who feel themselves entrusted with the commission of fulfilling the command of justice delivered to Israel of the Bible. Were it but a handful—these constitute the pith of the nation and the future of the people depends on them; for the ancient mission of the nation lives on in them as for the cotyledon in the core of the fruit. In this connection I must tell you that you are mistaken when you assume that in general the Jews of today believe in God and derive from their faith guidance for their conduct. Jewry of today is in the throes of a serious crisis in the matter of faith. It seems to me that the lack of faith of present-day humanity, its inability truly to believe in God, finds its concentrated expression in this crisis of Jewry; here all is darker, more fraught with danger, more fateful than anywhere else in the world. Neither is this crisis resolved here in Palestine; indeed we recognise its severity here even more than elsewhere among Jews. But at the same time we realize that here alone can it be resolved. There is no solution to be found in the life of isolated and abandoned individuals, although one may hope that the spark of faith will be kindled in their great need. The true solution can only issue from the life of a community which begins to carry out the will of God, often without being aware of doing so, without believing that God exists and this is His will. It may be found in this life of the community if believing people support it who neither direct nor demand, neither urge nor preach, but who share the life, who help, wait, and are ready for the moment when it will be their turn to give the true answer to the enquirer. This is the innermost truth of the Jewish life in the Land; perhaps it may be of significance for the solution of this crisis of faith not only for Jewry but for all humanity. The contact of this people with this Land is not only a matter of sacred ancient history; we sense here a secret still more hidden.

You, Mahatma Gandhi, who know of the connection between tradition and future, should not associate yourself with those who pass over our cause without understanding or sympathy.

But you say—and I consider it to be the most significant of all the things you tell us—that Palestine belongs to the Arabs and that it is therefore "wrong and inhuman to impose the Jews on the Arabs."

Here I must add a personal note in order to make clear to you on what premises I desire to consider this matter.

I belong to a group of people who, from the time when Britain conquered Palestine, have not ceased to strive for the concluding of genuine peace between Jew and Arab.

By a genuine peace we inferred and still infer that both peoples should together develop the Land without the one imposing his will on the other. In view of the international usages of our generation this appeared to us to be very difficult but not impossible. We were well aware and still are that in this unusual—even unexampled case, it is a question of seeking new ways of understanding and cordial agreement between the nations. Here again we stood and still stand under the sway of a commandment.

We considered it a fundamental point that in this case two vital claims are opposed to each other, two claims of a different nature and a different origin, which cannot be pitted one against the other and between which no objective decision can be made as to which is just or unjust. We considered and still consider it our duty to understand and to honor the claim which is opposed to ours and to endeavor to reconcile both claims. We cannot renounce the Jewish claim; something even higher than the life of our people is bound up with the Land, namely the work which is their divine mission. But we have been and still are convinced that it must be possible to find some form of agreement between this claim and the other; for we love this land and we believe in its future; and, seeing that such love and such faith are surely present also on the other side, a union in the common service of the Land must be within the range of the possible. Where there is faith and love, a solution may be found even to what appears to be a tragic contradiction.

In order to carry out a task of such extreme difficulty—in the recognition of which we have to overcome an internal resistance on the Jewish side, as foolish as it is natural—we are in need of the support of well-meaning persons of all nations, and we had hope of such. But now you come and settle the whole existential dilemma with the simple formula: "Palestine belongs to the Arabs."

What do you mean by saying that a land belongs to a population? Evidently you do not intend only to describe a state of affairs by your formula, but to declare a certain right. You obviously mean to say that a people, being settled on the land, has such an absolute claim to the possession of this land that whoever settles in it without the permission of this people, has committed a robbery. But by what means did the Arabs attain to the right of ownership in Palestine? Surely by conquest and, in fact, a conquest by settlement. You therefore admit that, this being so, it constitutes for them an exclusive right of possession; whereas the subsquent conquests of the Mamelukes and the Turks, which were not conquests with a view to settlement, do not constitute such in your opinion, but leave the former conquering nation in rightful ownership. Thus settlement by force of conquest justifies for you a right of ownership of Palestine; whereas a settlement such as the Jewish one—the methods of which, it is true, though not always doing full justice to Arab ways of life, were, even in the most objectionable cases, far removed from those of conquest—do not justify in your opinion any participation in this right of possession. These are the consequences which result from your statement in the form of an axiom that a land belongs to its population. In an epoch of migration of nations you would first support the right of ownership of the nation that is threatened with dispossession or extermination; but were this once achieved, you would be compelled, not at once, but after the elapse of a suitable number of generations, to admit that the land belongs to the usurper.

Possibly the time is not far removed when—perhaps after a catastrophe the extent of which we cannot yet estimate—the representatives of humanity will have to come to some agreement on the re-establishment of relations among peoples, nations, and countries, on the colonization of thinly populated territories as well as on a communal distribution of the necessary raw materials and on a logical intensification of the cultivation of the globe in order to prevent a new, enormously extended migration of nations which would threaten to destroy mankind. Is then the dogma of "possession," of the inalienable right of ownership, of the sacred status quo to be held up against the men who dare to save the situation? For surely, we are witnesses of how the feeling, penetrating deep into the heart of national life, that this dogma must be opposed, is disastrously misused; but do not those representatives of the most powerful states share the guilt of this misuse, who consider every questioning of the dogma as a sacrilege?

And what if it is not the nations who migrate, but *one* nation? And what if this migrating nation should yearn towards its ancient home where there is still room for a considerable section of it, enough to form a center side by side with the people to whom the land now "belongs"? And what if this wandering nation, to whom the land once belonged, likewise on the basis of a settlement by force of conquest—and who were once driven out of it by mere force of domination, should now strive to occupy a free part of the land, or a part that might become free without encroaching on the living room of others, in order at last to acquire again for themselves a *national* home—a home where its people could live *as a nation?* Then you come, Mahatma Gandhi, and help to draw the barriers and to declare "Hands off! This land does not belong to you!" Instead of helping to establish a genuine peace, giving us what we need without taking from the Arabs what they need, on the basis of a fair adjustment as to what they would really make use of and what might be admitted to satisfy our requirements!

Such an adjustment of the required living room for all is possible if it is brought into line with an all-embracing intensification of the cultivation of the whole soil in Palestine. In the present, helplessly primitive state of *fellah* agriculture the amount of land needed to produce nourishment for a family is ever so much larger than it otherwise would be. Is it right to cling to ancient forms of agriculture which have become meaningless, to neglect the potential productivity of the soil, in order to prevent the immigration of new settlers without prejudice to the old? I repeat: without prejudice. This should be the basis of the agreement for which we are striving.

You are only concerned, Mahatma, with the "right of possession" on the one side; you do not consider the right to a piece of free land on the other side—for those who are hungering for it. But there is another of whom you do not enquire and who in justice, i.e., on the basis of the whole perceptible reality, would have to be asked: this other is the soil itself. Ask the soil what the Arabs have done for her in 1300 years and what we have done for her in 50! Would her answer not be weighty testimony in a just discussion as to whom this land "belongs"?

It seems to me that God does not give any one portion of the earth away so that the owner thereof may say as God does in the Holy Script: "Mine is the Land." Even to the conqueror who has settled on it, the conquered land is, in my opinion, only lent—and God waits to see what he will make of it.

I am told, however, that I should not respect the cultivated soil and despise the desert. I am told that the desert is willing to wait for the work of her children: we who are burdened with civilization are not recognized by her any more as her children. I have a veneration of the desert; but I do not believe in her absolute resistance, for I believe in the great marriage between man (*Adam*) and earth (*Adama*). This land recognizes us, for it is fruitful through us, and through its fruit-bearing for us it recognizes us. Our settlers do not come here as do the colonists from the Occident, with natives to do their work for them; they themselves set their shoulders to the plow, and they spend their strength and their blood to make the land fruitful. But it is not only for ourselves that we desire its fertility. The Jewish peasants have begun to teach their brothers, the Arab peasants, to cultivate the land more intensively; we desire to teach them further: together with them we want to cultivate the land—to "serve" it as the Hebrew has it. The more fertile this soil becomes, the more space there will be for us and for them. We have no desire to dispossess them: we want to live with them. We do not want to rule, we want to serve with them.

You once said, Mahatma, that politics enmeshes us nowadays as with serpent's coils from which there is no escape however hard one may try. You said you desired, therefore, to wrestle with the serpent. Here is the serpent in the fulness of its power! Jews and Arabs both have a claim to this land; but these claims are in fact reconcilable as long as they are restricted to the measure which life itself allots, and as long as they are limited by the desire for conciliation—that is, if they are translated into the language of the needs of living people for them-selves and their children. But instead of this they are turned through the serpent's influence into claims of principle and politics, and are represented with all the ruthlessness which politics instills into those that are led by it. Life with all its realities and possibilities disappears as does the desire for truth and peace; nothing is known and sensed but the political parole alone. The serpent conquers not only the spirit but also life. Who would wrestle with it?

In the midst of your arguments, Mahatma, there is a fine word which we gratefully accept. We should seek, you say, to convert the heart of the Arab. Well then—help us to do so! Among us also there are many foolish hearts to convert—hearts that have fallen a prey to that nationalist egoism which only admits its own claims. We hope to achieve this ourselves. But for the other task of conversion we need your help. Instead, your admonition is only addressed to the Jews, because they allow British bayonets to defend them against the bomb-throwers. Your attitude to the latter is much more reserved: you say you wish the Arabs had chosen the way of non-violence; but, according to the accepted canons of right and wrong there is nothing to be said against their behavior. How is it possible that in this case, you should give credence—if only in a limited form—to the accepted canons, whereas you have never done so before! You reproach us, that, having no army of our own, we consent to the British army preventing an occasional blind murder. But in view of the accepted canons you cast a lenient eye on those who carry murder into our ranks every day without even noticing who is hit. Were you to look down on all, Mahatma, on what is done and what is not done on both sides—on the just and the unjust on both sides—would you not admit that we certainly are not least in need of your help?

We began to settle in the land anew, 35 years before the "shadow of the British gun" was cast upon it. We did not seek out this shadow; it appeared and remained here to guard British interests and *not ours*. We do not want force. But after the resolutions of Delhi, at the beginning of March 1922, you yourself, Mahatma Gandhi, wrote: "Have I not repeatedly said that I would have India become free even by violence rather than that she should remain in bondage?" This was a very important pronouncement on your part: you asserted thereby that non-violence is for you a faith and not a political principle—and that the desire for the freedom of India is even *stronger* in you than your faith. And for this, I love you. We do not want force. We have not proclaimed, as did Jesus, the son of our people, and as you do, the teaching of non-violence, because we believe that a man must sometimes use force to save himself or even more his children. But from time immemorial we have proclaimed the teaching of justice and peace; we have taught and we have learnt that peace is the aim of all the world and that justice is the way to attain it. Thus we cannot *desire* to use force. No one who counts himself in the ranks of Israel can desire to use force.

But, you say, our non-violence is that of the helpless and the weak. This is not in accordance with the true state of affairs. You do not know or you do not consider what strength of soul, what Satyagraha has been needed for us to restrain ourselves here after years of ceaseless deeds of blind violence perpetrated against us, our wives, and our children, and not to answer with like deeds of blind violence. And on the other hand you, Mahatma, wrote in 1922 as follows: "I see that our non-violence is skin-deep. . . . This non-violence seems to be due merely to our helplessness. . . . Can true voluntary non-violence come out of this seemingly forced non-violence of the weak?" When I read those words at that time, my reverence for you took birth—a reverence so great that even your injustice towards us cannot destroy it.

You say it is a stigma against us that our ancestors crucified Jesus. I do not know whether that actually happened; but I consider it possible. I consider it just as possible as that the Indian people under different circumstances should condemn you to death—if your teachings were more strictly opposed to their own tendencies ("India," you say, "is *by Nature* non-violent"). Not infrequently do nations swallow up the greatness to which they have given birth. Now can one assert, without contradiction, that such action constitutes a stigma! I would not deny however, that although I should not have been among the crucifiers of Jesus, I should also not have been among his supporters. For I cannot help withstanding evil when I see that it is about to destroy the good. I am forced to withstand the evil in the world just as the evil within myself. I can only strive not to have to do so by force. I do not want force. But if there is no other way of preventing the evil destroying the good, I trust I shall use force and give myself up into God's hands.

"India," you say, "is by Nature non-violent." It was not always so. The Mahabharata is an epos of warlike, disciplined force. In the greatest of its poems, the Bhagavad-Gita it is told how Arjuna decides on the battlefield that he will not commit the sin of killing his relations who are opposed to him and he lets fall his bow and arrow. But the God reproaches him saying that such action is unmanly and shameful; there is nothing better for a knight in arms than a just fight.

Is that the truth? If I am to confess what is truth to me, I must say: There is nothing better for a man than to deal justly—unless it be to love; we should be able even to fight for justice—but to fight lovingly.

I have been very slow in writing this letter to you, Mahatma. I made repeated pauses—sometimes days elapsing between short paragraphs—in order to test my knowledge and my way of thinking. Day and night I took myself to task, searching whether I had not in any one point overstepped the measure of self-preservation allotted and even prescribed by God to a human community, and whether I had not fallen into the grievous error of collective egoism. Friends and my own conscience have helped to keep me straight whenever danger threatened. Weeks have now passed since then and the time has come, when negotiations are proceeding in the capital of the British Empire on the Jewish-Arab problem—and when, it is said, a decision is to be made.

But the true decision in this matter can only come from within and not from without.

I take the liberty therefore of closing this letter without waiting for the result in London.

Sincerely yours,

Martin Buber

Notes

1. Lev. 25:23. [Notes to this selection are Buber's.]
2. Lev. 25:13.
3. Ex. 21:2.
4. Ex. 23:4ff.
5. Ex. 23:12.
6. Lev. 25:5–7.

19

Keep Faith!

(July 1938)

(Editor's prefatory note:)

Alarmed by the mounting pace of Jewish immigration and settlement which followed the Nazi rise to power, militant Arabs in Palestine, despairing of Britain's failure to help their cause, decided to stage a revolt. The first stage of the "Arab Revolt" was a six-month general strike which began in April 1936. The boycott of both the Jewish sector and the Mandatory government was accompanied by sporadic acts of violence which gradually developed into open rebellion. Guerrilla bands were organized throughout Palestine. After a pause, the revolt was resumed with greater intensity in 1937, and lasted to the summer of 1939.

Attacks by Arab bands on unarmed men, women, and children aroused within the Jewish community of Palestine a desire for revenge. The Yishuv's leadership, however, adopted a policy of *"havlagah"* (restraint): a firm resolve, motivated by both political and moral considerations, not to be provoked to indiscriminate reprisals against the Arabs. In July 1939 the *Irgun*, an underground military organization associated with the Revisionists, rejected the policy of *havlagah* and pursued massive retaliation against the Arab civilian population.

In the following article—published on 18 July 1938 both in the *Palestine Post* and, in Hebrew, in *Davar*, the daily of the Jewish Federation of Labor— Buber does not refer to any specific incident but to the attitude which he believed was encouraging the emergence of Jewish terrorism.

KEEP FAITH!

Confusion is on the increase in Palestine, and has reached a pitch where it is unbearable. It has begun to manifest itself in actions which should be repugnant to every Jew with an inkling of what Judaism and humanity are.

Our public bodies have made their statements. But we individuals, without office and without obligation, we also may not keep silent if we feel that the situation is past bearing, and it is right that we should speak out. For we know in our hearts that whatever calamity may threaten our people from outside, it cannot be destroyed unless it ceases to keep faith in itself [and its ideals]. Those of us who know what is at stake must unite against this faithlessness, and must speak as individuals for the sake of this unity.

Faith has been broken. Factions that had no power while faith prevailed, are now directing the breaking of faith in order that they may profit by it. They trouble the waters, for only where there is trouble is there a future for them. They are watched from the outside with no little satisfaction by those who wish that we may be led, in this fateful hour to compromise our cause so gravely that our own actions may be held against us.

It need not surprise us that success should attend the powers of darkness, that youths should be blinded and enter their service, and that the unseeing among the people should applaud deeds of brute force. The situation is weighing so heavily upon us that we can understand how daily more and more of our people join in the cry "If we cannot save ourselves from the wolves, then let us become wolves ourselves!"—forgetting, it seems, that we set ourselves a task in this country in order to become once again complete human beings.

We may understand their cry, I say, but do they show any understanding of our position? They do not. What do our admirers of force believe they can achieve by their deeds? Frighten off the aggressors? On the contrary, they create new and comprehensive hatred. It was for us to put the terrorist beyond the pale and to instil courage into the well-intentioned among the Arabs by our attitude, our speech, and our clearly professed readiness for agreement. Those who support violence are by their deeds helping to weld together against us the Arabs of this country and elsewhere. Or do they believe they can influence public opinion in Europe? They will only lose us sincere and valuable sympathies by using and so giving tacit sanction to a method that we have branded as inhuman.

We have nothing to gain from use of force and everything to lose. If the force-mongers are given free reign, we stand to bar the way to peace with the people with whom fate has decreed that we shall live and build up this country. The inwardness of this fate will not be revealed to us until we have faced the issue sincerely and in full earnestness. Great as this loss of contact would be, we have still more to lose within ourselves. Our movement draws its strength and meaning from the will to free Jewry from the conflict between a soul that recognizes truth and justice as the supreme treasures of this world, and a life in which this recognition cannot be translated into reality. Our movement has made it its task to offer the Jewish people a chance of ordering their lives in accordance with their principles. If we permit the rule of force, then our professed belief becomes hypocrisy, life is despoiled of its content, and our very soul is destroyed, while the conflict that was the unhappy fruit of exile is elevated as master in Zion, bringing death to our movement and catastrophe for our people.

Will those who preach force give us a new soul, a conscience-less, conflict-free wolf's spirit? We ourselves can only crush and silence our soul, but we cannot exchange it.

Faith has been broken. Some of those who might have exhorted the people to abandon their folly have instead helped to spread a halo of sanctity and heroism around the victims of misguidance, notwithstanding that he who kills, or wishes to kill, innocent people is neither saint nor hero, whether he claims to have acted in defense of his people or not. An attack of innocent persons cannot constitute defense, and those of the teachers of the nation who justify such actions are preaching against the Law. And moreover, they are helping to rob true defense of its honor.

We who are charging with faithlessness those who have indeed broken faith with the nation, do so as defenders. If a man enters the room where his child is playing, and sees a stranger point his rifle through the window, it is his right and duty to fire the first shot, and we may hope that he will find pardon. But if robbers enter his house to murder and pillage and make good their escape, right and justice will not admit of the sufferer waylaying a passing stranger, only because he is of the same blood as the criminal.

We believe in true defense. If this proves impossible, what then? He who cares for truth and justice will hold back. Beginning by showing the world that he knew how to defend himself, he must continue, and show now that he knows to abstain from injustice, and that there is such a thing as living truth and right. If the world does not rally to his side straight away, then it must do so at its own time.

This holding back and bearing of the world's indifference is called *havlagah* (self-restraint). We do not claim that he who practices this is a hero; but we do say that self-restraint is the real strength. Nor do we say of him who falls, not even if he is killed in the execution of his duty, that he is martyred; but we do say that he is a witness who has contributed indestructibly to the evidence of the truth and justice of our cause.

There can have been few hours of distress in the history of our people as bitter as these through which we are now passing, and never has the test been so stringent. Neither cunning nor force can help us now, but only strength to withstand the trial and keep faith.

But faith has been broken. Denude these actions of their mask of self-assertion, and know them for what they are. Faith has been broken with the Jew himself, with the tenets of Judaism and of humanity, faith has been broken with our task and our achievements, our aims and our methods, our movement and our people. Know this breaking of faith for what it is, and treat it accordingly. The ultimate and unconquerable disaster will threaten from within, and not without, if you stand by and let violence take its course.

Keep faith! There is no telling whether it will bring rapid reward. Even he who emerges from the trail unbroken may still have to endure and go on waiting in greatest bitterness. But he will live, and when the time for harvest comes, faith alone will walk over the fields and reap.

This is what I have to say to our own people. Whoever else cares to listen is welcome, but the message is meant for Jewish ears. To the rest of the world I say that we suffer in sympathy not only with our own wounded and bereaved, but with the wounded and bereaved of those Arabs who fell without raising their hands against us. The history of mankind began with brother killing brother, and fratricide has remained with us ever since, but still the love of man for his brother is the stronger power.

I said that "we" sympathize. Anxious hearts beat in unison up and down the country and though they have no slogans or program, a great feeling and a deep certitude unites them. They must unite, not into a party or society, but into an active, committed community.

20

Our Pseudo-Samsons

(June 1939)

(Editor's prefatory note:)

Militarily the Arab Revolt failed, but politically it did achieve its objective—the abrogation, by virtue of a White Paper issued by His Majesty's government in May 1939, of Britain's commitment to foster the development of a Jewish National Home in Palestine. With its foreclosure of future Jewish self-rule, severe restrictions on Jewish immigration and land purchase, the White Paper of 1939 was regarded by the Zionist movement as an act of extreme treachery, especially when the need of the Jewish people for a Home was never more acute. The Yishuv was outraged. Angry protest demonstrations were held throughout the country. For many, in particular the youth, the White Paper discredited the Jewish Agency's policy of self-restraint. The British, it was argued, had obviously been more impressed by Arab terrorism; the only way to rescind the White Paper was for the Jews to mount their own terror campaign against the Mandatory government. In this agitated mood the Irgun greatly expanded its ranks and activities. Shortly after the publication of the White Paper, it bombed government buildings in Tel Aviv and Jerusalem; other acts of sabotage and murder quickly followed. This sudden outburst of Jewish terrorism, Buber observed in the following article published in *Davar* on 5 June 1939, is animated by an understandable indignation. Nonetheless, the Yishuv should follow the example of the Jewish Agency in strenuously condemning these actions. The public, Buber urges, must not secretly admire the deeds of the self-styled Samsons of the Irgun. They are not heroes but petulant, morally and politically irresponsible "fools."

Our Pseudo-Samsons

Apparently there are young men in the Yishuv who fancy themselves to be contemporary Samsons. It seems they regard the placing of mines in the path of vehicles bearing innocent, defenseless non-Jews or attacking the homes of innocent, defenseless non-Jews as similar to Samson's exploits. They tell youths in the street that the time has come to act as Samson did; and if those youths want to be contemporary Samsons, all they have to do is learn from the speakers. It goes without saying that they find plenty of children who like listening to such things.

How is this to be explained? When we returned to our land after many hundreds of years, we behaved as though the land were empty of inhabitants—no, even worse—as though the people we saw didn't affect us, as though we didn't have to deal with them, that is, as if they didn't see us. But they did see us. They saw us, not with the same clarity with which we would have seen them had we been the veteran denizens of the land and another people came to settle in it in ever-increasing numbers; not with the same but with sufficient clarity, clarity that naturally only increased from year to year. We didn't pay any attention to this development. We didn't say to ourselves that there is only one way to forestall the results of this ever-increasing clarity of vision: to form a serious partnership with that people, to involve them earnestly in our building of the land, and to give them a share in our labor and in the fruits of our labor. We did not wish to believe those among us who sounded the warning.

Meanwhile, in any case, in the arena of world politics where we were suddenly needed, we had received the promise of protection for our undertaking [in Palestine] from one great power, a promise that the League of Nations had, as it were, confirmed. Wasn't that enough for us? We didn't say to ourselves that, in the world of politics in which we have lived for twenty-five years or more now, such promises are valid only as long as the political situation created by them exists unchanged and that we should prepare ourselves for the hour of change, bound to come sooner or later, with a different sort of guarantee: instead of a declaration—reality, the reality of a shared undertaking and of common interests with our neighbors in the Land. But we didn't want to believe those among us who sounded the warning. . . . And to whoever pointed to the growing Arab national movement, we responded that there was no need to take it into account—or that we would assuredly prevail. Therefore everything has happened as it did. Jewish terrorist gangs have perpetrated acts that our youth regard as Samson-like deeds. Perhaps there were those among the terrorists who saw themselves as contemporary Samsons, that is, if they knew anything of Samson. The question of whom they regard as the contemporary Philistines invading the country, the British or the Jews, requires no reply. I assume they mean both. I don't believe that there is a single person among us who sees these murderers as Samsons. Why? Because the Samsons of old fought face to face against a well-armed group that outnumbered them; because terrorism is not legitimate warfare. We refuse to regard them as heroes, but rather as madmen. I do not mean by that, however, madman in the heroic sense, i.e., a man thought to be mad but in reality a hero; no, I mean by madman someone who really has lost his wits, a real fool.

And our attitude to the Arabs? Almost all of us knew how to distinguish between the [Arab] terrorists and the Arab people. But there's no hope that the Arabs will be able to distinguish between our thugs and the Jewish people, for very long. And then how shall we arrive at an understanding with the Arabs? It is true that there are those among us who consider such an understanding unnecessary and even harmful; but only politicians of illusion such as they—who only know how to replace one old, broken illusion with another, equally ephemeral— only they could imagine that our Yishuv will exist forever without understanding and cooperation with the Arabs. At this critical hour, whoever encourages eruptions of blind violence, endangers the very existence of the Yishuv. Everything that has been built with such great labor and such great sacrifice, stone after stone, may be destroyed wholesale in the chaos to which these imagined Samsons lead us. Every blow they believe they strike at our enemies, strikes us. They deal in suicide; and not Samson's kind of suicide—he who killed three thousand Philistines as he died—but the destruction of everything cultivated by generations of dedicated, self-sacrificing *halutzim* [pioneers]. We have no right to commit this kind of suicide. "Thou shalt not murder" it is written. He who murders as these self-styled Samsons do, murders his own people.

Herein lies the foulest and most fraudulent deception of all: that it is possible to achieve redemption through sin, if the sin is at all intended from the beginning to redeem. If the people justifies the murder, identifies with the perpetrators, and thus accepts responsibility for the sin as its own, we will bequeath to our children not a free and pure land but a thieves' den to live in and raise their children in.

The order of the day is the whole Yishuv's battle against the White Paper. The White Paper not only belittles the demand for our people's survival and for the continued development of our work here, it ignores the interests of this country and the kind of peace needed here. What is needed is orderly, well-coordinated, and responsible opposition. This sort of opposition should not be expressed as the Arabs have expressed theirs or as the Irish have theirs. (Those among us who admire Irish terrorism forget that there are only two sides involved— apart from Ulster—in the Irish question, while there are three in ours.) The fact is that in this country, we, unlike the Irish, face the opposition of a majority population supported to a greater or lesser degree by 230 million Muslims. This fact reveals the fond comparison with the Irish to be just so much drivel. (By the way, Ireland did not achieve independence because of terror tactics, tactics that Lord Balfour among others fought most successfully, but because of England's sophisticated policy, the new imperialism of the "round table" that seeks centralized control through decentralization.) In our battle we must not do anything to cut our ties with England, since that will be an obstacle to any future agreement with the Arabs and will endanger the Yishuv's survival. We must continue to do whatever is required for the growth and flowering of our settlement work, nothing more and nothing less. As before, the ploughshare must remain our only weapon, the ploughshare without fear. We need fearless hoers of the soil and not throwers of bombs. We need leaders to guide us in our work, leaders who know what they want and how to achieve it; we do not need disturbers of the peace—what they disturb is our work.

21

And Today?

(March 1939)

(Editor's prefatory note:)

Anxious about the generally worsening situation, leading proponents in the Yishuv of Jewish-Arab amity allied themselves to found on 16 April 1939 the League of Arab-Jewish Rapprochement and Cooperation. The aim of the League, according to its program, was to unite "all those who recognize the need for Jewish-Arab rapprochement . . . and also all those who consider it necessary that the Palestine question be solved on the basis of economic advancement and freedom of national culture and social developments of both nations—Arab and Jewish—together."[1] The League had emerged from an earlier effort by its founding members to stimulate debate within the Yishuv on the urgency of Arab-Jewish understanding by the publication in Hebrew of two collections of essays on the subject. The first volume, entitled "At the Crossing of Our Ways" *(Al Parashat Darkenu),* was published in March 1939. Buber, who played a prominent role in the founding of the League, contributed to this volume a Hebrew translation of a selection of his previous writings on the Arab question. He concluded this selection, which appeared under the title "An Accounting," with a postscript, presented here, in which he addresses those who claim that it is too late for Arab-Jewish rapprochement.

Note

1. Cited in Susan Lee Hattis, *The Bi-National Idea in Palestine During Mandatory Times* (Haifa: Shikmona Publishing Co., 1970), p. 222.

And Today?

Some of you say, "So be it. We have erred, we readily acknowledge it; but now come what may, it is too late to have recourse to the way which you recommend. Today the fast rule of international politics and its hard consequences prevail. . . . And if today we have still to act, we can do so only within the prevailing situation and its exigencies, but our actions will perforce be different from that which you prescribe!"

No, surely not only today. It has been years now that you have been speaking thus. You are forever exclaiming, "Perhaps yesterday your advice was sound, but now it is no longer valid. Today it is no longer possible; it no longer holds true. Today everything has changed!" And thus today has become yesterday and yet another yesterday. But every situation results from another, and every single time you have stood on the wrong side; every single time you have increased the power of evil; every time what could at least have been justly done, was not done, and this inactivity influenced the future. Always, in every situation it is possible to do *something*, some correct undertaking, something which determines to some extent the face of the next hour, the character of the next situation. The conditions of action are constantly changing; there is always the obligation to do something else, something new, that is, to respond to a changing situation. But the correct response! You have always made tactical responses instead, not understanding that deliberating tactically always provides us with the wrong means, sacrifices the future for the sake of the moment, while we who absolutely need the future can achieve our aim only by consistent work for the future. The correct response is a reaction to the moment not from the moment, but from the future. This is what we have missed every single time. But we can still do it even today. To be sure, the situation has become much more difficult; conditions of activity have greatly worsened. We shall certainly have to choose a path along which there will be no shining successes. But it will be the right way. The new situation will also present us with an alternative, and the future will depend upon our decision to an extent which cannot be estimated in advance.

Today we can no longer say what we will have to do tomorrow. But already today it is possible to say what will have to be the basis of our future actions, namely, the truth grounded in an examination of the whole reality of Jewish-Arab life. If what we say here be true, and you who say "We have erred" admit it, then this is also the truth of today and tomorrow. Now, at this very moment, the main thing is to get off the tactical path and take upon ourselves the yoke of the truth. And even if falsehood should triumph in the world, even then there is no need to despair unless we tag along with the rearguard, in which case we shall have forsaken our future. While, if we resist the temptations of falsehood, if we recognize the futility of its might, if we refuse to allow the seal of success to displace the seal of faithfulness, then we need not despair. Perhaps tomorrow we shall have a choice between only two alternatives: either to blazon our standard with the colors of falsehood and go down to Hell as the most wretched of standard-bearers, with an empty cheer and boasting, or to watch over the lesser of the two seals of God, the human truth, and keep it in the ark of a hard life until the ruler shall arise who has delivered it into our hands and who will raise it up to the light of the new day.

22

Concerning Our Politics

(August 1939)

(Editor's prefatory note:)

The second volume sponsored by the newly founded League for Jewish-Arab Rapprochement was published in August 1939. It was prompted by what its editors deemed to be the myopic response of the Zionist leadership to the White Paper of May 1939. In his contribution to this volume, Buber focused on the major thesis of the volume, claiming that the endless harping on the perfidy of the British disclosed the fundamental weakness of Zionist policy. Rather than developing a political strategy consonant with the unique moral and social character of the Zionist colonization project, the Zionist leadership unimaginatively adopted the political principles of European colonization, and, accordingly, rendered the Zionist movement dependent on the might of an imperial power.

In presenting this thesis, Buber makes adumbrative reference to a distinction between "concentrative" and "expansive" colonization, a distinction which he had developed in an earlier essay.[1] An expansive colonization, he argues is typical of imperialism; it seeks to expand the power and interests of the metropolitan country, and should the native populations resist the colonizers—the emissaries of the metropolitan power—force and cunning are employed. A concentrative colonization, on the other hand, does not intrinsically serve an imperial power, but merely seeks to concentrate anew the members and moral and spiritual energies of a scattered, forlorn people. Zionist settlement in Palestine—with its emphasis on the return of the Jews to the soil and the renewal of their social and cultural autonomy—is thus fundamentally an undertaking in concentrative colonization.

In the present essay, entitled "Concerning Our Politics," Buber bemoans the fact that the Zionist leadership had failed to develop a political policy which would reflect and indeed give manifest expression to the profound moral forces that animate the concentrative settlement promoted by Zionism. This would have been a "great Zionism" *(Grosszionismus)*, instead of the prevailing unimaginative "petty Zionism" *(Kleinzionismus)* with its frenzied dependence on Britain, its emphasis on exclusive "Hebrew labor" (to the exclusion and harm of the Arabs) and on the creation in Palestine of Jewish demographic majority, protected by British bayonets, with the consequent estrangement and embitterment of the Arabs.

Note

1. Cf. Buber, "Selbstbesinnung" (1926), in Buber, *Der Jude und sein Judentum: Gesammelte Aufsätze und Reden* (Cologne: Joseph Melzer, 1963), pp. 488–500.

Concerning Our Politics

The basic flaw in our Zionist undertaking has been that we did not develop independent political methods for our unique type of settlement. At the same time as we took new paths in the very work of settlement and discovered new forms of economic and social organization that were appropriate for our purpose and the conditions of our enterprise, we accepted the colonial politics of the states of modern Europe, which was born under completely different circumstances and which did not fit our position at all. The great states and commercial companies directed their colonial efforts according to the orientation of nations well centered and seeking to expand. Their enterprise was based upon their continued readiness to intervene with military force that in technical power greatly exceeded that of the colonial population. Contrastingly, we are colonizing with the orientation of a completely scattered nation lacking a nucleus. Our aim is concentration, and we have no military power to fall back upon in the hour of need. The image of our renowned brigades, which have come to take the place of the so-called [Jewish] Legion, is but a romantic chimera. In a period of war, technically legions can only operate as an adjunct of real military might, and only insofar as it equips us technically, and only insofar as no other military power equips the masses of natives who oppose that settlement: in other words, so long as there is no change in global political conditions. We have pursued a policy of legions without any. That is to say, in our concentrated settlement effort, we depended on the support of the political power of an expansionist state. We have adopted the faulty assumption that an expansionist interest and a concentrative interest can coexist side by side in a natural alliance, as it were, which is unharmed by changes, even fundamental ones, in global politics. However, that is not the case. He who colonizes for the purpose of concentration needs the land of his concentration, and he is tied to it indissolubly, whereas the expansionist colonizer can clear out in an emergency or withdraw from a position that has become uncomfortable; he can change the order of his connections, reduce some, develop others—everything according to his needs. As soon as the global political situation changes and the British monarchy needs, either truly or according to its own lights, a second Egypt to the west of the Suez Canal—at that moment, we should expect that the government will try to get the Arabs, or some part of them, to supply that second Egypt. We cannot supply that need. Although I hold the opinion that the Arabs who can supply it will not in fact do so, it seems to me that at this time the British authorities do not perceive the relations of the Arab states among themselves correctly, and therefore they are not planning their strategies well. Nevertheless that does not at all change the fact that our present position is what it is. The complaint that they, the British, have betrayed us may have a certain propaganda value, but politically it is worthless. In the past we relegated the banner of Zion to a political interest, which needed it for its own purposes, and now we complain that those in charge of that interest no longer need the banner today, or, in their opinion, they no longer need it, for now they find it too costly—we complain that they interpret the contract that was signed to that effect in a manner consistent with their aim. Did we not know till now that the global politics of great powers presently follows (and, it seems, against its own will now) from considerations of profit and loss at the moment and not from the consideration of unshakable political principles? From that point of view there is no difference between the democracies and the dictatorships.

Our error lay in acting within the scheme of western colonial policies, which has only two parties, the one engaged in colonization and the one that suffers it. We acted within that scheme for our own purposes, which were so different that we were necessarily coopted on one side, that of the ruler, and we gave ourselves over entirely to its rule. The result was that we received the stamp of the agent of imperialism, although its cause was not at all linked internally to our own. Moreover, it is well known how precarious the position of agents is, with regard to both parties. We were considered the agents of imperialism even at a time when in reality this type of imperialism was no longer, and in its place has come a League of Nations for the purpose of preserving free trade in the world, a league better known by the old name of "imperium."

What ought we have done? We should have done two things. First, we should have achieved a single promise, a decisive one, from that power to whose hands they [the League of Nations] were about to deliver the mandate over the Land of Israel, with the explicit aim of helping to settle it—this promise: that it recognize the right of free Jewish immigration to the land and the free purchase of property there, and that it never do anything to infringe on that right. That simple, clear promise would have been impossible to undo by means of interpretation. Second, we should have obtained the acknowledgment of that right on the part of the Arabs, also a simple, clear acknowledgment. Both the acknowledgment and the promise should have been ratified by an official international body. That acknowledgment could, of course, only be put into effect if it were the product of negotiations on the basis of a comprehensive settlement program, a program in which sufficient expression was given to the essence and goals of our concentrated settlement. Such a program would not in justice be limited to the Land of Israel alone. But this center [of Jewish settlement] in the Land of Israel would require a wide expanse to support it. Such an expanse could have been created only by extending the productive basis to the Jewish communities of Arab lands. On the other hand, that means systematic expansion of Jewish property and Jewish labor in the economic upbuilding of the Near East. The historical fate of such cooperation in our annals has been that we have always been persecuted after working for the benefit of any nation. We would not have had to fear such a fate this time, if we had created a historical innovation, that is to say, if the center of our effort were an effective independent position, the Land of Israel. We should make clear to ourselves that the Land of Israel would in this way have become not only the organic center of the people of Israel, but also the organic center of a rising East.

It is reasonable to assume that such negotiation could not have been carried out with a few notables, and the acknowledgment that I have in mind could not have come in the form of a private letter from an Arab prince. We needed a counterpart in negotiations that would be balanced. If there were in reality no such counterpart, our duty was to demand one and to assist in its organization, a sort of official representative of all the Arabs. Of course it would also have been necessary to negotiate with representatives of the Palestinian Arabs themselves on our mutual enterprise. A major part of the conclusions of the program would have been to include them in the work of building up the land and to find in every area organizational forms for combining our interests. The *small* program that was suggested necessarily led to war against Arab labor;[1] whereas the *great* program would not only have permitted its participation in our enterprise, but would even have made it obligatory. This is also the case in the sphere of politics. The small program has led to emphasis on the need for becoming a majority in the land.[2] The great program would have taught that cooperation between peoples is possible, such that the question of numerical proportion no longer has decisive importance. In its essence our independent settlement policy would have created new political forms that would remain in power even after the Land of Israel became a member of a federal union of nations. But we did not develop an independent policy. We distracted ourselves from its necessity.

Everything I say here has already been said by me twenty years ago, partly in public, but the greater part in the committees of the Zionist Congresses and in the councils of Zionist groups. Nothing has been done. Today I accuse myself for being deceived then by prejudice against publicity, a common prejudice among us. It is probable that if at that time we, my friends and I, had overcome that prejudice, we would have been more influential. We held the decree of Zionist discipline higher than that of our own political understanding. That has proven to be a grave error.

When we come forward today and point to our suggestions and memoranda of that time, many argue against us: so be it; perhaps you were correct, but now everything has happened the way it did—now there is no way of coming to any agreement with the Arabs except for what amounts to renunciation, an agreement that entails abandoning the vital claim of our settlement; now nothing remains, come what may, except the supreme struggle, the struggle for our lives. That argument is no more than a fresh evasion of the highest task of a greater Zionism.

Cooperation is only possible on the basis of genuine trust, and we have trampled a thousand buds of trust. Certainly the task has become several times more difficult than it was, but it is not true that it has become an impossible one. The main thing is to set our hearts today in that *direction,* in which we must search, experiment, expand, and win souls. A great decision of that sort is productive. If we go in one direction and are not diverted, it will turn out that it is possible to move in that direction. It is not true that the idea of concentrative settlement can no longer find independent and wide political expression. It will find expression if we take it seriously. As soon as we truly recognize that this nation has no salvation except in creating a covenant and a comprehensive alliance between the two brother nations, we will attain the ability to show the Arabs too that that is the case. Through cunning nothing more can be done at the moment, but through truth we can accomplish everything.

Notes

1. The reference is to the policy of "Hebrew labor," which sought to create a comprehensive and autonomous Jewish economy in Palestine. This policy in effect meant the exclusion of Arab labor. Cf. Buber's note on the issue on p. 214.

2. On the official Zionist policy of creating a Jewish majority in Palestine, see selections 29 and 31.

23

False Prophets

(Spring 1940)

(Editor's prefatory note:)

Parallel to the formation of the League for Jewish-Arab Rapprochement and Cooperation, Buber and a number of his friends, most of whom had been associated with the by then defunct Brith Shalom—and who were also active in the League—established a journal, *Be'ayot Ha-Yom* (Problems of the Day), which appeared between August 1940 and November 1942. Dealing with contemporary issues from a humanistic perspective, the journal sought to be alert to the political needs of both the Jews and Arabs. In a special brochure, *La-Mo'ed,* issued for Passover 1940—a publication that preceded the formal founding of *Be'ayot Ha-Yom*—Buber contributed a long disquisition on the Biblical conception of "false and true prophets." Amid the scholarly detail of the article, there was the following message.

FALSE PROPHETS

. . . History is a dynamic process, and history means that one hour is never like the one that has gone before. God operates in history, and God is not a machine which, once it has been wound up, keeps on running until it wears out. He is a living God. He expresses his truth through his will, but his will is not a program. At this hour, God wills this or that for mankind, but he has endowed mankind with a will of its own, and even with sufficient power to carry it out. So, mankind can change its will from one hour to the next, and God, who is deeply concerned about mankind and its will and the possible changes it may undergo, can, when that will changes, change his plan for mankind. This means that historical reality could have been changed. One must rely on one's knowledge. One must go one's way and listen all over again.

. . . The true prophets are the true politicians of reality, for they proclaim their political tidings from the viewpoint of the complete historical reality, which it is given them to see. The false prophets, the politicians who foster illusions, use the power of their wishful thinking to tear a scrap out of historical reality and sew it into their guild of motley illusions. When they are out to influence through suggestion, they display the gay colors, and when they are asked for the material of truth, they point to the scrap, torn out of reality.

. . . False prophets are not godless. They adore the god "Success." They themselves are in constant need of success and achieve it by promising it to the people. The craving for success governs their hearts and determines what rises from them. They do not deceive; they are deceived, and can breathe only in the air of deceit.

The true prophets know the little bloated idol which goes by the name of "Success" through and through. They know that ten successes that are nothing but successes can lead to defeat, while on the contrary ten failures can add to a victory, provided the spirit stands firm. When true prophets address the people, they are usually unsuccessful; everything in the people which craves for success opposes them. But the moment they are thrown into the pit, whatever spirit is still alive in Israel bursts into flame, and the turning begins in secret which, in the midst of the deepest distress, will lead to renewal.

The false prophet feeds on dreams, and acts as if dreams were reality. The true prophet lives by the true word he hears, and must endure having it treated as though it only held true for some "ideological" sphere, "ethics" or "religion," but not for the real life of the people. . . .

24
Let Us Avoid Provocations!

(3 March 1940)

(Editor's prefatory note:)

Although the Zionist leadership greeted the White Paper of May 1939 with profound anger, they maintained a guarded optimism that it was merely an ephemeral gesture to appease the Arabs, and that His Majesty's government would postpone its implementation indefinitely. This conviction that the Anglo-Zionist alliance would be quickly restored was reinforced when, with the outbreak of World War Two in September 1940, the Yishuv immediately and with impressive effectiveness mobilized its economy and human resources on behalf of Britain's war effort.[1] The Yishuv's optimism, however, was suddenly dashed when on 28 February 1940, without warning, the Mandatory government issued Land Transfer Regulations, severely restricting, as stipulated by the White Paper of 1939, Jewish land purchase in Palestine. The Yishuv was stunned. With the tacit approval of the Zionist leadership, massive, illegal demonstrations were staged throughout the first week of March. In the ensuing violence seventy-four Jews were seriously injured, with two subsequently dying of the wounds, and more than two hundred others received lesser injuries; of the twenty-five British personnel hurt, five were seriously wounded.

In response to these events, Buber wrote the following letter, dated 3 March 1940, to the Executive of the Jewish Agency for Palestine and to the *Va'ad Ha-Leumi*—the National Council of the Yishuv. Having failed to receive a reply other than a perfunctory note from the *Va'ad Ha-Leumi* acknowledging receipt of the letter, Buber published it as an open-letter in *La-Mo'ed*, the Passover brochure of 1940, sponsored by the editorial board of *Be'ayot Ha-Yom* (see introduction to selection 23).

Note

1. Between 10 and 21 September 1940, close to 120,000 men and women in the Yishuv voluntarily registered for national service; this figure constituted 25 percent of the Jewish population in Palestine.

LET US AVOID PROVOCATIONS!
An Open Letter to the Yishuv's Leadership

Honorable Sirs,

Still under the impression of the events of the last few days, I turn to the responsible institutions of the Zionist movement and the Yishuv with the following questions:

1. Are you aware that, for as long as a parliamentary form of government has existed in Great Britain, street demonstrations have never influenced the parliamentary majority which supports the government? Are you aware, moreover, that nothing influences the decision-making circles in England more than the manifest skill exercised by

leaders of some sectors of the population in controlling the masses in time of upheaval? Do you realize that the conclusion to be drawn is that the recent demonstrations undermine the Jewish Agency's declared policies?

2. If, despite historical precedents, the Yishuv's leadership believes that the demonstrations may possibly achieve some parliamentary success, do they realize that the demonstrations will arouse the strongest resentment on the part of the Mandatory government? That, furthermore, this sort of pyrrhic victory will naturally bring in its wake Arab counter-demonstrations, such as occurred when demonstrations were held to protest Sir Arthur Wauchope's proposed legislation?[1] And that this will once again create a situation in which the rabble influences policy decisions? Does the Yishuv's leadership realize that Arab counter-demonstrations will be much more successful than our own, as long as there is a chance that the Near East may become involved in the War and as long as defense of the Allied armies' flanks is the order of the day. The Arab potentates have a greater or lesser degree of freedom of choice in this War. They, unlike us, have several options—to enter the War on England's side, to maintain neutrality, or even to ally themselves with one of Britain's enemies in the East—with, that is, one of the two anti-Semitic powers, Germany or Italy, or perhaps with anti-Zionist Russia.

3. Does the Yishuv's leadership actually believe that demonstrations at this time are an appropriate means of effectively influencing our own people? Or do they, on the contrary, believe that the demonstrations may nourish or even create illusions among the masses, illusions whose very existence is damaging and whose inevitable failure may cause the internal disintegration of the Yishuv?

4. Does the Yishuv's leadership believe that such demonstrations will not adversely affect—to a significant degree—the chances of arriving at an understanding with the Arabs, chances which have improved since the War began? If, as may be assumed from the Jewish Agency's establishment of a special committee on the Arab question, efforts have been made since the outbreak of the War to arrive at such an understanding, what then motivated the Yishuv's leadership to tolerate demonstrations which undermine their very own policies?[2]

5. If, as I have heard it said, the Yishuv's authorities deny responsibility for the demonstrations, are they aware that the youths who took to the streets did so in the belief that the signal was given by the Yi-

shuv's leadership? If the Yishuv's leadership knew this, what did they do to inform the youths that that belief was mistaken?

6. If the responsible institutions of the Zionist movement and the Yishuv do not accept responsibility for the demonstrations, who *is* responsible? Do the authorities wish to demand of whoever is responsible that they account for themselves? Do the Yishuv's leaders believe that, especially now, they can and should tolerate the existence of groups or individuals who do not belong to the leadership but who issue directives which are generally understood as proceeding from it? If, as I would guess, the Yishuv's leadership believes that this should not be tolerated, have they issued the necessary orders to prevent those groups or individuals from continuing their activities and subverting the official policies of the Yishuv?

With great esteem,

M. Buber

Notes

1. Sir Arthur Wauchope (1874–1947), High Commissioner of Palestine between 1931 and 1938, proposed in December 1935 the establishment of a Legislative Council for Palestine in which the Arabs would enjoy a majority. The Yishuv rigorously rejected this proposal.

2. At the Twenty-First Zionist Congress in Geneva in August 1939, an Inquiry Commission was set up "to examine Jewish-Arab relations in the political, economic, cultural, and social fields to determine the possibilities of collaboration between Jews and Arabs in all these branches of activity and to submit their conclusions and proposals to all the authorized institutions of the Zionist movement." Resolution no. 7 of the Twenty-First Zionist Congress; cited in S. L. Hattis, *The Bi-National Idea in Palestine* (Haifa: Shikmona Publishers, 1970), p. 222. The proposed Inquiry Committee was established in January 1940 under the auspices of the Jewish Agency. The majority of the members of the committee were active in the League for Jewish-Arab Rapprochement, and its report, submitted in September 1941, not surprisingly recommended the establishment of a bi-national federal state as the most equitable solution to the problem of Palestine. The Committee's report was, of course, ignored.

25
The Ichud

(September 1942)

(Editor's prefatory note:)

From its initial endeavors to promote social and cultural reconciliation between the peoples of Palestine, the League for Jewish-Arab Rapprochement and Cooperation had crystallized a political program for a bi-national state. This platform, of which Buber was one of the fourteen signatories, was formulated in June 1942 and presented as an alternative to the creation of the Arab state of Palestine implied by the White Paper of 1939 and to the demand for a Jewish state that since the Biltmore conference of May 1942 seemed destined to become the official Zionist policy. (Indeed, the Biltmore Program, discussed in full in the introduction to selection 30, was adopted as the official policy of the Zionist movement in November 1942.) The League's program was endorsed by *Ha-Shomer Ha-Tza'ir*, a Marxist-Zionist party of considerable strength and prestige within the Yishuv, and several smaller parties.

In light of the fact that these parties also joined the League *en bloc*, many independent members of the League now felt a need to organize themselves as a distinct political grouping. At the initiative of Judah L. Magnes a meeting of about one hundred individuals was convened in Jerusalem on 11 August 1942. At the conclusion of this meeting, the *Ichud* (Union) was established as a separate political party associated with the League. Its executive committee included, among others, Magnes, Henrietta Szold (1860–1945), founder of Hadassah (the American women's Zionist organization) and Buber. At the same meeting it was decided to adopt the monthly *Be'ayot Ha-Yom* as the organ of the Ichud, since its moving spirits were now members of the new organization. (See selection 23.) The journal—which reappeared in April 1944 under the shortened name *Be'ayot* (Problems)[1]—was to be published by Buber, and edited by his close associate Ernst Akivah Simon. The program of the Ichud, composed by Magnes, Robert Weltsch, and Buber, was published on 3 September 1942.

Note

1. With volume 7 (1948), the name of the journal was changed to *Be'ayot Ha-Zman* (Problems of the Time).

THE ICHUD

1. The Association Union (Ichud) adheres to

a. The Zionist movement insofar as this seeks the establishment of the Jewish National Home for the Jewish People in Palestine.

b. The struggle throughout the world for a New Order in international relations and a Union of the peoples, large and small, for a life of freedom and justice without fear, oppression and want.

2. The Association Union therefore regards a Union between the Jewish and Arab peoples as essential for the upbuilding of Palestine and for cooperation between the Jewish world and the Arab world in all branches of life—social, economic, cultural, political—thus making for the revival of the whole Semitic World.

3. The main political aims of the Association Union are as follows:

a. Government in Palestine based upon equal political rights for the two peoples.

b. The agreement of the steadily growing Yishuv and of the whole Jewish people to a Federative Union of Palestine and neighbouring countries. This Federative Union is to guarantee the national rights of all the peoples within it.

c. A Covenant between this Federative Union and an Anglo-American Union which is to be part of the future Union of the free peoples. This Union of the free peoples is to bear the ultimate responsibility for the establishment and stability of international relations in the New World after the war.

The Association Union is to cooperate with the League for Jewish-Arab Rapprochement, containing, as it does, representatives of organizations with varying points of view. It is also prepared to cooperate with other organizations and groups in specific projects.

26

In the Days of Silence

(1943)

(Editor's prefatory note:)

The Ichud was frequently vilified as traitorous for having raised a dissenting voice during the Yishuv's struggle against the White Paper. Occasionally, its members were ostracized, such as the writers Moshe Smilansky (1874–1953) and Shelomo Zemach (1886–1974). Each of these authors of renown had submitted an article to *Moznayim,* the literary organ of the Hebrew Writers Association published in Tel Aviv. Zemach's article had actually been accepted, set in type, and proof-read when he received notice that the editors felt "it was inappropriate at this time to publish his article, even though its literary merit cannot be doubted." The Ichud decided to publish Smilansky's and Zemach's essays in a special booklet, entitled "In the Days of Silence." In his foreword to this booklet, which follows, Buber tersely reminds the Yishuv of the distinction between dissent and disloyalty.

IN THE DAYS OF SILENCE

It has become characteristic of our society to assert directly or indirectly, verbally or by other means, that "there are certain things that should not be said or published because they are liable to endanger our national interests." Yet this in fact is the very question at issue: what are our national interests and how are they being endangered? Labelling individuals who hold different opinions as people who do not have the national interest at heart, or have insufficient regard for it creates a noxious atmosphere. The views expressed in the articles published here derive precisely from a deep concern that what is called "advancing our national interests" today is liable to place the real interests of the nation in grave danger. They derive from a deep-seated feeling that imagined interests must be confronted by real interests, and delu-

150

sion by reality. They derive from a dread of the fate towards which delusions are leading us. They derive from a very strongly felt need to sound a warning while there is still time.

It is quite true that those who seek to discourage expression have a different conception of what our national interests are. But what do they mean when they assert that the expression in public of a view different from theirs is liable to endanger our national interests? How can opinions expressed by individuals bring that about, as long as they remain within their own bounds, the bounds of individual opinion? To be sure, the government of a state, even the most democratic, has the right to prevent disclosure of state secrets; it has the right to prevent incitement to rebellion and sabotage, particularly at a time of emergency. But how can the knowledge that there are individuals who do not subscribe to the accepted definition of the interests of the Jewish people harm the view of those who are trying to limit expression? Do they really imagine that at present, when totalitarian systems are on the rise, the world sees reticence as proof that other opinions do not exist? On the contrary, where silence prevails, the world tends to visualize opinion that deviates from the official view of things as far more extreme than it actually is.

27

Do Not Believe It!

(June 1944)

(Editor's prefatory note:)

The Yishuv's opposition to the White Paper of 1939, especially its restrictions on Jewish immigration, was not merely motivated by ideological considerations, but also by a resolve to save as many European Jews as possible from the clutches of Hitler. The decision, embodied in the Biltmore Program, to demand the immediate establishment of a Jewish state in Palestine was prompted precisely by the feeling that only a sovereign Jewish state, beholden to no one but the Jewish people, would guarantee the free mass immigration of Jews to Palestine. The problem of Palestine, as Ben-Gurion emphatically put it, is almost exclusively "the problem of further Jewish immigration. . . . If Jewish immigration into Palestine depends on Arab consent [as implied by the White Paper], there will hardly be any Jewish immigration at all. It is vitally important politically as well as morally that our position on this crucial question should be made unequivocal. *Jewish immigration to Palestine needs no consent. We are returning as of right.*"[1]

The Ichud's initial hesitation to endorse this right not surprisingly aroused considerable antagonism. Indeed, it was moved in the Inner General Council of the Zionist Organization that the adherents of the Ichud be expelled from the movement. The proposal was rejected, but the Ichud was invited to submit a clarification of its position on the question of immigration. The Ichud complied, and on 5 October 1942 released a statement declaring that it was opposed to the "fixation" of the Jews as a permanent minority in Palestine and that it favored "the creation of a political and economic situation enabling the absorption of the greatest possible number of Jewish immigrants into Palestine."[2] The cherished goal of a large Jewish immigration, as the Ichud explained in subsequent statements, would be most effectively achieved if the Yishuv were sensitive to the genuine Arab fear of domination by a Jewish majority. The only way of satisfying Jewish needs and allaying Arab fears, the Ichud maintained, was bi-national parity within a single state.

In the following article, published in *Be'ayot* in June 1944, Buber elaborated the Ichud's position that, until a final disposition of the Palestine question, the rate of immigration should be regulated by the economic or "absorptive" capacity of the country so as not to exacerbate Arab fears of being inundated and excluded from the development of the country they share with the Jews. The essay itself was occasioned by the publication in the Hebrew press of a statement attributed to Chaim Weizmann endorsing the "maximalist," non-negotiable position on immigration. Buber was incensed by the joining of Weizmann's prestigious name with a position which, in Buber's judgment, the elder statesman of Zionism was far too sensible and politically astute to have supported.

Notes

1. Speech delivered on 5 October 1942. Cited in J. C. Hurewitz, *The Struggle for Palestine* (New York: Schocken Books, 1976), p. 164 (italics in original).

2. *Palestine Post*, 7 October 1942.

DO NOT BELIEVE IT!

The newspapers report that [Chaim] Weizmann said in a speech in London, "Only those for whom it is a question of life and death can decide on the matter of absorption [of Jewish immigration into Palestine]; nothing could be simpler."

When faced with the alternative of whether to doubt the experienced political wisdom of Weizmann or to distrust the newspapers, I prefer the latter, for who knows as well as Weizmann that every public utterance of the leader of a movement is a political utterance in the precise sense of the word. That is, by its very nature it is directed not only to the immediate audience, but is meant to influence the entire political world! And, supposing that this news is true, what influence will it have in the present situation? What will the men of the world of politics think when they hear that the Zionists now deny them the right to judge and decide what number of immigrants can be absorbed by this country at any one time according to economic and technical conditions? International polticians can only think that the Zionists no longer want to consider them participants in the negotiations over *aliyah* [Jewish immigration to Palestine], that the above-mentioned demand deprives the negotiations of their realistic basis.

Until now, the maximal Zionist demand for *aliyah* was considered to be based upon the fitness of the land to absorb immigration, which might, of course, be enlarged by our creative and fructifying enterprise. Now, instead of this version of Zionist maximalism, if this news report is correct, the rate of *aliyah* at any one time will be what is considered desirable in the opinion of the representatives of the Jews. And so there will no longer be an objective criterion (which, to be sure, naturally permits of various understandings, but may also bring about a relatively objective decision after joint consideration). But the matter will now be under the absolute authority of him for whom it is "a matter of life and death."

Would we not find it intolerable if, over another issue of international politics, the opinion of all the parties should be silenced except for the wish of the one whom the matter affects most? Would we not find it unthinkable that any international institution should accept such a principle? And if we do find its acceptance unthinkable, what is the political sense of expressing such an opinion? Could any intelligent and well-informed individual imagine that the expression of demands lacking any reality could aid our cause? And which of our comrades is more intelligent and better informed than Weizmann? Thus, when the press comes and asks you to believe that he said such things, my plain advice is "Do not believe them!"

Moreover, what should be done if not one but *two* parties are directly concerned with something and both of them claim that for them it is a matter of life and death? And what if, at the critical moment, one of them should demand everything and the other should refuse everything, and there should be not the slightest chance of compromise, for there can be no acknowledgment of the wish of anyone other than the one for whom it is a matter of life and death? To be sure, it may be that one party is speaking the truth and thus, for him, it really is a question of life and death, while the other is not speaking the truth, so that it is not a matter of life and death for him. But is there any possibility that an international institution would be able to decide about the truth or lack of truth of such claims in order to assign to one of the parties the absolute right to decide, while denying the other side even the slightest participation in the decision which affects it so directly? Do we think that such a possibility exists? And if we do not think so, what is the political sense of expressing this view? Do our respresentatives speak in order to banish from the minds of their audience with well-defined claims, the terrible doubts involved in the situation, or in order to act in the political sphere? And which of our people is like Weizmann for knowing the purpose for which he speaks? Thus, when the press mentions, as if Weizmann himself had spoken it, the simple sentence, "Nothing could be simpler," I repeat, "Do not believe them!"

28

Nathan Rotenstreich:
I Believed—Too Hastily?

(August 1944)

(Editor's prefatory note:)

Buber's essay on Weizmann elicited a critical response from a young philosopher, Nathan Rotenstreich, who although not a member of the Ichud was close to some of its leading members, especially Shmuel H. Bergman, Ernst Simon, and Buber. In contrast to his teachers and friends in the Ichud, Rotenstreich—who was to become one of Israel's most prominent philosophers—held that the establishment of a Jewish state must be a precondition for any compromise and accommodation with the Arabs. Only the attainment of Jewish political sovereignty, in his judgment, could secure the realization of the vital interests of the Jewish people which the current urgencies of Jewish history have rendered non-negotiable. Paramount among these interests was the right of free, unhindered Jewish immigration to Palestine. This perception of Zionist priorities, which was shared by most members of the movement, seemed to Rotenstreich so logically and morally compelling that, as he writes in the following critique of Buber, published in the August 1944 issue of the Ichud's journal *Be'ayot*, it is perfectly credible that the sapient Weizmann endorsed Jewish immigration (which, in fact, he did) as an unalienable right not affected by the politics of compromise.

NATHAN ROTENSTREICH: I BELIEVED—TOO HASTILY?

The recent issue of *Be'ayot* contains Martin Buber's words of warning not to believe the newspapers which wrote in Chaim Weizmann's name that "only those for whom it is a question of life and death can decide on the matter of absorption [of Jewish immigration into Palestine]; nothing could be simpler."

155

Buber gives two reasons for this warning:

1. Would you find it tolerable if, in any other affair of international politics, the opinion of all the parties should be silenced excepting the will of those whom the matter concerns most?

2. What is to be done if not one, but *two* parties are directly concerned with some cause and both contend that it is a matter of life and death for them?

It seems that these two arguments require clarification, I will then proceed to demonstrate that he who is tempted to believe that Weizmann said what he did, believed correctly.

We have seen with our own eyes and heard with our own ears that very vital matters are being taken out of the international sphere for, it is declared, they are more appropriately settled by the decisions of the nations themselves. [Accordingly], all we ever hear is that the decision concerning the regime of Italy is the concern of the Italian people—and this after, by the decision of that same Italian people, it was ruled for a generation by a regime which brought it to its present state.

Is not the alliance between Soviet Russia and England built upon this setting of limits which leaves the affairs of the regime and way of life to the peoples themselves and does not combine these matters with the interrelationship between the two peoples? In the case of Italy, Spain, and France, these declarations are the result both of convenience and of many other considerations, while others result from the realistic consideration that we must not seek too much, nor compare and draw parallels between peoples in every area. At any rate, here we must not lay down the principle which Buber did.

Yet the gist lies in the second reason, the claim of the vital interests of the two peoples. Herein lies the bone of contention between us and our neighbors, and the cause of the controversy within our own Zionist ranks. For in this area we demand that the nations make an unequivocal decision on which of the two causes is more vital; which is a matter "of life and death" and which is not among the primary needs of a people. We demand of the world that it make a decision on this issue; not a *compromise* on the fundamental questions, but a *decision* in favor of one of the parties. Every discussion of compromise, if it has any substance, can be entered into only on the basis of this decision and not before. Only after the peoples who possess the might, who speak of justice and the right to live, shall decide that our cause is the more vital, that it affects the fate of an entire people, and that it solves a worldwide problem (factors which are lacking in the cause of the Arab community of Palestine), only then shall we be entitled to claim that our cause will be accomplished with the authority of our people.

Buber warns us not to believe what Weizmann is reported to have said because he adhered to the concept of a double commitment in Palestine which fits a double interest. This is one of the proofs of how political slogans which are the result of convenience and blurring become moral principles and first principles. Yet one who battles for principles and is armed, as Buber is, with a talent for criticism and the ability to strip away the outer covering, must recognize what this distinction requires.

I do not know if Weizmann said what the journalists attributed to him. I believe that he said it, not because "nothing could be simpler," but because nothing could be more just.

29

An Additional Clarification: A Reply to Nathan Rotenstreich

(August 1944)

(Editor's prefatory note:)

During the period of their controversy Buber and Rotenstreich had been working together on the editing of a book of essays in honor of S. H. Bergman.[1] Their collaboration occasioned frequent discussions of their political differences. At one heated moment, Rotenstreich accused Buber of emphasizing exclusively the "personal Jewish problem," i.e., the existential and cultural problems faced by the Jewish individual in the modern, increasingly secular world, and of neglecting the "collective problem of the Jews," i.e., anti-Semitism. Chagrined by this accusation, Buber beckoned Rotenstreich to his home and passionately assured him that "he lives the Holocaust and the death of every individual in the camps."[2] By implication, he suggests in the following rejoinder to Rotenstreich, published, like the preceding selection, in the August 1944 issue of *Be'ayot*, that these emotions are irrelevant to the actual political situation in Palestine.

Notes

1. *Hagut: Philosophical Reflections in Honor of Shmuel Hugo Bergman on the Occasion of His Sixtieth Birthday* (in Hebrew), ed. by M. Buber and N. Rotenstreich (Jerusalem, 1944).

2. Letter, dated November 1980, from N. Rotenstreich to the editor.

AN ADDITIONAL CLARIFICATION: A REPLY TO NATHAN ROTENSTREICH

I see that there is need for further clarification of what I have written, although I had thought it was as clear as it needed to be, and that a word to the wise was sufficient. Surely, [Nathan Rotenstreich would agree] that we must distinguish between political affairs within the province of one nation, and political affairs in the international arena.

The affairs of a single nation, for example, its government, are generally regarded as subject to the sovereign decisions of that nation— only to the extent, of course, that those decisions do not directly affect the interests of other peoples. . . .

To be sure, in special [seemingly extenuating] political circumstances, for example, when it is necessary to prevent the break-up of an important and vital international alliance, it is possible [for any one of the nations concerned] to transfer a host of issues which obviously affect the interests of other peoples from the domain of international politics to that of the exclusive political considerations of a single nation. This may easily be done on the grounds of the fiction that other nations do not exist in terms of international law.

Whoever in the Yishuv contends otherwise, using examples from either the first or the second type of politics—national and international—is avoiding the facts determining the political reality of our life in Palestine. The problems involved in our existence in Palestine so manifestly affect the existence of other peoples that no one would regard these problems as belonging to the exclusive realm of national politics, and no one with an elementary grasp of politics would think that in "our case" there are [extenuating] political circumstances.

To be sure, when difficult negotiations are being carried out or are about to be carried out between one power and its rival, and one power has some objectives which it can give up for others which are truly important, and thus seeks something in exchange, our case is recalled from time to time. But whoever does not understand that on *that* chessboard not a single pawn is ever moved except to effect an exchange, is a victim of one of our favorite and most disastrous illusions. (Admittedly, such "illusions" were once truly necessary to us in order to prepare a territorial claim. But this has ended as it did and there is not the slightest sign that this argument will be revived.) We allow every cunning stratagem of international politics which serves our cause and our pride, and we attach our salvation to imaginary prospects which have no reality except that of a stratagem, sometimes only for an election campaign.

The basic defects of our foreign policy are that it is not based upon a recognition of the real interests of the peoples involved in the decisions [concerning the future of Palestine], nor upon a recognition of the real relationships of power, and that we demand (as Rotenstreich does) the right of sovereign decisions which exigent interests [could possibly] allow only in the aforementioned case of [extenuating] political circumstances.

Against this critique, some claim that we must demand much because we will, obviously, receive less than we demanded. But, to use the language of the marketplace, we must reply that we do not ruin the entire business if we ask for too little. Rather, the only result will be that our profit will be a little less. Whereas the entire business can be ruined if we demand too much, for then there is the foreseeable danger that the deal will not be concluded at all.

But let us set aside such commercial considerations and seriously consider expressions of the kind here under discussion. We shall then find that their meaning is, in fact, the demand that by international decision a certain minority shall be given the possibility, with no limits imposed by international supervision, of making itself the majority. Not only has this demand no historical precedent, but it is so far from international custom that, in my opinion, there will necessarily occur to any thinking person the question of what the real interests are of these or of other nations on which we base our demand, and with what we can compensate these nations whose real interests lie in a completely different direction [than our demand admits]. As far as I can see, there is no answer to this question.

30

Dialogue on the Biltmore Program

(October 1944)

(Editor's prefatory note:)

The Biltmore Program, as already indicated, was formulated as a strategy to combat the White Paper of 1939. It was initiated by David Ben-Gurion, chairman of the Palestine Executive of the Jewish Agency, and adopted by an extraordinary Zionist conference meeting in May 1942 at the Biltmore Hotel in New York City. Since no Zionist congress could be held because of the war, the Biltmore conference was in effect invested with the authority of a congress. Delegates from every American and Canadian Zionist organization were joined by all European and Palestinian leaders able to attend. As Ben-Gurion explained the program, which was formally endorsed by the Inner General Council of the World Zionist Organization in November 1942, Jewry could no longer depend on Great Britain. To alleviate the impending catastrophe facing European Jewry it was imperative that the Mandate be transferred to the Jewish Agency. "The Conference urges," the Biltmore Program, concluded, "that the gates of Palestine be opened; that the Jewish Agency be vested with control of immigration into Palestine and with the necessary authority for upbuilding the country . . . ; and that Palestine be established as a Jewish Commonwealth."

The ideological rationale behind the perennial Zionist demand that the Mandatory government allow unlimited Jewish immigration had been to has-

ten the creation of a Jewish majority in Palestine; now this demand was associated with the supreme moral task of rescuing European Jewry. Dissent on
the demand for mass immigration was thus no longer a matter of political
disagreement; it was now construed as betrayal of the Jewish people. In the
following "dialogue," published in the October 1944 issue of *Be'ayot*, Buber
portrays himself as a "traitor." He seeks to indicate to "the patriot"—the
proponent of the Biltmore Program—that current talk in the Yishuv about
the Gibeonites (see Joshua 9:27) is an implied admission that in the projected
Jewish Commonwealth of Palestine the Arabs will not only be deprived of
"collective political equality" (i.e., they will be rendered a minority), but will
also be subordinated to the economically stronger Jewish community. And if
this is not the intention of the patriotic proponents of the Biltmore Program,
then they apparently desire the partition of Palestine into separate Jewish and
Arab states, that is, the establishment of a smaller Jewish state immediately
rather than continue to strive indefinitely for the establishment of a Jewish
state in the whole of Palestine. This, many suspected (correctly as it turned
out), was indeed Ben-Gurion's secret motive. But "partition," Buber warns,
will lead to unprecedented and interminable strife with the Arabs.

DIALOGUE ON THE BILTMORE PROGRAM

Patriot: I wish to speak with you frankly and without bias.
Traitor: I'm willing.
Patriot: Tell me, why do you oppose the Biltmore Program?
Traitor: Why in principle or why practically speaking?
Patriot: Well, let it be from the point of view of principle.
Traitor: May I ask a question in response?
Patriot: Ask whatever you wish!
Traitor: Why do people talk so much about the Gibeonites?
Patriot: The Gibeonites?
Traitor: Yes, the hewers of wood and drawers of water.
Patriot: Do people really speak of them so much?
Traitor: Yes, especially since the Biltmore Program was announced.
Patriot: But how are the two matters connected?
Traitor: That is what I want to know, too.
Patriot: What . . . what do you mean?
Traitor: I mean that the period of the Gibeonites has passed—it had
            to pass.

Patriot: Yes, it certainly has passed.

Traitor: If it has passed, why do people speak of it so much?

Patriot: I don't understand what you're saying.

Traitor: You do understand.

Patriot: But . . . but you wanted to tell me why you are opposed in principle to the Biltmore Program?!!

Traitor: I've just told you.

Patriot: Do you really believe that the men who formulated the Biltmore Program intend to reduce part of the population to the status of second-class citizens?

Traitor: Of course, you don't intend to deny them anything but collective political equality. But if two nations live in the same state and one of them rules the other, and if the ruling nation's productivity is manifestly greater, if their skill and activity in the world economy is manifestly greater, the other nation will naturally be reduced to the status of second-class citizens in the state's economy, one way or another. This imbalance can be prevented only if the ruling nation deliberately tips the scales in favor of the other nation by adding the weight of its own moral force and ensures the other nation's full participation in its own economy. Once I thought that the Jewish people in our day were already capable of such an undertaking; but the ascendancy of the politics of the mob has taught me that I was mistaken.

Patriot: But why should what the mob does matter to you? Isn't it true that they do not determine policies?

Traitor: If so, why then do we court them so assiduously?

Patriot: Well, it's true, we do need the mob—so that we are entitled to speak in the name of the people; but it is not the mob that will determine what is to be done in the future when we implement the Program. Let the mob therefore interpret the Program as they will.

Traitor: But their interpretation is the one that affects lives, and for me life is the main thing.

Patriot: You are a strange man.

Traitor: How so?

Patriot: I argue politics with you and you respond with a lecture on morality.

Traitor: You argue about short-term politics and I speak to you of long-term politics. Short-term politics does not go well with morality, while long-term politics merges with morality at certain crucial junctures.

Patriot: This is not the right time to clarify such matters. And wouldn't it be better if we spoke more specifically about political issues?

Traitor: I'm ready.

Patriot: If so, tell me why on practical grounds you are opposed to the Biltmore Program?

Traitor: Because it is impossible for any length of time to build with one hand while holding a weapon in the other. One may be able to do this when building a wall, but when building a country is what's at stake, one cannot succeed at it for very long. One generation is entitled to pass on the builder's tools to the next generation, but not both the builder's tools and a weapon. If that is what nevertheless happens, both hands can do only poor work. And that means that soon no hand will be found to hold either building tools or weapon.

Patriot: If I understand you correctly, you start from the same basic assumption that we do—that the Biltmore Program can be implemented.

Traitor: No, it cannot be implemented.

Patriot: But didn't you just describe what you think will happen if it is implemented?

Traitor: No. When we spoke about matters of principle I told you why I opposed the Biltmore Program, on the assumption that it could be implemented—but it can't be. When we spoke about the practical side of the issue, I explained what I believe will happen when the most probable decision is made by those who have the power to determine [the fate of Palestine, i.e., the United Nations] . . . if the Jewish people stands firm by the Biltmore Program.

Patriot: And what will they decide?

Traitor: You know better than I do—partition.

Patriot: Where do you get that idea from?

Traitor: There are certain reasons to assume that in this case those in power will want to propose an alternative to the unacceptable Biltmore Program. It can be assumed that the alternative proposal won't be the continuation of the Mandate in a different form (with compromises in favor of freer immigration); and it certainly won't be the establishment of a bi-national state, because such a proposal would not be [regarded by you as] an adequate alternative to the demands of the Biltmore Program. What they will propose is partition, and I see that proposal resulting in an unprecedented catastrophe.

Patriot: But we will refuse to accept partition!

Traitor: There are many ways of refusing something. The decisive majority will accept it even as they say they refuse it. Haven't you taken care to ensure that the majority prefer the mirage of a state over any real oasis?

Patriot: Really, it's impossible to talk with you.

Traitor: That's right.

Patriot: Do you know what you are?

Traitor: Yes, I know—a traitor.

31

A Majority or Many?
A Postscript to a Speech

(May 1944)

(Editor's prefatory note:)

In light of the plight of European Jewry, the Ichud, as we have noted,[1] called for the *aliyah* or immigration to Palestine of as *many* Jews as possible. In a speech before the *Histadrut*, the General Federation of Jewish Labor in Palestine, Ben-Gurion ridiculed the expression "many" as meaningless, insisting instead on the term "majority." This bit of semantics, Buber argues in the following article published in May 1944 in *Be'ayot*, betrays a deliberate attempt to confound moral and political issues, i.e., the moral task of rescuing as *many* Jews as possible, and the political goal of creating a Jewish *majority* in Palestine in order to justify the demand for Jewish sovereignty in that country. By confounding the two issues, Buber implies, Ben-Gurion seeks to give his political goals the absolute form of unambiguous moral imperatives. But morally the political goal of a Jewish majority in Palestine, Buber asserts, is hardly unambiguous. Furthermore, politically Ben-Gurion's policy is not necessarily the wisest strategy for securing the future of Jewry in Palestine. Morally and politically, Buber suggests, the program for a bi-national state seems eminently sounder—not as an infallible formula, for as a political program it is open to criticism and revision, but as a "direction" leading the imagination beyond the concepts of "majority" and "minority," which are morally impalatable, especially to Jews, and equally beyond the political quagmire of mistrust and enmity between Jews and Arabs.

Note

1. See introduction to selection 27.

A MAJORITY OR MANY? A POSTSCRIPT TO A SPEECH

"The main issue," said Ben-Gurion in his speech before the Histadrut council, "is the question of *aliyah:* whether the masses of Jews will come to *Eretz Israel.*" But he added, "Not 'many'—for what does 'many' mean? . . . We want a majority." What majority means, according to his explanation, is a majority of world Jewry, that is, that the majority of the Jewish people will reside in the Land [of Israel]. But, of course, first and foremost, he means "majority of this country's population."

Many years ago [Joseph] Sprinzak formulated the slogan: "Not a majority, but many."[1] He too wanted the masses of Jews to come, but he interpreted masses literally as "many," not "majority." And he knew what he was saying when he emphasized "*not* a majority." Then Ben-Gurion came along and reversed the whole thing. Why and to what purpose?

The difference between Ben-Gurion's type of thinking and our way of thought stands out most clearly when one juxtaposes these two concepts: "many"—"majority." Our aim is that as many Jews as possible come to Palestine, while Ben-Gurion wants the Jews to become the majority in the country. Of course, "many" could be the same as "majority," but the connection is not logically necessary, because it is possible to conceive of a situation in which the majority is not many. In contradistinction to Ben-Gurion, we do not regard "many" as equivalent to "majority." "Many" is not a relative quantity, i.e., defined in relation to other quantities, but an absolute quantity. "Many" is a concept rooted in life's essential realities, while "majority" is solely a political concept. In fact, the term "majority" tells us that, in the realm of relations between nations, at decisive moments the power of decision rests with the majority which can determine the fate of the minority.

And this is not what we aspire to. Just as we do not want our neighbors to determine our fate, we do not want to be in the position of determining theirs. We thoroughly understand that they fear us; we understand this in the depths of our souls. To be sure, Ben-Gurion has declared that the Jewish state he aspires to, "our state," will be characterized by national justice and national equality. But can we expect the Arabs to accept that promise as a commitment limiting our future actions regarding them, a commitment that the generations of our descendants will fulfill in its entirety? The relations between national majorities and national minorities have not been encouraging up to now, and it is natural that the Arabs' trust in us is no greater than ours in them. Didn't Ben-Gurion himself point emphatically to the potentially catastrophic situation "if the majority does not want to recognize the needs of the national minority"? And isn't that necessarily true for both sides? Ben-Gurion goes so far as to say that no written promises can really guarantee any of the Jewish people's vital interests. Doesn't that necessarily apply to both sides? Shouldn't we be unflagging in our efforts to dispel the misgivings of the country's Arabs, lest we become responsible for determining their fate? We cannot accomplish this with words alone; our well-meaning declarations about the nature of the Jewish state we intend to establish will not induce them to agree to the change from a majority to a minority status. In their place, we, too, would not allow ourselves to be convinced by declarations alone to do that.

At one time, we declared it our desire not to subjugate, as a majority, and not to become subjugated, as a minority. We will not be able to transform that desire into a reality, influencing the relations between our neighbors and ourselves, if we do not dispense with the pursuit of attaining a majority [in Palestine]. Is it really necessary that the lives of two nations living together in one place depend on the solely political concepts of majority and minority? Has not the time come to try and put the problem in different terms? And isn't it possible that this particular location and our particular situation may be just the circumstances in which to begin trying? True, it is very difficult, very, very difficult; it demands tremendous daring, and in order to accomplish it courageous and independent thinking is required, capable of formulating new means to achieve new goals. But whoever knows our situation thoroughly, knows that we have no choice; only here, if anywhere, lies the true path—all other paths are deceptive. It may be that the programs for a bi-national state have till now been imperfect; if so, we must amend them. The main thing is not this or that program, but the direction in which we seek the solution—that and the earnestness of the search and the energy invested in it. We hold that the Ben-Gurion mode of thinking lacks this direction, this earnestness, this energetic searching. It does have a clear direction—but one that only leads down a blind alley. It is very serious, but it does not dare to leave the well-paved conceptual path of a "majority in the state" and invest a new solution to a new problem. It does have a wonderful energy, but it expends it wrestling with empty space. We hold that it moves in a closed circle: in order to become the decisive force (the "majority"), we must be given the decisive power (as if we were already the majority). This sort of thing is not common practice in the world of political realities. This demand, if it leads to anything, can lead only to partition of the country; that is, to the creation of a tiny Jewish state, thoroughly militarized and not viable. I am certain that Ben-Gurion today does not want partition; but I am no less certain that this is what will result from the usual bargaining process, if his demand (which is itself unattainable) is truly sounded by the entire Jewish people. I see several men on our side who would support that solution, since they have despaired of realizing more noble Zionism and are willing to accept something less, even if it is essentially as transient as the day-long life of a fly. We, however, do not despair; we know that there is no reason to despair if only we seek in the right direction.

Now Ben-Gurion argues, in opposing all the programs for the establishment of a bi-national state (whose form would take into account the given situation), that our situation is unique: "the essence of Zionism is its dynamism." He was right in saying this, since we do need large-scale and constant *aliyah*. He comes to this conclusion in particular from a consideration of the Jewish question [in the Diaspora], but it is equally true from the point of view of the life of the Yishuv, which in its present stage of development runs the risk of Levantinization without constant infusions of new blood. "What solution is there," asks Ben-Gurion, "in the formula of a bi-national state?" The solution lies precisely in this—that a formula is not sufficient; rather some fundamental arrangement beyond formulas is necessary. In other words, the right of [free] immigration—till, let us assume, numerical parity is reached (and this is something that will require great efforts on our part, much greater than all our efforts hitherto)—should be placed on a separate footing: it should be included in a "Magna Carta" that will form the basis for the growth of a Palestinian polity and will be guaranteed by the United Nations. We can obtain the right to Jewish immigration above numerical parity only by an additional agreement, after we have succeeded in the meantime in dispelling the Arabs' fears of a Jewish majority that will determine their fate . . . that is to say, only if the way we have found to neutralize the question of the majority will be supported by a suitably receptive psychological state on both sides. The principal means of accomplishing this is wide-ranging and intensive economic cooperation that reveals and creates a commonality of interests. The separate national economic systems should be replaced, as much as good economic sense allows, by one shared countrywide system, in whose success both nations are interested and whose shared development may well create mutual trust, that in turn will lead to far-ranging agreements. The cunning slogans and deceitful proclivities of politics often make it appear that there are contradictory economic interests here; this argument will not hold up in the face of unbiased examination. Again, that kind of unbiased examination can be attained only by action; here, too, courageous decisions are necessary—and they require liberation from routine thinking. The entry of the Palestinian polity into a federation of Greater Syria can provide vital assistance in bringing about the desired development. In such a federation, Jewish initiative and Jewish labor may have an enormous role to play. And what, it may be asked, if such a federation is not established? It will be much harder then to create an atmosphere of trust and understanding, but then, too, there will be a way—if only there will be a will.

Note

1. Joseph Sprinzak (1805–1959), a leader of the Yishuv.

32

Politics and Morality

(April 1945)

(Editor's prefatory note:)

Buber and the Ichud were frequently vilified as being naïve about the harsh realities of the world. In an imperfect world, riddled by the contradictory interests of nations and peoples, in a world in which force and power are, alas, the ultimate arbiters of public affairs, Buber's attempt to introduce universal moral considerations into politics was regarded as, at best, chimerical. In fact, with respect to the question of Palestine, it was deemed immoral, for Buber's and his friends' solicitude for the feelings and interests of the Arabs encouraged "defeatism," a weakening of morale and a crippling compromise of Zionist imperatives. In pursuit of the overarching need of the Jewish people for a home, "injustice" was indeed perpetrated against the Arabs—as many of the Ichud's opponents were prepared to admit—but in contrast to the suffering of the Jews to be alleviated, the hardship caused the Arabs is but a necessary "inconvenience." Buber's and the Ichud's failure to recognize this, it was maintained, was indicative of their political naïveté and the moral distortions attendant on their overzealous humanitarianism. Buber's response to these charges was given in the following article, which appeared in the April 1945 issue of *Be'ayot*.

POLITICS AND MORALITY

Life, in that it is life, necessarily entails injustice. Anaximander even believed apparently that the very fact of human existence is an injustice against the "whole," to all the other creatures, and we owe them atonement. Undeniably, there can be no life without the destruction of life. If we observe carefully, we shall note that everyone encroaches upon the living space of someone else at every moment. In fact, if one were to observe as carefully as the subject warrants, one would no longer be able to bear one's own life. A person commences to be truly human when he pictures to himself the results of his actions and, accordingly, attempts to encroach upon other creatures as little as is necessary. What the degree of necessity is in every single case—that, of course, is not easy to recognize, for formidable drives intervene here, endowed with great powers of deception: the thirst for possession and the hunger for power. One can, however, always come back to the recognition of what is actually necessary. We cannot refrain from doing injustice altogether, but we are given the grace of not having to do more injustice than absolutely necessary. And this is none other than the grace which is accorded to us: humanity.

The problem becomes more complex when we no longer consider our individual lives, but our lives in society. For here those formidable drives easily anaesthetize the mistrust our soul has acquired for their deceptive maneuvers. Every injustice whose nature was evident in our personal lives occupies a righteous position here. It is enough to say "we" instead of "I"—and we already have a ready-made easy conscience. The result is a situation in which as individuals we live humanely, but as members of a nation we live a life that is less than humane. This situation contains a fatal danger, not only to ourselves as individuals but also, in the nature of things, to the nation which we constitute. For the proportion of humane life to inhumane life in every nation is what ultimately determines not only that nation's value, but also its fate.

The migration and resettlement of a nation, or of large parts of a nation, in the conditions of the world today, a world in which there are apparently no viable empty regions, necessarily entail obvious "injustices" to another population, whose living space has been encroached upon—if not in the present generation, at any rate for future generations. With regard to the issue of "necessity," there is a crucial difference between expansive settlement, seeking to enlarge the borders of the property and rule of the colonizing nation, and concentrative settlement, in which a nation which has lost its organic center seeks to return to its origins. We, whose settlement is concentrative may weigh our "righteousness" in the scales against the "injustice" which we give rise to, especially in this crucial moment, unprecedented in human history. For since large portions of our people's expanse were shattered, the task of renewal, the need for regeneration which is the property of an organic center, has become correspondingly greater. But here again, the main point is recognizing limits. If one has the intention of driving people who are bound to the soil out of their homeland, then one has exceeded those limits. Here we confront an inalienable right, the right of a man who cultivates the earth to remain upon it. I shall never agree that in this matter it is possible to justify injustice by pleading values or destinies. If there is in history a power of righteousness that punishes evil-doing, it will intervene here and react. Transfers of population effectuated by conquerors have always been avenged; and this shall be done to the nation that attempts to answer evil with evil. I seek to protect my nation by keeping it from setting false limits.

At this juncture, as my experience tells me, some readers will throw down the book and cry out against me: "If that is the case, then all of your words about morality are nothing but a cloak for defeatism!" These days it is the custom to accuse those of us who see the truth and wish to lay it bare, either of dumb humanitarianism or of defeatism. Both of these concepts come from the same batch of pathetic slogans by means of which a political outlook that has lost real power tries to acquire the semblance of power. I only ask that the slogans not be used separately, but at the same time. For at the same time I am fearful for the future of the Jewish person as a human being and for the future of our settlement, a daring attempt, beset by many dangers, to renew that Jewish person. I am fearful both politically and morally. That is my defeatism. And I state that the Zionist outlook is only a means of reaching a goal. That goal is the rehabilitation of the Jewish person. I must constantly examine and reexamine that means to see whether it is serving that end. You may call that my dumb humanitarianism.

We frequently hear that one should not introduce moral categories into political discourse. This is true in that every political consideration is essentially the evaluation of the effectiveness of certain means for achieving a public end, and the means must definitely be fittingly adapted to the end. However, if the political end itself has a "moral" character, and if "immoral" means only appear to serve the achievment of that end and, in fact, actually move us away from it—then what is the answer? By "immoral" I mean here that a person commits or is prepared to commit an act of injustice greater than is necessary and that he sees the necessary limits not where they truly are, but where his thirst for possession and his hunger for power persuade him to see them. One should not introduce moral themes into political considerations. Granted. But if immoral politics are also bad politics, then what is the answer?

We are accustomed to viewing morality and politics as two parallel lines which only meet at infinity. That is to say, they do not meet at any point in our physical world. Thus it is concluded that one must distinguish between the two areas as strictly and exactly as possible. Of course, it is self-evident that one should not prevent politicians from making use of moral concepts and claims in their speeches and declarations in order to create the impression, certainly a desirable one, that there is actually no contradiction between politics and accepted morality. By the same token, however, it is self-evident that for a politician to take those principles and claim seriously and actually that he acts in accordance with them while composing his political programs would be considered dangerous and silly. There is a grain of truth in that opinion: since politics is the adaptation of means to ends in public matters, there cannot be, with regard to a decision being made, any criterion other than the effectiveness of the means for achieving those ends. Nevertheless, this does not mean that there is no room for moral motives in political decisions. It does mean that moral motives have right of entrée only insofar as they are directed towards achieving goals. In order that these words not be misunderstood, one must consider these three truths:

1. By its very nature, setting a goal transcends the boundaries of politics, although it must be based on the recognition of political facts. Setting a true political goal (that is, not merely announcing the program of a ministry or something of that nature) always plumbs the depths of history and taps the primary forces which determine the life and death of peoples. This means there is a "moral" dimension to the setting of political goals—not as an independent principle, but by its deepest roots linked to those of any spiritual essence [i.e., any genuine human endeavor].

2. Achieving a goal depends on laws fundamentally different from those which determine what we call a political "achievement." There is nothing that impedes the achievement of a goal and distracts one from it more than so-called "achievements," which rise up before the goal and obstruct it. Then not only the naturally short-sighted see merely the closest achievement, feasible at the moment; also the few

who started off with a burning vision of a certain true goal lose themselves in pursuit of achievement. In their pursuit they even exploit their vision as propaganda. And, of course, in that pursuit there is no guiding principle, only tactical maneuvers. This is not the case with a path directed at a goal.

3. "A goal will only be reached if the means is already dyed with the same hue as the goal" (Gustav Landauer). All those who strive for regeneration by degenerate means only increase degeneration. Even if "rebirth" is blazoned on their banners, those banners will disappear in the end—or they will be lowered and rolled up.

The "penetration" of Jews into *Eretz Israel* is not "an immoral action." But if, as it continues, that penetration becomes corrupted, then despite our impressive "achievements" we shall lose sight of our goal, the reason for that penetration. Our stand is not "inferior" to that of the Arabs. But woe unto us if we should adopt a stand which is inferior to our goal!

33

Our Reply

(September 1945)

(Editor's prefatory note:)

The Ichud was reviled by most elements of the Zionist community of Palestine, from Mapai, the Socialist Zionist party which dominated the Jewish Agency, to the *Irgun*, a clandestine military organization ideologically linked with the right-wing Revisionist movement. The Irgun—whose supreme command was assumed by Menahem Begin in May 1944—gained its élan and increasing popularity through its proud refusal to compromise on one iota of what it regarded to be Zionist priorities; and, indeed, it fought for its conception of Zionism with ferocity and daring, often resorting to terrorism, first against the British and later against the Arabs.

In the July 1945 issue of its underground monthly, *Herut* (Freedom)—distributed illegally as wall-posters—the Irgun attacked the Ichud. In this passionate critique, the anonymous author refers to the Ichud as an organization of "moralistic" professors from the Hebrew University of Jerusalem. This august university, the author sarcastically notes, is appropriately situated on Mt. Scopus—in Hebrew, *Har Ha-tzofim*, literally, the Mount of the Beholders or Observers:

With respect to the problems that face the nation and its youth, [the professorial denizens of Mt. Scopus] are indeed observers [*tzofim*]. Their conscience is quiet; their soul is tranquil. . . . They are not party to what takes place below: they reside above on the heights of a moral Olympus, from whence they raise their voice—quiet, refined, reproachful.

What is their point of view? In a word: Compromise! Compromise in their opinion is the purpose of life; it is divine wisdom without which there is no existence and progress. Proof? These professors are not at a loss to adduce biological, sociological, economic, political, and historical proof that compromise is the principal path of human development. Accordingly we in the Land of Israel ought to suggest and seek *at any price* compromise. Otherwise our cause is lost.

It is difficult to argue with omniscient professors. But nonetheless we who are ignorant of learning believe that they make a fundamental error of historical fact and principle. Let us begin with the Jewish tradition, an allegiance to which our intellectuals pride themselves. To be sure, the Torah recommends compromise, but only when it comes to minor matters. But with respect to major issues of fundamental significance which shape the character of both the nation and the individual, the Torah knows no compromise. "Do not take unto yourself other gods"—this is the cardinal moral commandment which was given to our solitary nation so we would not compromise ourselves with idolatrous nations. . . . And what did this commandment cost us? Anguish. Nonetheless we did not compromise. And if there were periods in our history in which "reason" and convenience prompted parts of the nation to accommodate themselves to the environment, then there appeared prophets—not professors!—who damned the "compromisers" and condemned "compromise." No, we did not know compromise. And not only did we refuse to compromise with the idolatrous peoples, we did not desire that they compromise with us. Hence, we rejected proselytism. . . . From the days of yore until this very day this is the path of the Hebrew nation. Thanks to it—and only thanks to it—we continue to exist, despite everything, as a nation. Were it not for our refusal to compromise we would have long ago been assimilated among the Gentiles. To be sure, this path has bestowed upon us incomparable suffering. Surely, we [Jews] may amend Descartes famous saying: "I suffer, therefore I exist."

[A similar refusal to compromise, moreover, is also the source of all significant developments among the Gentile nations.] . . .

[Furthermore, any compromise with "the British overlords of Palestine" and the Arabs will in effect aid Hitler in his efforts to annihilate our peoples.] It is therefore not surprising that we reject the morality of the observers [*ha-tzofim*], the professors of Mt. Scopus [*Har Ha-tzofim*]. We the flesh of the flesh of the slaughtered [Jews of Europe], we the blood of their blood. And what is more important, we the spirit of the spirit of the martyrs of Israel in the past, the present, and the future. . . . In matters of supreme importance we do not and will not know compromise. We rejoice that He who gave to his people eternal life gave us the moral strength to suffer, but not to capitulate to evil. This is the path of life for the nation that chooses life. . . . [1]

Buber's reply on behalf of the Ichud was published in the September 1945 issue of *Be'ayot*.

Note

1. "The Voice of a Child." *Herut*, No. 48 (5 July 1945), p. 2 (Hebrew).

OUR REPLY

The things we are bound to fight for are clarity, the coordination of knowledge and conviction, and political rectitude. By political rectitude I mean refusal to put up with brittle illusions after their brittleness has been recognized; and refusal to issue declarations involving claims that are known to be unrelated to the facts and incapable of realization. The fanatical adherent may achieve a certain effect and a certain amount of influence on the political stage, so long as his faith is genuine; but the fragments of a faith once broken can have no political effect, because no inner power is attributed to them any more.

It is clear from a survey of the situation that the "official" polemic against us has really lost its basis. The polemics of the right-wing opposition continue, but they are being carried on at such a low level that there is no need for us to deal with them. However, outside the "parliamentary" conflict, in certain youth circles which deserve attention in view of their personal sincerity, the kind of criticism which is truly fundamental is crystallizing just now. This calls for a further fundamental clarification on our part.

This kind of criticism begins on a definitely personal note. It is based on the supposition that we "are for the most part recruited from Mount Scopus *(Har Ha-tzofim)*"; which is untrue, as far as the great majority of us is concerned. It then goes on to state that they are indeed "*tzofim*" (observers), who take no part in life here below, but are content to lift up their "quiet, refined, reproachful" voices from the height of the "moral Olympus."

This critic errs. He seems to imagine that only the man who cries aloud suffers. But such is not the case. Those who suffer most deeply have ceased crying. As long as we cry, we do not know how to help. Those who have been in hell, and have returned to the light of day again, have learned to speak quietly and clearly. For it is only in this way that the truth can be spoken, and there is nothing that can help us except the truth. And truth is rather unpalatable at times. Sometimes it is harder to speak the truth than to lose control, lash out and call upon others to do the same. But he who knows the truth, the truth that alone can help us, is compelled to speak out, no matter whether a whole people is listening or only a few individuals.

This criticism, however, goes further and undertakes to prove that what we are saying is not the truth at all. It bases itself on the supposition that we are following the road of compromise, without reservation and as a matter of principle. But neither is this true. All we maintain is that there are situations for which compromise provides the only way out, and that everything depends on being able to recognize such situations when they eventuate. We do not believe compromise to be "the high road of development," but we are of the opinion that we must not shrink from it if, in a given situation, compromise, and compromise alone, can lead us to the high road. Compromise as such is neither good nor evil; if or when it is fitted by its nature and content to save our cause, and if there is no other way of salvation, then it is good. By its nature and its essence it must only be adopted if it is in harmony with our cause; it must not threaten our cause's foundations or falsify its maxims while appearing as its savior. We had to ponder this; we had to confront the nature of compromise with the nature of our cause. And when the result we reached was found to be a positive one, it was our bounden duty to say so, to affirm publicly the bitter truth that in a uniquely difficult situation there can be no easy way out. We had to say that the way of claims and declarations, the way of losing control and lashing out, cannot save us, but only the hard way that leads through compromise to real service of this country. For that indeed is our goal: to be able to work in peace, with all our might. That is the high road, and there is no other way.

Now the critic would try to teach us, with the help of a long list of grandiose examples, beginning with the Prophets and Socrates and ending with the Encyclopaedists and George Washington, that in all "great, fundamental matters" compromise is inadmissible. In reality these examples, if they are subjected to a careful historical examination, merely go to show that what is most important is to make a practical distinction between the absolute and the relative. In all matters touching the absolute, compromise must be ruled out. But for the sake of the absolute, it is permissible and defensible to act within the sphere of the relative as the situation demands; provided always that compromise is not in conflict with the claims of the absolute. In a catastrophic situation Jeremiah, in order to save Israel and the Torah, proposed a way out which amounted not only to a compromise, but to downright submission—a solution which I myself could never have brought myself to propose. Socrates knew no compromise when he was called upon to testify to the truth; but his disciple Plato did not betray the master when, his ideal Republic having turned out to be unrealizable, he proposed an alternative scheme. The men of the French Revolution, who were spurred to action by abstract principles and a lust of power based upon them, rather than by a combination of ideas and a correct diagnosis of the situation, defeated their own ends. Our critic is ready to quote examples "from Prometheus to Gandhi." Well, as to the politics of Prometheus, I am not sufficiently well informed. In any case, tradition records curious compromises he made with the gods—though, no doubt, in this he deceived his partners. The mention of Gandhi surprises me even more; for if he is to succeed, it will only be on the basis of a compromise with the Moslems.

Naturally, everything depends on making the right compromise at the right time. But that is exactly what I am talking about. There are people among us who appear to be guided in their attitude by the lunatic motto of "the twelfth hour being past," meaning that there is nothing to lose any more. Our critic is not one of them. He will not cease fighting, against the whole world, if need be. He has elected to follow the path of "heroism." This heroism prompts him, not to look in front of him or around him, but to rush about and lash out in all directions. This heroism is not the heroism of Prometheus, but that of Don Quixote, but a tragic Don Quixote, tragic in the fullest sense of the word.

Our reply to this youth stricken with tragic blindness is based on a presupposition which touches on the absolute and brooks no compromise. This premise is the faith, which no catastrophe can shake, that a great future awaits the people of Israel. For this people, the guardian of such an inheritance and the possessor of such powers, there can be no question of simply ending its life as one of the "small nations." Even as we see it today, tragically reduced, crushed and violated as it is, a creative task is waiting for it still. Today it is up to us to recognize the beginning of this task, for it is an hour that offers labors such as few other hours in history have imposed; and in conjunction with the rise of the Near East, in whose most important center the remnant of Israel is gathering. This task cannot be solved in isolation; in isolation, surrounded by hate and distrust, it cannot even be imagined. To win a truly great life for the people of Israel, a great peace is necessary, not a fictitious peace, the dwarfish peace that is no more than a feeble intermission, but a true peace with the neighboring peoples, which alone can render possible a common development of this portion of the earth as the vanguard of the awakening Near East.

During the quarter century we have so far had at our disposal we have not laid the foundations of that peace, either economically or politically. On several occasions when peace seemed to come within our reach, we did much to prevent it. Our economic life was built up as a barrier rather than as a point of contact,[1] and our policy, instead of producing a constructive plan working towards an equilibrium, only submitted to the Powers' claims for greater rights than were compatible with the realities of the situation.[2] No doubt there were occasions when Zionist leaders if not in practice, at least in their formulas, drew certain conclusions from their realization of the fact that it is impossible to live in a house of cards. But their experience that declarations, and declarations alone, were sufficient to score success after success, made them lose sight of reality. At the present moment, however, precisely because foreign policy is more to the fore than at any other time, and because we shall not be able to evade the necessity for a solution much longer, we can see on the political horizon the hour when a firm hand will put us back on the *terra firma* of reality and confront us with the question: what proposals have you to make for the peaceful development of the Near East?

Even those who are most favorably disposed towards us will be compelled to pose this question; and they will be forced to ask it because it is we who come to them with claims. Those who even then have nothing to say beyond the mere repetition of trite claims of the past will find they do not enjoy a sympathetic audience. Everything will depend on whether another answer, a true one, will have matured in us by that time.

Notes

1. The reference is to the policy of *'avodah 'ivrit* (Hebrew labor), which sought to create a comprehensive and exclusive, that is, autonomous, Jewish economy in Palestine.

2. Buber is referring, or course, to the Biltmore Program.

34

The Meaning of Zionism

(March 1946)

(Editor's prefatory note:)

Great Britain increasingly lost its resolve to administer the Mandate for Palestine. On 13 November 1945, British Foreign Secretary Ernest Bevin and United States President Harry Truman announced simultaneously in London and Washington the formation of an Anglo-American Inquiry Committee to explore alternatives to the British Mandate, and specifically to consider the pressing plight of the Jewish survivors of the Nazi holocaust and the possibility of their immigration into Palestine. After visiting various camps for Jewish "displaced persons" in Europe, the Anglo-American Committee, composed of six American and six British representatives, went to Palestine in March 1946 in order "to hear the view of competent witnesses and to consult representative Arabs and Jews on the problem of Palestine." The Zionist Actions Committee, representing the Executive of the World Zionist Organization, forbade any Zionist group to appear independently before the Inquiry Committee. Eager that its program for a bi-national state be considered, the Ichud decided to break Zionist "discipline" and to send three of its members— Judah Magnes, Moshe Smilansky, and Martin Buber—to present its position to the Inquiry Committee. In introducing his colleagues before the Committee, Judah Magnes explained the intention of his delegation's testimony as follows:

> . . . Professor Buber will [first] present a brief paper on what our Zionism means to us and why we so ardently believe in the return to Zion. I shall then try to bring out some points of our written statement. Mr. Smilansky will in the course of the discussion want to emphasize two points, first, that Jewish-Arab cooperation is possible, and, second, that there is sufficient land in the country for the absorption of a large Jewish immigration. . . . Professor Buber and I wish to make it clear that we are not speaking in the name of the Hebrew University. There are various opinions there as elsewhere. We are speaking as residents of the country and as Jews who feel it to be their duty to give voice to a view which, though differing from the official Zionist program, is nevertheless shared, as we know, by large numbers of the population.

THE MEANING OF ZIONISM

BUBER: Mr. Chairman,[1] it is impossible to survey the problem you are trying to meet without an understanding of the very roots of Zionism. For only through this understanding will the observer realize that he faces something quite different from the well-known national antagonisms, and therefore that methods other than those of political routine are called for.

Modern political Zionism, in the form it has taken during my nearly fifty years of membership in this movement, was only prompted and intensified, but not caused by modern anti-Semitism. Indeed, Zionism is a late form assumed by a primal fact in the history of mankind, a fact of reasonable interest at least for Christian civilization. This fact is the unique connection of a people and a country. This people, the people Israel, was once created by the power of a tradition that was common to some semi-nomadic tribes. Together these tribes migrated, under very difficult conditions, from Egypt to Canaan because they felt united by the promise to them of Canaan as their "heritage" since the days of the "Fathers." This tradition was spectacular and decisive for the history of mankind in that it confronted the new people with a task they could carry out only as a people, namely to establish in Canaan a model and "just" community. Later on, the "prophets"—a calling without any historical precedent—interpreted this task as obliging the community to send streams of social and political justice throughout the world. Thereby the most productive and most paradoxical of all human ideas, Messianism, was offered to humanity. It placed the people of Israel in the center of an activity leading towards the advent of the Kingdom of God on earth, an activity in which all the peoples were to cooperate. It ordered every generation to contribute to the upbuilding of the sacred future with the forces and resources at their command. Had it not been for this idea, neither Cromwell nor Lincoln could have conceived his mission. This idea is the origin of the great impulse that, in periods of disappointment and weariness, ever and ever again encouraged the Christian peoples to dare to embark upon a new shaping of their public life, the origin of the hope of a genuine and just cooperation among individuals as well as nations, on a voluntary basis. But within the people that had created it, this idea grew to a force of quite peculiar vitality. Driven out of their promised land, this people survived nearly two millennia by their trust in their return, in the fulfillment of the promise, in the realization of the idea. The inner connection with this land and the belief in the promised reunion with it were a permanent force of rejuvenation for this people, living in conditions which probably would have caused the complete disintegration of any other group.

This serves as an explanation of the fact that, in the age of national movements, Judaism did not simply create another national movement of the European type, but a unique one, a "Zionism," the modern expression of the tendency towards "Zion." In this age the hostile forces which, consciously or not, see in Judaism the Messianic monitor, quite logically attacked it more and more violently. Yet simultaneously, in Judaism itself, a great regeneration had started. Out of an inner necessity this movement of regeneration chose for its aim the reunion with the soil and, again out of an inner necessity, there was no choice other than the soil of Palestine and its cultivation. And with an inner necessity the new Jewish settlement on this soil centers in the village communities which, in spite of their differing forms of organization, all aim at the creation of a genuine and just community on a voluntary basis. The importance of these attempts surpasses the frontiers of Palestine as well as of Judaism. Given the chance of unhampered development, these vital social attempts will show the world the possibility of basing social justice upon voluntary action. Sir Arthur Wauchope who, as High Commissioner [of Palestine] in the years 1931-1938 had the opportunity of acquainting himself with this country and this work, was right in pointing out that these "astonishingly successful" communal settlements are an example of cooperation for the whole world and can be of great importance for the foundation of a new social order.

At one time the productive strength of the people of Israel in this country was a collective strength in the most sublime sense. Today the same might be said of the productive strength which the returning Jews have started to display in this country. It is the productive strength of a community directed towards the realization of real *community*, and as such, it is important for the future of mankind. Mankind is fundamentally interested in the preservation of a vital and productive Jewish people, such as can grow if fostered by the unique connection of this people and this country.

From this the principle of Zionism results. It concentrates in Palestine the national forces fit for renewing their productive strength. This principle again results in the three irreducible demands of Zionism. They are:

First: Freedom to acquire soil in sufficient measure to bring about a renewed connection with the primal form of production, from which the Jewish people had been separated for many centuries and without which no original spiritual and social productivity can arise.

Second: A permanent powerful influx of settlers, especially of youth desiring to settle here, in order incessantly to strengthen, to amplify, and to revive the work of reconstruction and to protect it from the dangers of stagnancy, isolation, and the forms of social degeneration particularly threatening colonization in the Levant.

Third: Self-determination of the Jewish community about its way of life and the form of its institutions, as well as an assurance for its unimpeded development as a community.

These demands, formulated simply in the concept of a "National Home," have been recognized, but not yet adequately understood, by large parts of the world. The tradition of justice, which I have mentioned and which must be realized within every community and between the communities, makes it clear that these demands must of necessity be carried out without encroaching upon the vital rights of any other community. Independence of one's own must not be gained at the expense of another's independence. Jewish settlement must oust no Arab peasant, Jewish immigration must not cause the political status of the present inhabitants to deteriorate, and must continue to ameliorate their economic condition. The tradition of justice is directed towards the future of this country as a whole, as well as towards the future of the Jewish people. From it and from the historical circumstance that there are Arabs in Palestine, springs a great, difficult, and imperative task, the new form of the age-old task. A regenerated Jewish people in Palestine has not only to aim at living peacefully together with the Arab people, but also at a comprehensive cooperation with it in opening and developing the country. Such cooperation is an indispensable condition for the lasting success of the great work, of the redemption of this land.

The basis of such cooperation offers ample space for including the fundamental rights of the Jewish people to acquire soil and to immigrate without any violation of the fundamental rights of the Arab people. As to the demand for autonomy, it does not, as the greater part of the Jewish people thinks today, necessarily lead to the demand for a "Jewish State" or for a "Jewish majority." We need for this land as many Jews as it is possible economically to absorb, but not in order to establish a majority against a minority. We need them because great, very great forces are required to do the unprecedented work. We need for this land a solid, vigorous, autonomous community, but not in order that it should give its name to a state; we need it because we want to raise Israel and *Eretz Israel* to the highest level of productivity they can be raised to. The new situation and the problem involved ask for new solutions that are beyond the capacity of the familiar political categories. An internationally guaranteed agreement between the two communities is asked for, which defines the spheres of interest and activity common to the partners and those not common to them, and guarantees mutual non-interference for these specific spheres.

The responsibility of those working on the preparation of a solution of the Palestine problem goes beyond the frontiers of the Near East, as well as the boundaries of Judaism. If a successful solution is found, a first step, perhaps a pioneer's step, will have been taken towards a juster form of life between people and people. . . .

AYDELOTTE:[2] . . . I would like to ask a question of Professor Buber. Did I understand you to say, sir, that the majority of the Jews do not, in your opinion, favor a Jewish State in Palestine?

BUBER: I think that state and majority are not the necessary bases for Zionism.

AYDELOTTE: I gathered that, but I thought I saw the sentence in your paper to the effect that the majority of Jews do not favor a Jewish State.

BUBER: You see, there are no statistics for it. A great part of Jewry cannot tell what it thinks about it. We have no communication with them, but I think a very great part of the Jewish people think a Jewish State is necessary for Zionism.

AYDELOTTE: You think a great part of the Jewish people think a Jewish State is necessary?

BUBER: Yes, a great part think—a very great part—think it is necessary—that a Jewish State is necessary.

AYDELOTTE: The sentence I was referring to in your paper is as follows: "As to the demand of autonomy, it does not . . ." I beg your pardon, I think I misunderstood your sentence. Thank you very much.

Notes

1. The chairmanship of the Inquiry Committee alternated between the British and American chairmen. This particular session was conducted by the British chairman, Sir John E. Singleton, Judge of the King's Bench Division of the High Court of Justice, London.

2. Frank Aydelotte, member of the Inquiry Committee. At the time he was the director of the Institute for Advanced Study at Princeton, New Jersey.

35

A Tragic Conflict?

(May 1946)

(Editor's prefatory note:)

In its report, published on 1 May 1946, the Anglo-American Inquiry Committee in effect endorsed the concept of a bi-national state in Palestine.

> It is [the report states] neither just nor practicable that Palestine should become either an Arab state, in which an Arab majority would control the destiny of a Jewish minority, or a Jewish state, in which a Jewish majority would control that of an Arab minority. In neither case would minority guarantees afford adequate protection for the subordinated group.... Palestine, then, must be established as a country in which the legitimate national aspirations of both Jews and Arabs can be reconciled without either side fearing the ascendancy of the other. In our view this cannot be done under any form of constitution in which a mere numerical majority is decisive, since it is precisely the struggle for a numerical majority which bedevils Arab-Jewish relations. To ensure genuine self-government for both the Arab and the Jewish communities, this struggle must be made purposeless by the constitution itself.[1]

The Ichud, of course, was elated by this report. In a sanguine and somewhat self-congratulatory mood,[2] the Ichud called a conference of its members to determine its future actions in light of this dramatic endorsement of its program.

In his opening address to the conference, which was convened in May 1946, Judah L. Magnes spoke of the need for the creation of institutions and forms of administration, even prior to the constitution of the bi-national state projected in the Inquiry Committee's report, that would render that constitution feasible by fostering a sense of shared community between Jews and Arabs. Buber followed Magnes with an address, reproduced here, in which he focused on the *political* significance of such an endeavor.

The conflict between Jews and Arabs, Buber observes, is frequently said to be a tragic one, that is, the interests of both are presumed to be irrecon-

cilable. Buber holds this to be an erroneous perception. To be sure, the conflict between Jew and Arab is real, but politics narrowly bound to the interests
of one's group exacerbates and, indeed, perpetuates the conflict. It creates, in
Buber's words, "a *political* surplus conflict." The Ichud seeks to de-politicize
the conflict by grounding it in the "domain of life"—as opposed to politics—
by which he means the matrix of everyday life which ultimately requires that
people learn to live together, that they compromise and reconcile differences
in order to affirm life itself.

Notes

1. Cited in *Palestine: A Study of Jewish, Arab, and British Policies*, published for
the Esco Foundation for Palestine (New Haven: Yale University Press, 1947), vol. 25
pp. 1225 f.
2. The testimony of *Ha-Shomer Ha-Tza'ir* in support of bi-nationalism, however,
also had a powerful effect on the Inquiry Committee.

A TRAGIC CONFLICT?

We have convened at a time in which we sense clearly that the steps
we have taken have brought us somewhere, that we have traveled further than we had anticipated—but we still do not know where our
steps have led us. Nor will that be made any clearer by the discussions
we will hold at this conference, for unknown factors are involved and
we must wait until they become fully manifest. But one thing is clear:
now is not the time to thrash about in one and the same place; it is
time to go forward. More precisely, further steps must be readied. We
will be speaking about this in this gathering and Dr. [Judah] Magnes
will have some proposals to present before you. I have no wish to antic-
ipate him in this matter, I only want to say a few words on the innermost and most general importance of the steps we are taking. This
importance I see centered in a certain outlook, which Dr. Magnes
stressed in his opening address to this conference and in his replies to
questions. It is, I think, a fundamental outlook to which we all are
bound. Dr. Magnes stated that institutions and forms of administration
must be developed in this country which by their nature will perforce

lead to a situation whereby the "demands of life itself" will bring about a genuine pact between the Jews and Arabs of this country. Life, he said, can produce such a pact. In my view what he said is of the most fundamental importance, important for our direct concern but also, beyond that, important for world peace.

We often hear it said that the Jewish-Arab problem in this country is by its nature a true dilemma, a tragic conflict to which there is no genuine solution, no way of arriving at an unambiguous situation. The fear that this is indeed the case could even be heard in the remarks of several members of the Anglo-American Inquiry Committee. This fatal error derives from the fact that the demands of life have been preempted—and concealed from the sight of the concerned parties—by the demands of politics.

To a certain extent there are real conflicts of interests between all groups—national, religious, economic, social—which live together. As long as these conflicts are dealt with within the domain of life itself, solutions are found. These solutions may take the form of negative compromise with both sides narrowing their demands, but may also take the form of positive, synthetic, creative compromise, that is, the creation of new life circumstances which require cooperation and make it possible. Matters are different if the conflicts pass from the domain of life to the domain of politics, and are different to the extent that politics overpowers life. What then happens is what I call political "surplus" conflict. Politics, seeking to retain its domination of life, has an interest in treating the interests of the various groups as if they were irreconcilable. But since this in fact is not so, politics has to make it so. And it accomplishes this by heightening the real conflict of interests to the point that it becomes non-real, albeit furnished with all the terrible force of political illusion. The politics of a group produces within its members a sense of a conflict with proportions much greater than those of the real conflict, and accords it a different, seemingly absolute, character. The difference between the real conflict and the politically induced imagined conflict is what I have referred to as political "surplus" conflict. Although this surplus has real vital influence only on the politically active part of the group, by political propaganda this segment gains total hegemony over all the others; that it, it achieves the dominance of life by politics.

The present Jewish-Arab situation, which appears to be without solution, emerged from a development of this sort in both camps.

When I first came to this country eight years ago a wealthy Arab merchant described the situation to me in a way somewhat naïve but fundamentally correct. "Both of us," he said, "your friends and mine, could have reached an agreement, because we want to develop this country into something and you want to develop it into something. We could have done this more successfully together than with each side working separately. We could have agreed to join forces to develop this country into something. But among us there are people and among you there are people who are interested in preventing such an agreement. They are the politicians. And who knows, they may yet bring things to such a point that we won't even be able to speak with one another as we are now doing." How quick they were to bring that about!

What must we who understand the situation and want to change it do? Are we to forego political work because of its insidious nature? That would be to abandon life totally to the grip of politics. No. What we must do is to launch a politics of de-politicization. We must do political work in order to induce a cure of the present sick relation between life and politics. We must fight against the excessive growth of politics, must fight it from within, from a position within politics' own domain. Our objective is to eliminate the political surplus conflict, the imaginary conflict, to bare the real interests, to make known the true bonds of the conflict between interests. This objective, however, we know cannot be accomplished only by explaining the truth. By itself the truth is not strong enough to undo the work of political propaganda nor to break the suggestive power of political illusion. The only hope is to establish institutions which accord supremacy to the demands of life over the demands of politics and which thereby provide us with a real and substantial base from which to explain the truth. Dr. Magnes alluded to institutions of this sort. In this way positive, synthetic, creative compromise will be attainable.

I was recently encouraged in this by what an Arab leader of the postal workers said during a strike: "Away with all those who introduce [extraneous] political issues." That is a healthy feeling, it is an opening to the victory of life over politics.

It can be argued: Who do you expect to set up institutions of this sort? Are not those to whom you turn themselves the representatives of political powers, the representatives of vast political groups whose leaders, even if unwittingly, play the same political game, the game of constantly introducing political surplus conflict? How can they be expected to break the vicious cycle?

There is, it seems, only one answer to this argument—for if it is raised in earnest it encompasses all political powers everywhere in the world. And while this answer is based only on hope, without this hope we are liable to despair of the future of the human race. It is the hope that within those powers are individuals, individuals of influence and responsibility, who see as we do that the hegemony of politics leads to destruction, and like us are dedicated to preventing it. It is to them that we turn when we insist that life be given its due. The destiny of this country and this people, and the destiny of countries and peoples in general, today depends on the force of truth in their hearts. The hope we pin on them and on their tie with us will help us find the strength and the direction for our next steps.

36

It Is Not Sufficient!

(July 1946)

(Editor's prefatory note:)

The British government greeted the report of the Anglo-American Inquiry Committee with considerable consternation and, despite its undertaking to the Committee, disregarded its recommendations. The Jewish Agency was not much more enthusiastic; indeed, the only aspect of the report which won its warm endorsement was the recommendation that 100,000 Jewish refugees be immediately admitted into Palestine. When Britain announced in early June 1946 its rejection of this specific recommendation, the newly formed Jewish Resistance Movement responded by blowing up the bridges linking Palestine with the neighboring states. The Jewish Resistance Movement was established in the fall of 1945 by the Haganah, the underground army under the tutelage of the Jewish Agency, together with the Irgun and other Jewish armed groups in order to exhibit, through coordinated attacks against British military installations, the Yishuv's determination to resist Britain's policy. The Mandatory government reacted to the latest action of the Jewish Resistance Movement by summarily arresting all the members of the Jewish Agency Executive who were in the country at the time. Other repressive measures against the Yishuv soon followed. Tensions reached a new height when, on 22 July 1946, the Irgun, acting alone, blew up the central government offices in the King David Hotel in Jerusalem, resulting in the deaths of eighty people, government officials and civilians, Britons, Jews, and Arabs. Appalled, the Jewish Agency called upon the Jews of Palestine "to rise up against these abominable outrages," and ordered a halt in armed operations against the British.

In the following article, published in the Tel Aviv Hebrew daily *Ha-Aretz* on 26 July 1946, Buber elliptically refers to the bombing of the King David Hotel and to the Jewish Agency's condemnation of the act. By countenancing violence—again an elliptical reference, undoubtedly to the Jewish Resistance Movement and the legitimacy accorded by it to the terrorism of the Irgun— the leadership of the Yishuv, Buber suggests, is implicated in the Irgun's murderous act.

IT IS NOT SUFFICIENT!

No, it is not sufficient.

It is not sufficient that we express our abhorence. We must admit that we too have a part in the very deed that arouses our repugnance.

All of us, all individuals who, by virtue of their position or influence, participate in the leadership and guidance of our unfortunate Yishuv— we are all accomplices in this crime.

We were not wise enough to found our Yishuv on the idea that the redemption of Zion cannot be achieved but by the rule of the sacred law. This law, whose essence is respect for the life, property, and honor of one's fellow human beings, has been borne by the Jewish people throughout the lands of its dispersion. Here, in the very land which was Jewry's goal in all its wanderings, the people have dispensed with that law. And we have allowed this to happen because we did not elevate that law above all else, because we did not make it into an unimpeachable power.

We did not teach the generations growing up here to distinguish between true lessons learned from history and false teachings that use history illegitimately. It is a false teaching that the rebirth of a people can be accomplished by violent means. The way of violence does not lead to liberation or healing but only to renewed decline and renewed enslavement. We did not inculcate this central principle in our schools. Thus we witness what has occurred. Criminals exiled to Australia become responsible human beings with a sense of social justice, while the people who came to Zion under a holy banner have become criminals.

Now there are voices calling loudly for the Yishuv to condemn this crime. Too late!! Yesterday was the appropriate time for that call to be heard—and it was not heard, neither yesterday, nor the day before, nor at any time in the past until today.

We have no right to say "our hands have not shed this blood nor have our eyes seen [who did it]." We saw what was happening and yet we did not say what had to be said. Why then do we "wash our hands over the beheaded calf in the stream," proclaiming our innocence?[1]

These events will bring what they will in their wake. We must repent and change our ways, whatever will happen now, lest an even greater catastrophe befall us. It is our obligation to elevate the sacred law [of life] to ensure that it not be undermined, that the people as a people protect it from all subverters.

It is too late for mere words; it is not too late for deeds.

Note

1. Reference is to Deuteronomy 21.

37

A Plea for Clemency

(August 1946)

(Editor's prefatory note:)

In response to the bombing of the King David Hotel, the Mandatory government redoubled its efforts to apprehend Jewish terrorists and to destroy their organization. Typical of the severe measures pursued by the British was the summary trial before a military court and the sentence of death passed on a gang of eighteen members of the Irgun caught in early August 1946.[1] Buber and six other members of the Ichud were signatories to the following appeal, dated 21 August 1946, to the High Commissioner for commutation of the sentence passed on the Irgun youth.[2]

Notes

1. They had taken part in the blowing up of the Haifa Railway Workshop on the very night that the bridges surrounding Palestine were destroyed. The four girls in the group were sentenced to life imprisonment.

2. On 30 August 1946 their sentence was indeed commuted to life imprisonment. Buber wrote or signed several such appeals, on behalf of Jews and Arabs, during the period of the Yishuv's struggle against the British.

A PLEA FOR CLEMENCY

Jerusalem
21 August 1946

Your Excellency,

We the undersigned respectfully submit an appeal to Your Excellency to exercise clemency in the case of the eighteen young men sentenced to death by the Military Court in Acre on 16th August.

We abhor terrorism in all its forms and have fought terrorism to our utmost capacity since it first raised its head within the Jewish community. As far back as 1939 we and others appealed successfully to the Jewish community against terrorism when the first individual acts of violence occurred. We are determined to continue this fight and redouble efforts to stamp out terrorism wholly, endeavoring to do this by interpreting the political situation to the Jewish community and by explaining once again the moral principles on which Zionism is based. Despite all obstacles and setbacks we hope that our work will be successful because fundamentally the Jewish community as a whole, both on account of its historic tradition and its sad experience in its struggle for survival, has no real belief in violence.

The youths who have been carrying out acts of violence we regard as misled. Their deeds are not so much through their fault as the result of circumstances and of an atmosphere which has been created. That, of course, does not absolve them from punishment. But, particularly in view of their youth and since, other than members of the group itself, no one happily was killed as a direct result of their action, we submit that Your Excellency should exercise the prerogative of lightening their sentences.

We have stated above our constant opposition to terrorism. We might add that in 1930 some of the undersigned, under similar circumstances, made an appeal to the then High Commissioner to commute the death penalty for twenty-three Arabs then sentenced for the murder of members of the Palestinian Jewish community. We appealed then, as we appeal now, to the Head of the Government of Palestine, in the belief that, long as the way may be, education and persuasion are more likely to bear fruit in the long run, whereas capital punishment creates "martyrs" in the eyes of the surviving members of the offending groups and of some elements of the community as a whole.

Respectfully yours,

Martin Buber et al.

38

Two Peoples in Palestine

(June 1947)

(Editor's prefatory note:)

In June 1947, during a visit to Europe, Buber was invited by Dutch radio to present his views on the Palestine question. Buber took the occasion of this fifty-minute lecture to weave many of the themes we have encountered in his writings—the insidious hegemony of the political principle, the meaning of Zion and Zionism, the prospects of Arab-Jewish cooperation, a bi-national state in Palestine and its socio-economic *and* spiritual conditions—into a comprehensive statement of his vision of an amicable future for Jews and Arabs in their common homeland.

Two Peoples in Palestine

I

In coming to speak to you about Palestine, I would like first to share with you a perspective on this subject—which is of such importance to the entire world—that is not generally presented in newspapers and journalistic books. In addition, I would like to make use of the example of Palestine to illuminate the pernicious effects of an evil which afflicts humankind perhaps more than any other evil. I am referring to the current exaggeration, indeed glorification, of politics in our world, of its absolute domination, out of all proportion to what is truly important in life.

The domination of politics is not always apparent, for it has insinuated itself into every area of life, taking in each realm a different form, dressing up in all manner of disguises, and speaking in the specific language and terms of each realm. People think, for example, that it is the economic principle that outweighs all other considerations in determining what occurs in contemporary society. This supposition, however, is quite unfounded, and it is only because the political principle has infiltrated economic life and undermined its foundation that this attitude prevails. The vital and healthy foundation of any economy is comprised of the inner urge to create goods that are of benefit to humanity and that further our cooperation with other men, our brothers, whose relationship to us rests upon a basis of common assumptions and similar goals. This healthy foundation, however, has been pushed aside by greed for futile dominion and by competition that knows no bounds. If the motto of a natural economy is "to create what is needed," then the motto of an economy that has become dominated by politicization is "to achieve more than what is needed."

In every place and in every realm the society of men, infected by the domination of the political element, seeks to achieve more than what it truly needs; and the political chimera has so confused all of mankind that they have become entirely unable to distinguish between "what is truly needed" and "more." And so all are fighting all—not for "what is truly needed," but for the sake of this same "more." And since they no longer recognize any higher authority that might adjudicate between them, there is no longer anything to stand in the way of their descent towards common destruction.

II

Almost seventy years ago, Jews began settling in Palestine. The external impetus for this was given by persecution and pogroms, but these constituted no more than a kind of stimulus that served to awaken deep inner forces and energies, whose roots lie in the very beginning of time. With this deep inner motivation the people of Israel seeks to renew its relationship with the land of its earliest beginnings, and to become once again, by virtue of this renewed tie, an organic, healthy, united people, after thousands of years of dismemberment and dispersion.

In order to understand this impetus correctly, you must set before you the fact that the Jews are not a people like all others—whether or not the Jews care to acknowledge this. They are a unique phenomenon, unlike any other: a society in which peoplehood, on the one hand, and faith, on the other, have been melted down together and refined into a unity that cannot be sundered. And that faith has been bound up from its beginning with this land—the same land to which the Lord of the Universe Himself sent this people—that they might elevate it to perfection, and that it, the land, might in turn bring about their own perfection—and that these two perfections together might bring forth the *atchalta degeulta*, the beginning of Redemption, the onset of "the harmonization of the world under the sovereignty of God."

It is true that this great role was never fulfilled, and the tie between people and land was broken for thousands of years. Furthermore, a sizable portion of the Jewish people lost its faith, at least consciously so. Yet the unconscious force of this faith remained so strong that it sustained the people's impetus for wandering in that historic hour when they set their faces towards their ancient homeland. Whether or not the settlers recognized this, it was the desire for the renewal of a "godly society" that lay at the root of their motivation.

III

Throughout these seventy years, the generations of Jewish settlers have worked their land with unparalleled enthusiasm and energy. They have made it bear fruit and turned it into a land of blessing and plenty—and just as much have they fructified themselves and aroused in their midst forces they had not known existed. One can easily understand how, in the midst of all this activity, so full of energy and imbued with creativity and willingness to sacrifice, they did not take sufficient note of one important fact: that Palestine already had another population, which sees and feels this land to be its homeland—even if this feeling is dimmer, simpler and more inchoate than that of the Hebrew pioneers. These, of course, are the Arabs, who have dwelt in this land for something like thirteen hundred years. The crucial challenge of planned cooperation between the two peoples in developing the land has not been discussed with sufficient clarity on either side—and nor, of course, have any measures been undertaken with the vigor necessary to bring about this vital cooperation.

Even so, good foundations for active cooperation between the two peoples in creative activity and in developing the land have not been lacking. The first of these foundations are historical: they have their source in the common origin of the two peoples; their languages are closely related, and the tradition of their common father, Abraham, binds them from the earliest days of the Semitic race. Their customs, too, have many common and related aspects, especially if one considers the ways of the Oriental Jews who have made their permanent home in Palestine for many generations. It is no coincidence that, of all the long days of the exile, it was the Spanish-Arabic period that saw a blossoming of spiritual and philosophical creativity among the Jews.

A second basic foundation that was in existence and could have facilitated cooperation is the love for their homeland that the two peoples share. We have already noted that this love is more passive among the Arabs; yet it could have been developed among them as well to the point where they were drawn to take an active part in a great joint undertaking to make the land bring forth its fruit. True, the Jews, who lived for hundreds of years in the West, absorbed much more of its culture and way of life than did the Arabs dwelling in Palestine, are a bridge between East and West. It is true, too, that there is a great difference between the two populations in their pace of life and work; and one can easily understand that certain elements of the veteran population had no desire to make undue haste about bringing new life to the wilderness, and saw in the pioneering work of the immigrants who were coming to the land an alien phenomenon that was being forced upon them against their will.

Even so, there is no doubt that the possibilities for cooperation, flowing from the two peoples' common origin and shared task, could have overcome all of these obstacles—were it not for the intervention of the political element. Even now, in every place where the Arab village population has not yet been affected by politicization, neighborly relations, peace, and brotherhood reign between Jewish and Arab farmers, and they give each other a great deal of generous mutual assistance. The irrigation and fertilization projects of the Jews have not only benefited the Arab peasants, but also brought credit to the Jews in their estimation; and the places are many where these peasants have eagerly learned the methods of farming and intensive agriculture that the Jews were wholeheartedly willing to teach them. I have on several occasions been an eyewitness to celebrations in Jewish villages in which Arab neighbors participated not only as honored guests, but also out of a feeling of profound joy that testified to a genuine feeling of brotherhood.

We cannot, it is true, disregard the fact that certain of the basic elements of the Jewish settlement enterprise have worked against cooperation, without their intentionally working directly against the Arabs. The healthy principle that the Jewish people must return to productive work, for instance, drew after it the circumstances in which Arab work forces often were unable to find enough room for themselves in the labor market that was created by the Jewish enterprise. Even so, they would surely, by inner necessity, have chosen to take the path towards a joint Arab-Jewish economy, had not the political element, that same desire to achieve more than what is truly needed, been active on both sides, sowing obstacles and difficulties in both camps. The slogans of statehood have been voiced with increasing volume, calling on the one side for an Arab state, and on the other for a Jewish one. Let us examine the degree to which these demands and slogans are justified by the real needs of the two peoples.

IV

The Jewish people, which is renewing itself at this juncture in the history of Palestine, is in need of a strong and developed autonomy. It needs not only the opportunity freely to preserve and develop its ancient/modern Hebrew culture, but also the opportunity to determine for itself and to develop freely those social forms that will facilitate social renewal in a spirit of harmony and cooperation. The Arab people in Palestine is also in need of strong and developed autonomy. But it is not necessary that either of these peoples ever prevent or interfere with the free growth of the spiritual and social values of the other.

On the Jewish side, one more need, which has two parts, must be added. Jewish immigration to Palestine must be allowed, in numbers commensurate with the economic capacity of the country to absorb it, in order to prevent the stagnation of the settlement enterprise and to enable it to fulfil its purpose—the creation of a center and homeland for world Jewry of the dimensions required by the present circumstances of the Jews. In addition, the acquisition and settlement of land must be permitted to an ever-increasing extent, in order to prevent undermining at its very base this enterprise, which is renewing the people by reestablishing the relationship of the Jewish person, who had become economically unproductive in exile, with the land and the working of it.

Yet these two requirements must be realized in such a way that no

injury is done to the fulfillment of the real needs of the Arab population. The dimensions of the real needs of both sides and the extent to
which their demands are justified must therefore be reexamined and
redetermined from time to time; and this must be carried out jointly,
in an atmosphere of mutual trust which has its source in the cooperation between the two peoples. The continuous growth and domination
of the political element has interfered to an ever-increasing extent with
the creation of this mutual trust, whose achievement, though it might
not have been easy in any case, would not have proved impossible.

What is really needed by each of the two peoples living one alongside the other, and one within the other, in Palestine is self-determination, autonomy, the chance to decide for itself. But this most certainly does not mean that each is in need of a state in which it will be
the sovereign. The Arab population does not need an Arab state in
order to develop its potential freely, nor does the Jewish population
need a Jewish state to accomplish this purpose. Its realization on both
sides can be guaranteed within the framework of a joint bi-national
socio-political entity, in which each side will be responsible for the particular matters pertaining to it, and both together will participate in
the ordering of their common concerns. The demands for an Arab state
or a Jewish state in the entire Land of Israel fall into the category of
political "surplus," of the desire to achieve more than what is truly
needed.

A bi-national socio-political entity, with its areas of settlement
defined and limited as clearly as possible, and with in addition economic cooperation to the greatest possible extent; with complete equality of rights between the two partners, disregarding the changing
numerical relationship between them; and with joint sovereignty
founded upon these principles—such an entity would provide both
peoples with all that they truly need. If such a state were established,
neither people would have to fear any longer domination by the other
through numerical superiority; and Jewish immigration in accordance
with the capacities of the country to absorb it—and this depends upon
the broadening and intensification of production, which, as I have said,
is necessary to the Jewish settlement enterprise and an indispensable
condition for its growth and for its very existence—Jewish immigration
could no longer be seen by the Arabs as endangering their very existence. And on the other hand, since the freedom of self-determination

and the opportunities it needs to develop itself would be guaranteed to the Jewish population in this bi-national socio-political entity and grounded upon a firm and unshakable foundation, there would no longer be anything to prevent this entity from joining the federation of Arab states; and this in itself would give the Arab population an additional guarantee of its status.

V

Today, with politicization reaching pathological, almost catastrophic dimensions, this route appears to be blocked. Yet I truly and firmly believe that it has not yet become totally impassable. If the gateway to it is to be broken open, however, two great and unconventional actions must be undertaken, the one economic-technical, and the other political-spiritual.

When I say "political" in this connection, I am, of course, referring not to the negative sense in which I used it earlier when speaking about the undue politicization that has come to dominate our lives, but rather to the great and positive sense, the Platonic significance, of this idea: the spirit which builds and gives form to society and the state. At the same time, too, I am employing the most elevated sense of the term "technical," as it were its highest tier: that realm in which the technical aspects of life are formed and determined by the spirit, by the will of the spirit to create all-encompassing, fruitful, and lasting peace among the peoples on the face of the earth.

The technical-economic activity of which I am speaking is a comprehensive undertaking to develop the country. Its central feature would be a huge irrigation enterprise, which on the one hand would multiply several times over the amount of land that can be worked agriculturally, and on the other would supply energy to an extensive local industry and guarantee it a central standing in the economy of the Near East.

Such an undertaking would stimulate and advance the economic life of the whole of Palestine. From being a divided territory made up of a dynamic Jewish element and an Arab element that is still fundamentally static, it would come to be a united land humming with intensive productivity.

In order to accomplish this, the Arab population must, of course, be incorporated in this undertaking to the fullest extent, not only in reaping its benefits, but as a working and active partner. It is worth noting that such participation is integral, as far as I know, to every plan for such an enterprise that has been worked out on the Jewish side. If it should indeed be implemented, the ways in which the greater part of the population lead their lives would be changed, and along with this there would be a fundamental transformation in the relations between Jews and Arabs. This depends, of course, on all stages and all parts of this enterprise being carried out in the proper spirit of partnership, solidarity, and cooperation. The commonality of interests between the two peoples, which has been clouded and obscured by the politicization of which I spoke, must be uncovered and revealed to all; it must be heightened to bring forth a joint productivity sustained by shared love for this wonderful land.

VI

The second undertaking, which I called spiritual-political, must go hand in hand with the work of building up the country. In order to clarify its nature to you, however, I must say a few words about an important factor of which I have not yet spoken, and which even now I raise not without hesitation. Up to this point I have presented these two peoples to you as though the relations between them depended upon them alone. However, this is most definitely not the case. The truth is that these relations have increasingly been influenced—an influence which has been fundamentally negative—by the complex of international political concerns. In this case, as in many other instances of quarrels and conflicts of interest among peoples, this international political complex has drawn the conflict between Jews and Arabs into the churning interplay of its forces and made use of it for its own ends.

If there existed in our days a real supra-national authority, whose role was to discuss, to conciliate, and to settle conflicts, it could do work of great value in such cases. But there is no such superior authority, and all of international life exhausts its energies to no purpose in wars over dominion and rule, acquisition and possessions that are ultimately barren. The "great powers" thus see in conflicts among the smaller peoples not suffering which they must work together to end, but interesting complications which can be exploited very nicely in the great struggle for supreme dominion over all. The small peoples themselves, dominated by politicization, try on their part to exploit this exploitation to their own advantage. In this desperate, vicious circle, conflicts become more and more intensified. All of this has come to pass in the relations between Jews and Arabs, and at the present time it is occurring seventyfold before our very eyes.

We who fear for the future of man, who was created in the image of God, can do more in the face of this situation than await the appearance of the spirit for good in politics, which is not allowed by the evil spirit dominating the political world today to shine forth and show itself. This spirit, which undoubtedly lives on in the hidden depths of all that is happening in the world, is the spirit of building and forming in the political realm, the spirit of truth, justice, and peace in the relations between peoples.

The problem of Palestine, of Arab-Jewish relations, is one of the most difficult political problems of our time, perhaps the most difficult of them all. Let this problem be a touchstone by which the world shall be tried. From among all the peoples, men of inspiration must arise, men who are of impartial mind and who have not fallen prey to, or become entangled in, the war of all against all for dominion and possession. Such men must come together to pave the way for these two peoples to work together to overcome this complicated situation. But they must also concern themselves with the future that lies beyond the present hour.

Until that joint socio-political body that I described to you is established, let the administration of the common affairs of the two peoples be in the hands of a joint supreme council of their representatives, in which several members of that circle of impartial men of which I spoke shall also take part. These men must work for the development of solidarity, cooperation, and mutual trust between the two peoples, and they must also restrain those factors that give rise to strife, which will in the nature of things burst forth from time to time to endanger the young social entity.

Can such a spiritual-political enterprise be initiated and successfully carried out? This is the great question, the touchstone for mankind. The destiny of Palestine and the destiny of all mankind are presently bound up with one another by a hidden tie, fraught with danger but also with hope.

39

Can the Deadlock Be Broken?

(July 1947)

(Editor's prefatory note:)

In the summer of 1946 Buber visited London where he participated in a round-table discussion on the Palestine problem. The discussion was chaired by Richard H. S. Crossman, a Labour M.P. who was a member of the Anglo-American Inquiry Committee. Also participating in the discussion were Thomas Reid, a Labour M.P. who served in the Woodhead Commission of 1938 (which had concluded that the partition of Palestine was impracticable), and Edward Atiyah, a Lebanese Christian who headed the Arab Office in London (which had been established by several Arab governments in conjunction with the Arab League). Excerpts of the discussion, which was sponsored by the London magazine *Picture Post* are presented here.

CAN THE DEADLOCK BE BROKEN?

CROSSMAN: So we can get agreement on this point, that in the past the failure has been the failure of the British Government and the League of Nations to face up to the issue in Palestine one way or the other, and if we do not face up in the future to the fundamental issue we shall not add anything to the solution of the problem, whichever way it goes. There has been a great deal of discussion about an agreed solution between Jew and Arab. Is it sheer moonshine for a statesman to say that he is looking for an agreed solution between the existing organizations on both sides?

ATIYAH: I think an agreement between the Arabs and the Zionists is absolutely impossible.

BUBER: I think it is now somewhat difficult, but not impossible.

ATIYAH: It is quite impossible because the conflict is between the indigenous people of Palestine, who are in the majority, who are determined to keep their country and want independence immediately, and a group of Jews—not the whole of Jewry—who regard Palestine as theirs by right and who want to come in in unrestricted numbers and have a Jewish National State. Between the two armies there can be no compromise.

BUBER: Political organizations can be changed, and can change their opinions. The real question is not one of organization but of reality. Nor is it a question of majority and minority.

CROSSMAN: You do not believe in counting heads in Palestine?

BUBER: No: nor in any other country. But there is an urgent need to find a new political form for the living and working together of two peoples.

CROSSMAN: The question we put to you, put bluntly, is, if we wait for an agreed solution between the Jewish Agency and the Higher Committee of the Arab League, have we got to wait till Doomsday?

BUBER: If you put the question so, I have no answer to it. I think what is the real obstacle is the morbid obsession with purely political terms, which does not allow these two people to come to an understanding on the basis of their real common interests.

REID: It is quite hopeless to expect political Zionists and political Arabs to agree. It would not pay them politically, from a narrow point of view, to lower their demands to outside powers.

ATIYAH: It is not only the Arab politicians who would never agree to a Zionist solution, but the whole Arab people.

CROSSMAN: Do you feel that on the basis of an imposed solution, cooperation might be possible?

BUBER: Everything depends upon the kind of solution. If it is a sound one, bringing the two peoples together in their common interest, a solution, even if imposed, will do what must be done.

ATIYAH: It is not only an imposed solution that offers a chance of cooperation. There is one alternative, that every foreign influence should be withdrawn completely from Palestine and the Arabs and the Jews left alone to come to terms or fight it out. This may not be a very desirable solution, and the condition it involves may be unrealizable, but if it could be tried a natural equilibrium would be reached, possibly after a fight. If the Zionists could no longer depend on foreign armed assistance they would realize that it was essential for them to cultivate the goodwill of the Arabs.

CROSSMAN: . . . This brings us now to our concluding stage of asking ourselves what, in our view, is the sort of solution which a commission could give, and which the Great Powers could impose. Readers will want to know what sort of solution could be, first, just and, second, feasible.

BUBER: A solution giving to either side the right of domination would lead to a sudden catastrophe. The only solution that would not lead to a catastrophe, but only to a difficult situation for some time, is the creation of a bi-national state. That is, putting Jews and Arabs together in a kind of condominium and giving them the maximum of common administration possible in a given hour. They would have equal rights, these two nations, as nations, irrespective of numbers.

CROSSMAN: In a State where there was such a parity there would be deadlock on any vital issue and that would mean no Jewish immigration, because every issue over which there was a deadlock would be one on which no action would be taken.

BUBER: I mean the constitution of the State should be based on the right of immigration by the Jews until there is an equal number, but there should be equality at once, not only of individuals, but of nations.

REID: On what grounds would the Professor justify immigrants coming into a country until they were equal in numbers with the indigenous population?

BUBER: I think that Judaism cannot live without becoming an organism with a living center, and not only for itself, but for mankind it should live on. Arabism is not faced with a similar alternative [between life and death].

ATIYAH: I think a bi-national State on the basis of absolute parity is either unnecessary or impossible, because unless there is enough goodwill on both sides such a State will end in deadlock and complete paralysis. If there is enough goodwill there is no need for such an elaborate scheme.

BUBER: Then the question of majority arises and that is what I am trying to avoid. In the last thirty years the possibilities of an agreement between Jews and Arabs have deteriorated as a result of growing politization. I do not see any solution other than depolitization as far as possible. This means replacing the slogans on the site of reality and building upon it.

.   .   .

REID: I have been greatly impressed by the sincerity and moderation of the Professor's views, but he said earlier that he does not believe in counting heads to get a majority, and yet when he comes to a solution he insists that emigration must go on until Jews equal the Arabs.

BUBER: I am not interested in formulas. You can say if you prefer: the Jews have a right to immigration as far as the economic conditions allow.

.   .   .

CROSSMAN: I personally think that Dr. Buber's solution, the so-called bi-national State, is a figment of the constitutional imagination. If they work together, you don't need it, and if they don't work together the constitution doesn't work. With regard to Mr. Atiyah, I happen to agree that the immediate objective has got to be independence, but for *both* Jews and Arabs. . . . I do not like partition because I think it is wicked to divide that small country, but I see no other way of getting responsibility into the hands of Jew and Arab, and of recognizing the rights of Jewish immigration into Palestine.

BUBER: Unfortunately, time is not sufficient to discuss the question of partition. I am against it because I am for a living and productive Palestine.

CROSSMAN: Would you rather have partition than an Arab independent state?

BUBER: Of course, but only because I think it is the lesser evil. You said a bi-national state in your view would not work. This is an argument that has been used many times against that kind of thing. Secondly, I am for, and not against, a bi-national Palestinian state entering as an autonomous member into a Syrian confederation.

CROSSMAN: On the Syrian Confederation at least we have reached agreement.

40

The Bi-National
Approach to Zionism

(1947)

(Editor's prefatory note:)

In an effort to broaden its constituency and increase its influence, the Ichud published in 1947 a volume of essays in English, entitled *Towards Union in Palestine: Essays on Zionism and Jewish-Arab Cooperation*, edited by Buber together with Judah L. Magnes and Ernst Simon. Most of the essays were translations of articles which previously appeared in *Be'ayot*. Buber, however, wrote an essay especially for the occasion and which served to introduce the volume. In this essay, reprinted here, Buber offers an overview of the ideological motives and program of the Ichud.

THE BI-NATIONAL APPROACH TO ZIONISM

When some years ago, a group of Jews from Jerusalem and elsewhere in Palestine combined their efforts in founding the *Ichud* (Union) Association, and later created the monthly *Be'ayot* as its organ, the main problem occupying their minds was the one usually referred to as the Arab question. This problem consists in the relationship between Jewish settlement in Palestine and Arab life, or, as it may be termed, the intra-national basis of Jewish settlement.

The *intra-national* approach is one which starts out from the concrete relationship between neighboring and inter-dependent nations, when considering the given economic and political facts and when considering decisions within their domain; the *international* view, on the other hand, gives predominance to the necessarily more abstract relations between civilized nations as entities. It is one of the most important characteristics of our revolutionary age that intra-national considerations are gaining in significance, when compared with international ones. As long as tbe traditional colonial policy, the "legitimate" rule over the destinies of remote peoples, was undisputedly maintained, the intra-national point of view was denied its natural precedence. With the growth of self-confidence in the nations and with their increasing desire for self-determination, concrete geographical conditions became absolutely and relatively more important factors. Especially was this the case where historical connections existed and where new possibilities were opened up for the joint erection of a new cultural and social structure. This accounts for the fact that international politics soon became the scene of a dispute between the colonial point of view and considerations of neighborliness. It may be assumed that this state of affairs will only suffer a radical change in the course of a future stage of global development, when the actual and all-embracing cooperation between the nations, brought about by an enormous calamity, will give concrete substance to international activity.

Jewish settlement in Palestine, which was embarked upon in order to enable the Jewish people to survive as a national entity, and which, in its social, economic and cultural aspects, constitutes an enterprise of universal significance, suffered from one basic error, which handicapped the development of its positive features. This basic error consisted in the tribute paid by political leadership to the traditional colonial policy, which was less suitable for Palestine than for any other region of the globe and certainly less fitting the Jewish people than any other nation. Hence, political leadership was guided by international and not intra-national considerations. Instead of relating the aims of the Jewish people to the geographical reality, wherein these aims had to be realized, the political leaders saw these aims only against the background of international events and in their relation to international problems. Thus, Palestine was embedded in international entanglements and attempts towards their solution, isolating it from the organic context of the Middle East, into the awakening of which it should have been integrated in accordance with a broader spiritual and social perspective.

Whoever pointed to this state of affairs as constituting a decisive factor in the shaping of the future, had to realize that the Zionist public and their leaders were, in this respect, blind to reality. This blindness was bound to prove fatal. To a large extent, this attitude and its practical consequences are responsible for the fact that the self-confidence and desire for self-determination prevailing among the Arab population of Palestine have found a militant form of expression.

At a time when colonial powers are forced into the defensive and have to give up position after position, even a nation with big-power backing could dare to settle in a country the population of which is maturing politically, only if it were sincerely bent on creating a real community of interest with that population; if it were prepared, at the price of inevitable sacrifices, to make the development of the country a joint concern; if it would enable the partner to cooperate actively in the enterprise and make him share the advantages gained. This applies in a still greater measure to a nation which cannot count on big-power support and which has to be careful not to mistake what is only the ephemeral interest of this or that big power, for genuine backing. What was needed at the outset of the settlement enterprise—in any case at the initiation of the modern one, undertaken with an international perspective—was a clearly defined program of *do ut des* (give and take). Such a program should have provided for the collective integration of the backward Arab population, as a whole, into Jewish economic activities and should have secured, in exchange, the indispensable demands necessary for the survival of the Jewish people as a national entity: free immigration, free acquisition of land, and the right of self-determination. What was actually put into practice, even when it seemed to answer real necessity, as was the case with the principle of "Jewish Labor,"[1] was bound to have results almost contrary to the above program. In these circumstances, those in the Arab camp who wanted to shape the awakening Arab national movement in a negative, defensive manner, instead of allowing it to develop positive and social features, which would have threatened their interests, had an easy task.

In this faulty development of the Arab movement, as well as in our own, another characteristic feature of our age becomes dreadfully apparent: the hypertrophy of political factors as compared to economic and cultural ones. This world of ours should, by dint of gigantic problems, be forced to bury phraseology and give way to matter-of-fact reality. Such a state of affairs should make politics only the façade of the economic and cultural structure. This façade has only to represent the economic and cultural structure, and not to exercise an influence impairing it. But instead of contenting itself with this rôle, the political principle claims to be the only decisive and active one. Hence, whenever real, that is, essentially economic clashes of interests between two nations occur, it is not the actual extent of the divergences which determines tbe struggle, but the exaggerated and over-emphasized political aspect of these divergences. Nurtured by fictitious political ideas, this surplus factor has become more powerful in the public arena than economic realities themselves, since in any emergency these economic factors cannot act but through their political agents, and, therefore, have to put up with and pay for the latter's encroachments. While the real conflicts might be easily solved, political fictions precipitate the crisis, by adding the emotional surplus; the crisis, in turn, increases the power of professional politicians. Such is the vicious circle.

It is frequently claimed that power lies with captains of industry, but this would only be true in unaffected conditions. More often than not are conditions affected by the mass intoxication with fictions, without which, it seems, most people can no longer go on in this dreadfully complicated world. In between come the catastrophes, that is, the time when the fictions become reality, because they were allowed to reign supreme. The power of professional politicians over the intoxicated masses is almost unlimited, although in the hour of catastrophe they have to share this power with military or gang leaders, unless they manage to unite both these functions—as, for instance, by holding one post officially and fulfilling the other function de facto, only. The "Jewish-Arab Question" has indeed become a classical example for all this.

What are we to call the Cassandra of our time? Whether we choose the proud name of "spiritual elite" or the somewhat contemptuous reference to "certain intellectuals," it comes to the same. I am referring to those who, equally free from the megalomania of the leaders and from the giddiness of the masses, discern the approaching catastrophe. They do not merely utter their warnings, but they try to point to the path which has to be followed if catastrophe is to be averted. This path is not unalterably defined. With history slipping farther down the dangerous slope, they have to change the plan and adapt it to the remaining possibilities. They do not prattle about the goal, they want to attain it. Thus, they have to analyze reality in its changes, brought about by the suggestive interplay of political fictions, in order to arrive at a correct appreciation of facts; in order to reach their target eventually. Since they are out to realize these aims in fact and since they refuse to accept hopeless, heroic gestures as a substitute for the triumph of the national rescue work over immense obstacles, they are called defeatists. Because they remain faithful to the ideal and do not allow its replacement by the Asmodeus of a political chimera, they are looked upon as quislings. Because, day and night, they summon up all inner forces so as not to submit to despair, and because they invoke the helpful power of reason, they are described as men whose hearts are left cold by the misery of their people.

Such are the convictions and such the fate of the group of men in whose midst *Ichud* and *Be'ayot* came into being.

Does this Cassandra act? She, too, only speaks. She does not act because she is not authorized to do so and because at this juncture action without authorization would be madness. But her speeches are as many deeds—because they point to the path. The history of the present and the coming generations will prove that her speech was action and the road indicated, the only one leading to Jewish revival in Palestine.

We describe our program as that of a bi-national state—that is, we aim at a social structure based on the reality of two peoples living together. The foundations of this structure cannot be the traditional ones of majority and minority, but must be different. We do not mean just any bi-national state, but this particular one, with its particular conditions, i.e., a bi-national state which embodies in its basic principles a *Magna Charta Reservationum*, the indispensible postulate of the rescue of the Jewish people. This is what we need and not a "Jewish State"; for any national state in vast, hostile surroundings would mean premeditated national suicide, and an unstable international basis can never make up for the missing intra-national one. But this program is only a temporary adaptation of our path to the concrete, historical situation—it is not necessarily the path itself. The road to be pursued is that of an agreement between the two nations—naturally also taking into account the productive participation of smaller national groups— an agreement which, in our opinion, would lead to Jewish-Arab cooperation in the revival of the Middle East, with the Jewish partner concentrated in a strong settlement in Palestine. This cooperation, though necessarily starting out from economic premises, will allow develop-

ment in accordance with an all-embracing cultural perspective and on
the basis of a feeling of at-oneness, tending to result in a new form of
society.

Essential prerequisites for such an agreement are the two principles,
which I have described as decisive for the immediate future of mankind: the precedence of economics over politics; and that of the intra-
national principle over the international one.

The cleansing of the Jewish-Arab atmosphere is much more difficult
today than it was only a few years ago. Above all, this is the result of
an entirely fictitious program, which does not comprise any possibility
of realization, and which relinquishes the realistic Zionism of toil and
reconstruction—the Biltmore Program. This program, interpreted as
admitting the aim of a minority to "conquer" the country by means
of international maneuvers, has not only aroused Arab anger against
official Zionism, but also made all attempts at bringing about Jewish-
Arab understanding suspicious in the eyes of Arabs, who imagined that
these attempts were concealing the officially admitted real intentions.
Yet, even today, such a cleansing of the atmosphere—an indispensible
preliminary condition for the establishment of agreement—is not
impossible. This can only be done, however, on the basis of the primacy
of reality. It is necessary to create conditions which will prove that the
common interests, now overshadowed by political considerations, are
more real, more vital than the differences hitherto so successfully
emphasized by the professional politicians on either side. This is what
J. L. Magnes, when giving evidence before the Anglo-American Committee of Inquiry, defined as reaching agreement "through life and not
through discussion." The realities of life should be given a chance to
force the walls of political fictions. Magnes was right in going as far as
to hope for an "agreement among the political leaders" themselves.
Life, when given a chance, will prove strong enough to force a new
line of action upon the politicians. The evil does not lie with politics as
such, but with its hypertrophy.

Equally important for the intended agreement is the precedence of
the intra-national principle over the international one. Prevailing Zionist policy hitherto adhered to the axiomatic view that international
agreement had to precede, no, determine the intra-national agreement
with the Arabs. It is imperative to reverse this order: it is essential to
arrive at an intra-national agreement, which is later to receive international sanction. This order will recommend itself also to the Arabs,

even if today their political leaders refuse to admit it, because the Palestinian State they aim at will, in the present international situation, only come about if demanded jointly by Jews and Arabs—that is, only after Jewish-Arab agreement will have been established.

In the present state of world politics, the intra-national principle tends more and more to assume a constructive role, while it remains for the international principle only to sanction the results of the former. In other words: as a consequence of agreements between nations, super-national structures will of necessity come into being, based, from without, upon common economic interests and joint economic action, and cemented inwardly by the singleness of purpose in the cultural and social domains. Within this common concern of two or more nations, economically unified and culturally diverse, the political activities will partly be the joint action of all and partly the result of the separate action of each group; but all this diversity of effort will be moulded into a whole, by a great vision, shared by all and creative. Finally, these new social structures will be fitted into a super-territorial pattern, corresponding with our present "international" principle, but more vital and more active.

In the Middle East, no such larger integration will come about without a genuine agreement between Jews and Arabs and its international sanctioning. In the same manner, the essential Jewish demands can only be realized by way of such an agreement. Only if the Jews are able to offer the world peace in the Middle East—as far as this depends upon them—will the world concede those demands to Jewry. For one thing is certain: not only this or that Great Power needs a peaceful Middle East, but the nations of the world at large.

Since we embarked upon our struggle against fictitious political thinking, the power of these fictions over the Yishuv has, it seems, been increasing continuously. First, a program was drawn up that could not be realized by political means; when this became apparent, a desperate and foolhardy section of Jewish youth resorted to violence—which is more vain still. The whole history of national movements, in which revolutionary and violent measures play no small part, was invoked to serve as a lesson that was no lesson—for it is evident that lessons drawn from history can only be applied if the particular character of the situation has been recognized; the weight of the interested powers, assessed; and the interplay of forces between and within these states, as they affect the particular problem, analyzed. But this very investigation—an essential preliminary—was not undertaken; had it been, it would have laid bare the absurdity of a policy of violence in our situation.

It should, of course, be borne in mind that genuine despair was prevailing, brought on by an action of extermination never before experienced by any other nation, as well as by the indifference of the world in the face of this action. Yet, despair does not usually render judgment more keen; rather does it lead to an intoxication by political fictions. Professional politicians here, as elsewhere, have made all the despair, all the misery of the nation, the demand for rescue, so many factors in their calculation. It is not the calculation that matters, however, it is reality; and the politicians of the world power most interested, instead of watching reality, had their eyes pinned on to these calculations. By so doing, they heightened the feeling of despair, especially since after an action of extermination of this kind, the poor human soul is inclined to see extermination lurking everywhere.

Nevertheless, the feeling continues to spread over the Yishuv that something is wrong with official Zionist policy; that irretrievable opportunities have been lost. The number of those, who re-examine their position, is growing. Our painstaking efforts have not remained without result. It is now of the utmost importance to prevent this disillusionment from developing into destructive pessimism and to shape it into constructive resolution. More emphatically than ever has it to be shown that a solution is still possible. To bring this solution about will be more difficult and less satisfactory now than at any earlier stage, but its realization is still within our reach: it will bring us back to our path of constructive work.

To point to the way and to aim at the solution in the present and more difficult conditions is a task which can only be fulfilled by dint of a supreme effort. To this end, we seek allies everywhere and appeal for their support.

Note

1. That is, the principle of that all hired labor, both in industry and agriculture, should be exclusively Jewish; first, because only thus can Jewish immigration to Palestine be absorbed into the economy of the country, and new jobs be created for additional Jewish immigrants; second, because Arab labor, for the most part not organized in trade unions, is cheaper, and hence may undermine the Socialist Zionist principle of employing organized labor only. [Buber's note.]

41

Let Us Not Allow the Rabble To Rule Us!

(January 1948)

(Editor's prefatory note:)

In February 1947 the British government requested the United Nations to relieve it of the Mandate. On 29 November, the U.N. General Assembly accepted the recommendation of the international committee appointed by the U.N. to terminate the Mandate and to partition Palestine into two independent states—Jewish and Arab. On the morrow of the U.N. vote, Palestine was embroiled in a virtual civil war between the Jews and Arabs. In the following article, an open letter published on the editorial page of the Tel Aviv daily *Ha-Aretz* of 29 January 1948, Buber together with his co-signatories Judah L. Magnes and D. W. Senator (1896–1953; an administrator of the Hebrew University and member of the Ichud), appealed to their fellow Jews, especially in Jerusalem, to desist from indiscriminate violence against Arabs.

LET US NOT ALLOW THE RABBLE TO RULE US!

The struggle in our land is erupting into barbarous violence that has spread with lightning speed and spares neither the old nor women nor children. Only a few weeks ago, the Tel-Aviv Municipality was able to declare that no peaceful and peace-loving Arab had anything to fear when walking the streets of the city. Today any Jew who dares to walk through an Arab neighborhood risks death—and so does any Arab who enters a Jewish area. While it has happened and does happen that Jews are saved by Arabs and Arabs by Jews, sometimes at great personal risk, the cases of murder of innocent people are increasing in number—murder committed in full view of the public, and even of the police.

A short while ago a Jewish physician was murdered by Arabs in Qatamon [a largely Arab quarter of Jerusalem] when he came with his car to help a Jewish family move its belongings. A few days ago, two Arabs were murdered by a Jewish mob in Mea Shearim [a Jewish quarter of Jerusalem]. The Arabs, who were passing through in a lorry with their belongings, were moving from Lifta [an Arab village on the outskirts of Jerusalem] to a quieter Arab neighborhood. Till this very day we have not heard a single word from Arab or Jewish authorities condemning these base deeds. A psychosis of war is spreading among us, a psychotic fear that turns every foreign-looking passerby into a criminal, a murderer, an enemy. In this pathological state, the rabble turn on and kill all strangers passing by. We appeal to the Jerusalem community. We appeal especially to our Jewish brothers: Let us not desecrate our name and our honor! For if we go the way of the incited mob, not only will we achieve nothing substantial, we will exacerbate an already worsening situation, deepen hatred, and evoke additional ruthless and indiscriminate reprisals. We appeal to the Jewish authorities and public opinion and demand that they employ all means to prevent attacks and reprisals by incited mobs. We demand that the men of the peoples' militia [*Mishmar Ha'am*] be given strict orders that will strengthen them in their difficult task and enable them to keep the peace in the Jewish areas, under all circumstances and at all costs. We demand that clear and strict instructions be given to the populace, forbidding and punishing all attacks and robberies in the city's streets. Every case of a suspicious-looking stranger must be brought to the local headquarters of *Mishmar Ha'am*, and there only, where the matter will be dealt with responsibly and in a cool-headed manner.

Let the recent deplorable events serve us as a grave warning. Let us not allow the rabble to rule us! Let us not destroy with our own hands the moral foundation of our life and our future!

42

A Fundamental Error
Which Must Be Corrected

(April 1948)

(Editor's prefatory comment:)

The United Nation's decision of 29 November 1947 to partition Palestine was greeted by the Zionist movement with singular enthusiasm. "Our right to independence, ... now ... confirmed in principle, must [forthwith] be translated into fact," declared the National Council of the Yishuv.[1] The Jewish Agency launched a diplomatic offensive to ensure the quick institution of the partition; it also immediately set out to prepare the Yishuv administratively, politically, and militarily for statehood. In mid-December 1947 Britain announced that it would comply with the U.N.'s decision and unanticipatedly declared it would terminate its Palestine Mandate as soon as 15 May 1948. The imminence of statehood and the military threat posed by the Arabs drew the Yishuv together, uniting all parties from the communists to the ultra-Orthodox Agudat Israel. The Ichud was an exception. Convinced that the partition of Palestine would lead to war between the infant Jewish state and the Arabs, the Ichud vigorously endeavored to alert Jewish opinion to the dangers of pursuing statehood.

In the following article, published on 1 April 1948 in *Be'ayot Ha-Zman*,[2] Buber warned that the rush for statehood which began with the Biltmore Program of 1942 was suicidal. It was based, he argues, on the erroneous premise that a Jewish state in Palestine would coincide with Britain's imperialistic interests and therefore ultimately earn its support. But clearly this was not the case, and thus the present crisis in which the Yishuv was abandoned to its folly and the terrifying wrath of the Arabs engendered by their fear that the Jews, borne by the ambition for statehood, wished to dominate them. Moreover, the rush for statehood violated the wisdom that had hitherto guided the Yishuv, namely, that the organic, gradual development of the moral and material resources of the Yishuv was the soundest way of assuring the realization of the pristine goals of Zionism. Political sovereignty, surely at this juncture in history at least, would endanger the Zionist enterprise.

Notes

1. Cited in J. C. Hurewitz, *The Struggle for Palestine* (New York: Schocken Books, 1976), p. 310.
2. Formerly *Be'ayot*, which with volume 7, 1948, adopted the name *Be'ayot Ha-Zman* (Problems of the Time); otherwise the journal remained unchanged.

A FUNDAMENTAL ERROR WHICH MUST BE CORRECTED

" ... If only the Jews had worked silently for twenty years ... !"

(a high-ranking British officer, 1938)

The fundamental error of our political leadership was to think that a speedy decision on the political status of the Yishuv was in the interests of Zionism. Without a doubt, this error is a consequence of a false analogy. We profited from the [geo-political] situation wrought by World War II; from this, the Zionist leaders concluded that it was also possible to exploit the situation created by World War II. But they failed to notice the main difference between these two situations. As part of her expansionist policy [in World War I] Britain needed us in order to justify the Palestine Mandate, whereas [during the last war] she sought nothing more than to save the basis of her economy. Hence, she was interested in ensuring the long lines of communication, and this we were not capable of doing for her.

From this blindness to the situation comes, apparently, the feverish haste with which we tried to get the declaration of a Jewish state—as if this were the last time it were possible to put the Zionist program into practice. This feverish haste is what pushed us into the crisis in which we find ourselves today.

In fact, the main thing is for us to gain *time* to develop the Yishuv. As everyone knows, in the areas of *aliyah* [i.e., prior to the White Paper of 1939 which severely restricted Jewish immigration and land acquisition] and settlement, we have not accomplished more than a part of what we had to do during the years when we had plenty of freedom to act. When we lost this freedom, we began to delude ourselves into thinking that in order to restore it, we must hurry and expedite the determination of the [ultimate] political status of the Yishuv in order to ensure perfect freedom in the form of a Jewish state.[1] Thus, instead of calm, persevering organic work, we have a breathless political card game in which we have staked everything on a single card.

In order to gain the freedom to develop the Yishuv, there is no need for a Jewish state. For the sake of the Yishuv's development, we need but the assurance of that rate of immigration which we are actually capable of absorbing into our economy; of that amount of settlement which our [material and moral] resources are actually capable of carrying out; and of that measure of independence required to establish and administer this immigration and settlement. Had we claimed this, we would certainly have attained it without endangering our future— which is what we did by our "achievement" of four months ago [i.e., the U.N. vote of 29 November 1947 in favor of the partition of Palestine].

To be sure, in order to ensure the Yishuv's development, one decisive factor was necessary: the faith on the part of the Arabs that our aim was not to rule them in this land. This faith we lost with the Biltmore Program which they necessarily interpreted as outsiders. Afterwards, when we supported partition, it was not understood [by the Arabs] that we were thereby giving up the Biltmore Program (which envisioned Jewish rule over all of Palestine) as a final goal, nor did we take sufficient care that it should be so understood.

To be sure, it is much easier to lose the faith of others than to dispel their suspicions. Nonetheless, it can be done, but at this late date any delay is terrible. Yet it cannot be accomplished by stratagems, but solely by decisions of conscience. Our goal must be changed. We must rid not only our declarations but also our hearts of every intention of becoming the majority at any time. If we do not, we shall not be able to bring about a change in the present course of events.

We must clearly declare what is necessary for us and what is not necessary. We need time and freedom for our enterprise, and not in order to gain the upper hand. We need *aliyah*, settlement, and communal independence, not in order to become stronger than others, but solely that we shall be able to shape our lives. In order to do this, there is no need for a Jewish state; rather, there is need of a treaty [with the Arabs] based on faith. And faith is not to be had except by a real change in our goals and its forthright revelation.

Note

1. The reference is to the Biltmore Program; see introduction to selection 30.

43

Zionism and "Zionism"

(May 1948)

(Editor's prefatory note:)

Disregarding the mounting pressure from Western powers, particularly the United States, to postpone the establishment of statehood, the Yishuv under the leadership of David Ben-Gurion proclaimed on 14 May 1948 its independence, reconstituting itself as the State of Israel. Amid the exultation that gripped most of the Yishuv, Buber declared in the following article—published in *Be'ayot Ha-Zman* of 27 May 1948, less than two weeks after the infant state's Proclamation of Independence—political sovereignty to be a perversion of the Zionist ideal of national rebirth. To be sure, from the very beginnings of Zionism there was a tendency to view the goal of the movement as the political "normalization" of the Jewish nation. But the quest to be a nation like all other nations, Buber insists, is tantamount to national assimilation, and, moreover, it betrays the true vision of Zionism. By sponsoring the rebirth of the Jewish people *within* the Land of Israel, "true" Zionism seeks to restore to Judaism its pristine vocation of serving the "spirit"—the source of universal truth and justice—through the "natural life" of the nation. Further, true Zionism, which eschews the way of "normal," egotistical nationalism, realizes that the return to the Land does not require its conquest, nor the subjugation of its non-Jewish inhabitants.

ZIONISM AND "ZIONISM"

From the beginning, modern Zionism contained two basic tendencies which were opposed to each other in the most thoroughgoing way, an internal contradiction that reaches to the depths of human existence. For a long time this contradiction was not felt except in the realm of ideas. However, since the political situation has grown increasingly concrete, and the need for decisive action has arisen alongside it, the internal contradiction has become more and more real, until, during recent years, it has attained shocking actuality.

One can comprehend the two tendencies at the origin as two different interpretations of the concept of [national] rebirth.

One tendency was to comprehend that concept as the intention of returning and restoring the true Israel, whose spirit and life would once again no longer exist beside each other like separate fields, each one of which was subject to its own law, as they existed during the nation's wandering in the wilderness of exile, but rather the spirit would build the life, like a dwelling, or like flesh. Rebirth—its meaning is not simply the secure existence of the nation instead of its present vulnerability, but rather the experience of fulfillment instead of our present state of being, in which ideas float naked in a reality devoid of ideas.

On the other hand, the second tendency grasps the concept of rebirth in its simplest meaning: normalization. A "normal" nation needs a land, a language, and independence. Thus one must only go and acquire those commodities, and the rest will take care of itself. How will people live with each other in this land? What will people say to each other in that language? What will be the connection of their independence with the rest of humanity?—all these questions are of no interest to this interpretation of rebirth. Be normal, and you've already been reborn!

In fact these two tendencies are only a new form of the pair that have been running about next to each other from ancient times: the powerful consciousness of the task of maintaining truth and justice in the total life of the nation, internally and externally, and thus becoming an example and a light to humanity; and the natural desire, all too natural, to be "like the nations." The ancient Hebrews did not succeed in becoming a normal nation.

Today the Jews are succeeding at it to a terrifying degree.

Never in the past have spirit and life been so distant from each other as now, in this period of "rebirth." Or maybe you are willing to call "spirit" a collective selfishness which acknowledges no higher standards and yields to no uplifting decree? Where do truth and justice determine our deeds, either outwardly or inwardly? (I said "inwardly" because unruliness directed outwards inevitably brings on unruliness directed inwards.) This sort of "Zionism" blasphemes the name of Zion;

it is nothing more than one of the crude forms of nationalism, which acknowledge no master above the *apparent* (!) interest of the nation. Let us say that it is revealed as a form of *national assimilation,* more dangerous than individual assimilation; for the latter only harms the individuals and families who assimilate, whereas national assimilation erodes the nucleus of Israel's independence.

From the clear recognition of these tendencies, which stand in opposition to each other, derives the principal political question confronting us as we dig out the roots of the political problems of our day.

The self-realizing tendency says: we wish to return to the earth in order to acquire the natural foundations of human life which make the spirit real. We do not wish to return to any land whatsoever, but to that land in which we first grew up, since it alone may arouse historical and meta-historical forces into action, coupling spirit with life, life with spirit. This land is not, today, devoid of inhabitants, as it was not in those times in which our nation trod upon it as they burst forth out of the desert. But today we will not tread upon it as conquerers. In the past we were forced to conquer it, because its inhabitants were essentially opposed to the spirit of "Israel." Moreover, the danger of paganization, that is to say, the danger of subjugating the spirit to the rule of the instincts, was not entirely averted even by conquest. Today we are not obliged to conquer the land, for no danger is in store for our spiritual essence or our way of life from the population of the land. Not as in ancient days, today we are permitted to enter into an alliance with the inhabitants in order to develop the land together and make it a pathfinder in the Near East—a covenant of two independent nations with equal rights, each of whom is its own master in its own society and culture, but both united in the enterprise of developing their common homeland and in the federal management of shared matters. On the strength of that convenant we wish to return once more to the union of Near Eastern nations, to build an economy integrated in that of the Near East, to carry out policies in the framework of the life of the Near East, and, God willing, to send the Living Idea forth to the world from the Near East once again. And the path to that? Work and peace—peace founded upon work in common.

In contrast to this view of Zionism, the "protective" tendency makes only one demand: sovereignty. That demand was expressed and presented in two different forms, one beside the other. The first form crystalized around the "democratic" concept of the majority: we must endeavor to create a Jewish majority in a state that will include the whole land of Israel.[1] It was evident that the meaning of that program was war—real war—with our neighbors, and also with the whole Arab nation: for what nation will allow itself to be demoted from the position of majority to that of a minority without a fight?

When that program was revealed to be illusory, a program of tearing off took its place.[2] That is to say, tearing one part of the land away from the rest, and in the torn off portion—once again, a majority, and the thing's name would be a Jewish State. They frivolously sacrificed the completeness of the land which the Zionist movement once set out to "redeem." If only we can attain sovereignty! The life-concept of "independence" was replaced by the administrative concept of "sovereignty." The watchword of peace was exchanged for that of struggle.

This thing was done during a period when the value of the sovereignty of small states is diminishing with frightening rapidity. Instead of the aspiration of becoming a leading and active group within the framework of a Near Eastern Union, there has come the goal of establishing a small state which is endangered in that it stands in perpetual opposition to its geo-political environment and must apply its best forces to military activity instead of applying them to social and cultural enterprises.

This is the demand for which we are waging war today.

Fifty years ago, when I joined the Zionist movement for the rebirth of Israel, my heart was whole. Today it is torn. The war being waged for a political structure risks becoming a war of national survival at any moment. Thus against my will I participate in it with my own being, and my heart trembles like that of any other Israeli. I cannot, however, even be joyful in anticipating victory, for I fear lest the significance of Jewish victory be the downfall of Zionism.

Notes

1. The reference is to the Biltmore Program; see introduction to selection 30.
2. Here Buber is alluding to the Palestine Partition Plan supported at the time by the Zionist leadership; see introduction to selection 42.

44

On the Assassination of Count Bernadotte

(September 1948)

(Editor's prefatory note:)

After the outbreak of war between Israel and its Arab neighbors in May 1948, the United Nations appointed a Swedish diplomat, Count Folke Bernadotte (1895–1948), as a special mediator between the contending parties. He arranged several abortive cease-fires and made several proposals for a solution to the Palestine crisis. Eager to satisfy the Arabs, while preserving the concept of a Jewish state, Bernadotte proposed territorial concession to the Arabs, including granting them sovereignty over Jerusalem (which the U.N. Partition Plan envisioned as an international city). On 17 September 1948, while on an inspection tour of Jerusalem, Bernadotte was ambushed and assassinated in the Jewish section of the city. The assailants were never caught, but they were believed to be members of the outlawed Stern Gang, a terrorist group which had broken with the Irgun in 1940.

   In the following hitherto unpublished essay, apparently written just after the assassination of Count Bernadotte, Buber laments what he believes to be the secret but pervasive adulation of the murderous act as a heroic deed on behalf of Jewish rebirth.

On the Assassination of Count Bernadotte

A recent event has revealed to us that this Yishuv is not on course for the abyss; indeed, it is already right at its edge. I say "revealed to us" but who is this "us"? Those who see what is to be seen are frightfully few. The way the man in the street speaks of what happened is even worse than what actually happened. Those with sight must therefore speak the truth more forcefully than would be necessary were the situation different. And wherever the truth is spoken, even in a small circle of friends, it must be uttered as if addressing the nation. And what needs to be said is this: murder and attempted murder will never produce life, never produce rebirth. He who dares to murder in the name of his people kills the buds of the future of that people. And he kills more of those buds to the extent that his people, those around him, confirms him by not repudiating him. To abhor the murder in official pronouncements is not genuine repudiation. What is of real importance is what is said in private conversation; what is of real importance is what beats in people's hearts; what is of real importance is genuine public opinion. And here the repudiation is lacking. Where are those who rise up against the criminals who, wherever their word is heard, declare in full voice or in whisper, as the moment demands: "Woe unto them who call evil good!"? The time has come once again to hurl at the events of the day the words of the prophet: "righteousness lodged in it, but now murderers."

He who argues against us says: "For our good and just cause we are compelled to fight, for our good and just war we are compelled to take upon ourselves this crime, and the future generations of our people will exonerate and bless us." To him I reply: These acts of vile murder will bring our people nothing but damage and contempt. They will not frighten a people so proud that no enemy ever intimidated it; they will only provoke it and incense it against us. If Jews are really involved in what happened, in future generations that people will say: "It was in those days that the Jews conspired to kill the representative of the King." And this memory will influence the lives of these peoples. If Jews are really involved in what happened, the future generations of our people will not exonerate but will condemn, not bless but curse the perpetrators of these deeds.

The heads of those perpetrators, or those assumed to be, they are today adorned, in the eyes of the man of the street, with a false splendor, a halo of a debased romanticism. All those who in the crisis years did not desire what was right and failed to prepare for it raise the real or imagined murderers to the rank of heroes and standard-bearers of the people. But murder from an ambush is vile and abominable; all murder is wicked and criminal, and murder in the name of a people only shatters that people's life and hope for life. In the commandment "Thou shalt not kill" can also be heard the commandment "Thou shalt not kill the soul of your people."

45

Let Us Make an End to Falsities!

(October 1948)

(Editor's prefatory note:)

Hours after Ben-Gurion proclaimed the establishment of the State of Israel, Egyptian war planes bombarded Tel Aviv. The armies of five Arab states had joined Palestinian irregulars in an attempt to thwart the Jewish state at birth. Buber, however, insisted in the following article, published in *Be'ayot Ha-Zman* of October 1948, that it would be disingenuous to claim that "we Israelis" are the innocent victims of Arab aggression. "The truth of the matter" is that Zionist political ambition is viewed by the Arabs as the primal aggression. Self-righteous protestations are thus irrelevant and politically asinine; the challenge is to change the Arab's image of Zionism.

LET US MAKE AN END TO FALSITIES!

It is characteristic for modern warfare that each of the two fighting sides is convinced his is a war of defense. Since the masses of a people take part in battles, they cannot be kept in the field in the name of their fatherland for a long period of time unless they can believe that they are being attacked and therefore fighting for their lives. To be sure, such conviction is easily created and sustained; even between individuals no real quarrel can arise unless each party feels that he is the injured one. How much more so then in the sphere of mass psychology and hypnosis.

Daily we read in our press that the war in which we are engaged is one of defense, because, surely, we have been attacked. And we do not see the facts as they are in reality. Two thousand years ago there lived in this land a people that did great things, and when this people was scattered over the world it maintained its inner bond with it. In our era, however, another people has lived in this same land which has created no extraordinary things, but it did simply live there, it culti-vated the soil as if no modern technique existed, kept its ancient cus-toms as if there were no modern civilization, and spoke its own lan-guage, without concern for a literature.

At the end of the last century small groups of the former people that grew ever larger infiltrated into this land with the intention of there establishing a basis for its concentration. The more political demands became attached to their colonization work, the more there appeared in the latter people signs of dissatisfaction, of opposition, and of hostility. At first the Arabs received the penetration with tolerance and even favor, out of an instinctive feeling of partnership in the devel-opment of the country, although here and there the fear arose that such growth might adversely affect their way of life. But as time passed the fear became crystallized in conviction that the newcomers were going to undermine their entire existence—and if not theirs, then that of their descendants. And now, when the first of these peoples has passed over from declarations to deeds and has moved the United Nations into granting it political power in the important part of the country, the conflict has broken out.

True, the conflict could not have become acute if the big powers, as always, had not exploited the mood of the people; without that it would not have acted. And now—we say—"we have been attacked." Who attacked us? Essentially, those who felt that they had been attacked by us, namely by our peaceful conquest. They accuse us of being rob-bers. . . . And what is our answer? "This was our country two thousand years ago, and here it was that we created great things." Do we gen-uinely expect this reason to be accepted without argument? Would we do so were we in their place?

Enough of all this! Let us make an end to these ambiguities. The truth of the matter is that, when we started our infiltration into the country, we began an attack "by peaceful means." We did so because we were forced to, in order that we might reestablish an independent, productive and dignified life for our people. Since such a venture could only succeed in the long run by agreement with the other nation, everything depended upon our capacity to convince them—by action, not talk—that in essence our attack was no attack at all, thus awakening in them the instinctive belief in our community of interests.

What, then, should have been our road in the sphere of action? On the positive side: to develop a *genuine* community of interests by including this other people in our economic activity. And on the negative side: to hold back all proclamations and political action of a unilateral nature, i.e., the postponement of all political decisions until that community of interests had found its true practical expression.

On the basis of these plain facts, and not on any empty slogans, let all who know the meaning of responsibility seek their own hearts as to what we have done, and what we have left undone.

46

Gideon Freudenberg: War and Peace. An Open Letter to Martin Buber

(December 1948)

(Editor's prefatory note:)

Buber's implied equation of Zionist political policy with Arab military aggression against the infant State of Israel elicited an impassioned rebuke from one of his most avid admirers in the Yishuv, Gideon Freudenberg (1897–1978). Freudenberg, who joined a Moshav (a cooperative farm) upon his emigration to Palestine from Germany in 1936, tirelessly sought to introduce Buber and his teachings into the cultural life of the Moshav movement. He later worked closely with Buber in the "Seminar for Adult Education," founded by Buber in 1949. In the following article, published as an open letter in the December 1948 issue of *Be'ayot Ha-Zman*, Freudenberg addresses Buber as an aggrieved disciple, claiming that Buber's offending article, "Let Us Make an End to Falsities," ultimately betrays the moral weakness inherent in the "plan" that Judah L. Magnes in the name of the Ichud presented to the Anglo-American Inquiry Committee in 1946. This "plan" for a solution to the Palestine problem called for a system of complete parity between Jews and Arabs in government, and for numerical parity of the population of the two peoples, with restrictions on Jewish immigration once demographic equality had been attained. This latter provision Freudenberg finds to be a cardinal flaw in the Ichud's program, for it not only indicates a willingness to limit the Jewish right to free immigration to Palestine, but implies that insistence on this right is not a preeminent moral necessity. Freudenberg thus takes exception to Buber's insinuation that Zionist policy, based precisely on the unimpeachable right of Jewish immigration, is a morally reprehensible act of aggression.

GIDEON FREUDENBERG: WAR AND PEACE: AN OPEN LETTER TO MARTIN BUBER

I

At this very moment when we are involved in a bloody conflict, I read your article "Let Us Make an End to Falsities" with the utmost seriousness. I read it—and was shocked.

You assert in your article that "day after day we read in the press that this war is a war of defense, for we were attacked." But "the truth is"—I find it difficult even to copy your words—"that we began the attack . . . ," though by "peaceful means," and it was our duty "to have brought the Arabs to understand . . . that at bottom our attack was no attack."

Do you really believe that the words "a war of defense" or "we were attacked" are on people's lips *because* they appear "day after day in the press"? Do I have to point out to you and stress that these words express a sincere, spontaneous feeling, heartfelt in the truest sense of the word? This, of course, is no proof that the feeling is justified, and you are fully entitled to think and to proclaim that there are no grounds for it and to demonstrate, if you are able that it is merely the result of distortion, the source of which lies in political ambitions, lust for power, etc. I find it strange that in so grave a matter Martin Buber employs, so to speak, an *argumentum ad hominem*, contrasting the conflicting viewpoints contained in the words "we were attacked" as against "we began to attack" by the terms "falsities" and "simple facts." Does not Buber the politician know what Buber the philosopher knows so well, namely, that in this world there are no "simple facts"— not even in the exact sciences!—because everything is subject to interpretation and the individual can do no more than demonstrate, if he is able, that his interpretation is the correct one.

II

Conflicting judgments about the present war are not related to the difference between "falsities" and "simple facts" but arise from two opposing interpretations; in support of their respective positions, both sides search in vain for something resembling a mathematical proof. It is this difference of interpretation which separates you from us and forms a dividing line not only between you and the "activists" of all parties but between you and *thousands of Jews* who regret no less than you do that we have reached the present pass and who feel as you do that grave mistakes have been made and continue to be made with regard to our attitude towards the Arabs; thousands who supported and continue to support your battle to end [Jewish] terrorism and to uphold the moral integrity of the Zionist venture; thousands who agreed with the sharp criticisms which you, as an intellectual standing virtually alone against the current of accepted opinion, voiced during the past several years, but who did not agree with certain political proposals based on the plan of the late Dr. Magnes which were put forward by people connected with the Ichud. And you know why: they, and I among them, found it impossible to agree of their own volition to grant the Arabs the right to limit or stop Jewish immigration—as was implied in the Magnes plan and not merely with reference to the future, once parity had been attained regarding the number of Jews and Arabs in the country.

As a refugee who fled from Hitler like many others, I was unable to agree, for reasons of conscience as well as for emotional reasons, that the gates of Eretz Israel be closed again after I had entered the country. I cannot buy peace in Eretz Israel—peace for myself and for my children—at the expense of my brother who is still abroad. For it is clear that even if from now on we were to act as cautiously as possible towards the Arabs in accordance with your demands, we could not be sure that in the future they would allow immigration to continue and would permit us to take in refugees when, heaven forbid, a new oppressor the likes of Haman[1] makes his appearance in the diaspora. Furthermore, there was not much likelihood that even recognition of the practical benefits of the Magnes plan—which, had it been accepted by both sides, would have allowed the immediate immigration of hundreds of thousands of Jews, and without war—could have overcome emotional resistance.

What I have said regarding the peace that the Magnes plan was purported to bring about holds to an even greater degree with respect to the war. Are you really so sure that only by means of the Magnes plan, by the means of limiting immigration in the future, could it have been averted? Is it just idle and empty presumption in your view that even today, despite all the mistakes we have made, there would have been no war had the powers, particularly England, wanted to prevent it and had they tried to promote peace between the two peoples? It is true that "on a hundred occasions" you warned "against the path taken by official Zionism which leads inevitably towards war" (as my friend N. Hofshi[2] wrote in *Be'ayot Ha-Zman*, 29 October 1948) and the war broke out! Meaning? That "you were proved right because the outcome has borne you out," to quote Lessing.

It is my view that the rejection of the Magnes plan by the great majority of the Yishuv is grounded—knowingly or not—in that same emotional resistance and not in ambitions or in a nationalistic spirit or in political or party maneuvers. And even if such unjustifiable factors as these operate among our people and have operated in the past, I don't think that they were the factors that were capable of generating the unlimited devotion and the heroism which the younger generation is now showing:

> To defend what is in the process of being created, to defend the revival [of one's people] against violent gangs, this too is war, if you want to call it that, but war that is fundamentally and radically different from all other wars.
>
> Contemplate the silent graves in Galilee and in Judea and you will hear the first sounds of the blasts of the ram's horn before which the walls of Jericho fell down.

These were the words written by a great Jewish spiritual leader thirty years ago, to commemorate the death of those who lost their lives in the first clashes between our defense forces (the men of the "Shomer" organization) and the Arabs. I remain faithful to these words even if it be the case that you, Martin Buber, who wrote them then no longer abide by that view.[3]

III

With regard to the present conflict, I don't think there is any point in delving into the question: who started the attack on the local population of the country, whether it was the patriarch Abraham, or Joshua bin-Nun's forces, or the Arabs under Omar, or the Turks, or the British under Allenby—I don't know. But I do know that the Jews who came to settle the land—from the pioneers of the Second *Aliyah* down to "Youth Aliyah" organized by the late Henrietta Szold—would strongly reject the notion that by their labor, by drying swamps, building roads, removing stones to make land fit for cultivation, and building villages, they began an attack on the Arabs. Nor did their neighbors, the Arab farmers who made their living from the land just as they did, consider them invaders or enemies. And surely you cannot believe that "an attack by peaceful means" of this kind can in any way justify a counterattack by non-peaceful means, an attack by bloodshed. If there is any point to the question "who attacked," it is clear that the bloodshed was begun by the Arabs, in 1921, 1929, 1936, and also in 1947.

Whoever wishes to probe the question "who is to blame" must also take care not to disregard the legal issue. An international institution of the highest authority, which you certainly do not dispute, decided on something. I am sure that had we wished to reject that decision as not being binding, which was proposed by the Revisionists, in whose view the decision was unjust towards us, you would have been strongly opposed. And you could have looked for support to Socrates, who accepted his sentence of death without accepting the justice of it, out of an overriding concern for the preservation of law and order, without which human life, society, and the coexistence of nations would be impossible. But when the Arabs, the Arab leaders, tried by force to reverse a U.N. decision, no censure of their action was expressed by you; you understand the Arabs because "they felt that they had been attacked by us." That sort of reasoning, I think, could be used to justify any offender, for example, someone who robs money from a publicly owned bank because he feels—and perhaps rightly so!—that the existing capitalist system of law and order has unjustly deprived him of his share of the national wealth.

There is no justification for the bloody attacks by the Arabs even if they felt themselves attacked by us. It is true that had we not immigrated to the country they would not have felt that way. But it does not follow from this that we are to blame because they felt themselves attacked. If we are partly to blame for it, it was not because we had immigrated to the country but because of our behavior once we had entered the country. And certainly we alone are not to blame that they felt themselves attacked. And it was they who began a vicious campaign of murderous ambushes, killing women and children; to which you say: Is it any wonder that the Arabs lost control of themselves after we had, so to speak, entered their home and had declared that from now on it would be our home (as asks N. Hofshi)? In my view, that sort of question should not be asked; otherwise, one can just as well ask another question, namely: With all that happened to the Jews (which hardly needs an effort to recall), is it any wonder that they lost control of themselves and killed English soldiers and officials? This kind of thinking must be rejected; murder is murder and I cannot make any distinction in favor of the Jews or in favor of the Arabs. The Arabs launched an attack against our lives and our possessions not in order to realize any political program designed to bring about justice, such as the Magnes plan or the U.N. resolution, but in open pursuit of the aim of putting an end to Zionism and of robbing us of the fruits of more than fifty years of labor and of our last hope of survival and national revival.

In 1936, the leaders of the Yishuv declared a policy of restraint and this policy was adhered to by all sections of the population—apart from the dissidents, who were few in number then. Even during the bitter years following the Second World War and up until December 1947, when the dissidents grew in number and were active in carrying out their reprehensible operations, no attacks were carried out on the lives of Arabs to my knowledge. And even in December 1947, when the Haganah was strong and prepared for battle, a week of Arab attacks that cost us many precious lives went by without any active response on our part. Only after the Haganah issued a grave warning which it circulated among the Arabs with no effect did that organiza-

tion launch a campaign of "active defense." And all of these actions—
which include unjustified actions and vicious actions—and even atroc-
ities which were carried out by the dissidents or by the Haganah or
our regular army, as well as the fact that thousands of innocent Arabs
suffered more than the gangs of Arab aggressors—all this cannot alter
our assertion that we were attacked and that we are engaged in a war
of defense to protect what is in the process of being created and what
is being revived.

That is my interpretation of contemporary events. And if you have
a different interpretation, let each of us respect the other's opinion. We
will acknowledge our differences, we will debate the issues and examine them as far as it is humanly possible to reach the truth. But let us
not confound the main points in dispute and the nature of these differences by categorizing an opponent's view as nothing but "falsities,"
that is, "empty slogans."

IV

Believe me, Professor Buber, I am (and you know me) by no means a
person who is inclined to underrate your views. My only purpose is to
make you realize that the extremism of your article "Let Us Make an
End to Falsities" will only repel the thousands of Jews I mentioned who
cherish peace, thousands whom you could have welded together under
your guidance, not to bewail our tragic involvement in this war nor to
do penance for our past mistakes, but for the sake of the future, for the
sake of tomorrow's peace.

We are still at war but the danger of the annihilation of the Yishuv,
the annihilation of our national venture, has miraculously passed.
Another danger, however, still remains: the danger of the annihilation
of the soul of our venture, the soul of Zionism, which is threatened by
the spirit of violence, the spirit of nationalism, and the spirit of militarism. This danger is also widely recognized within the parties in
power, and we all know that danger automatically increases with every
military victory, glorious and gratifying as they may otherwise be and
with every political gain which follows a victory. We had expected you
to call us to battle against this danger, against this evil spirit, against
Jewish expansionism, against robbery and plunder, against anti-Arab
discrimination, against the destruction of their villages, and for the
return of the refugees. We had expected you to call us to battle against
hatred and vengeance! Thousands of farmers, workers, and other peo-

ple, who hate war and never wanted it, even if you are correct in saying that they did not do everything possible to increase the chance that it could have been averted, are ready to enlist in this battle. For the sake of peace, they are willing to give the Arabs whatever rights they may demand in every sphere of public affairs and the economy, except for the right to limit Jewish immigration. Today these thousands are scattered and their voice and their influence can hardly be detected. And you, a pillar of strength, who steadfastly remained at the Jerusalem front and who bore all the suffering of six months of siege, shelling, and hunger, you, Martin Buber, whose destined role in life, as all your work testifies, is to be a guide and leader to these thousands—can it be possible that you have little regard for them and refuse to recognize them as allies until they own up and confess: "We have sinned, we are to blame for the blood that was spilled!"? Are only those who warned against the fire, or who are willing to admit that they caused it, fit to engage in rescue work? Good or bad, the Magnes plan is a thing of the past, just like the Biltmore Program, and there is no way of turning the clock back. But the way is clear for another plan. The way is clear, although there are many obstacles along it, for building a land of peace for the Jews and the Arabs who want to live within its borders, a land of righteousness and justice for our people, the kind of land the fathers of Zionism—Moses Hess, Leo Pinsker, and Herzl—dreamt about and foretold.

And for this land of peace, our pioneering youth will give their vigor and their lives—because this was the land they wished for and the land for which they gave their lives in battle.

Notes

1. The preeminent symbol of Jewish oppression, Haman was an official in the court of Ahasuerus who, according to the Scroll of Esther, conspired to kill all the Jews of Persia. The eventual frustration of his evil designs gave rise to the holiday of Purim.

2. Nathan Hofshi (1889–1981) was one of the founders of Moshav Nahalal of which Freudenberg was a member. A radical pacifist, Hofshi was active in both Brith Shalom and the Ichud.

3. Cf. *Jiskor, Ein Buch des Gedenkens an gefallene Wachter und Arbeiter im Lande Israel,* trans. by Gerhard Scholem, intro. by Martin Buber (Berlin: Jüdischer Verlag, 1918), p. 4. "Jiskor"—May He [God] remember—is the first word of the Hebrew memorial prayer for the deceased. The book, originally published in Hebrew in 1914 and in Yiddish in 1915, commemorated those *halutzim* who died defending Jewish settlements from Arab marauders.

47

Facts and Demands: A Reply to Gideon Freudenberg

(*circa* January 1949)

(Editor's prefatory note:)

Freudenberg's attack on Buber appeared in the last issue of the Ichud's journal *Be'ayot Ha-Zman* before administrative and financial difficulties forced it to close. Hence, Buber's reply was not published. This reply, in which he carefully delineates the nature of Zionism's *political* aggression against the Arabs, is presented here for the first time.

FACTS AND DEMANDS: A REPLY TO GIDEON FREUDENBERG

You say that there are no such things as simple facts, there are only interpretations. I disagree with that view, and I have always disagreed with it, in my capacity as a "philosopher" and in that capacity in particular. It is a fact that in 1789 the French Revolution occurred; an interpretation of that event is that it was essentially a political revolution, just as calling it a social revolution is an interpretation. It is a fact that at the present time there is a conflict between Eastern Europe and Western Europe, and anyone who tells you that the conflict stems from an urge for "ideological" expansion is merely interpreting that fact, and anyone who tells you that the explanation lies in an urge for "imperialistic" expansion is doing the same. This is not the place to take up the general problem, but regarding the immediate issue I am prepared to explain more precisely what the principal facts are, and I hope you will recognize that in the main they are genuine facts.

The first fact is that at the time when we entered into an alliance (an alliance, I admit, that was not well defined) with a European state and we provided that state with a claim to rule over Palestine, we made no attempt to reach an agreement with the Arabs of this land regarding the basis and conditions for the continuation of Jewish settlement. This negative approach caused those Arabs who thought about and were concerned about the future of their people to see us increasingly not as a group which desired to live in cooperation with their people but as something in the nature of uninvited guests and agents of foreign interests (at the time I explicitly pointed out this fact).[1]

The second fact is that we took hold of the key economic positions in the country without compensating the Arab population, that is to say without allowing their capital and their labor a share in our economic activity. Paying the large landowners for purchases made or paying compensation to tenants on the land is not the same as compensating a people. As a result many of the more thoughtful Arabs viewed the advance of Jewish settlement as a kind of plot designed to dispossess future generations of their people of the land necessary for their existence and development. Only by means of a comprehensive and vigorous economic policy aimed at organizing and developing common interests would it have been possible to contend with this view and its inevitable consequences. This we did not do.

The third fact is that when a possibility arose that the Mandate would soon be terminated, not only did we not propose to the Arab population of the country that a joint Jewish-Arab administration be set up in its place, we went ahead and demanded rule over the whole country (the Biltmore Program) as a fitting political sequel to the gains we had already made. By this step, we with our own hands provided our enemies in the Arab camp with aid and comfort of the most valuable sort—the support of public opinion—without which the military attack launched against us would not have been possible. For it now appears to the Arab populace that in carrying on the activities we have been engaged in for years, in acquiring land and in working and developing the land, we were systematically laying the ground work for gaining control of the whole country along with its Arab population.

The fourth fact, which again concerns the international aspect of the matter in a most immediate and direct way, cannot be explained here, but I am prepared to explain it fully in a private conversation.[2]

Given the four facts I have mentioned, we face the danger that peace, when it comes, will not be peace; that it will not be real peace, which is constructive, creative, which leads to productive friendship and calls forth great cultural enterprises, the kind of peace that we need; instead, it will be a stunted peace, no more than non-belligerency, which at any moment, when any new constellation of forces arises, is liable to turn into war. And when this hollow peace is achieved, how then do you think you'll be able to combat the "spirit of militarism," when the leaders of the extreme nationalism will find it easy to convince the young that this kind of spirit is essential for the survival of the country?

The battles will cease—but will suspicion cease? Will there be an end to the thirst for vengeance? Won't we be compelled, and I mean really compelled, to maintain a posture of vigilance forever, without being able to breathe? Won't this unceasing effort occupy the most talented members of our society? Won't the work of Jewish revival in which we are engaged undergo intense suffering, suffering of the most dangerous kind? "Every one with one of his hands wrought in the work, and with the other held his weapon" (Nehemiah 4:11)—that way you can build a wall, but it's impossible in that way to build an attractive house, let alone a temple.

You, Gideon Freudenberg, speak about the thousands who you say are waiting for me to call them "to battle against this danger," namely the internal danger of "the spirit of violence, the spirit of nationalism, the spirit of militarism." Yet where were those thousands when immediately after what happened at the King David Hotel I published what I did?[3] Where were they when we, people from the Ichud and our friends, published in these pages what it was possible to publish "against robbery and plunder, against the anti-Arab discrimination, and against the destruction of their villages"? How few were the voices of encouragement! Though there were people who came to my house whom I had not expected and said whatever they said, they came secretly. However, if those thousands do in fact exist, and they really and truly share the concern you have expressed, let them come, let them make their voices heard, and we will sit down together, we will examine the bitter reality, together we will look into the actual basis of the facts—as painful as this will be—and together we will search for a way out, if such a way exists. "Redemption" of an external kind can be paid for with the blood of our sons. Internal redemption can only be bought by gazing directly at the brutal face of truth.

Notes

1. See selections 2 and 3.
2. Buber may have had in mind covert actions by the Israel Defense Forces to encourage the flight of Arabs from Israel. His circumspection would then have been prompted by the military censor.
3. See selection 36.

48

On the Moral Character of the State of Israel: A Debate with David Ben-Gurion

(March 1949)

(Editor's prefatory note:)

On 10 March 1949, David Ben-Gurion, who led the provisional government of the State of Israel, was installed as its first elected Prime Minister. Some two weeks later he convened at his home in Tel Aviv a meeting of a score of the country's most prominent intellectuals—authors, poets, academics—to confer on what should be the moral and spiritual direction of the nascent state. Buber, who was one of the first to address the meeting, challenged Ben-Gurion's assertion that the government *per se* has no direct role in shaping the moral character of the state. While agreeing with the Prime Minister that intellectuals have a vital task to perform in building the society, especially in the field of education, Buber insisted that the government's policies with regard to issues that have a moral dimension help mold the moral and spiritual character of the nation. Hence, he called upon the government of the State of Israel to consider the moral implications of its policies toward the Arabs; the immediate challenge was to initiate a just and quick solution to the Arab refugee problem—the hundreds of thousand of Arabs who abandoned their homes in what was to become Israel and fled to neighboring Arab counties and to parts of Palestine later occupied by Jordan and Egypt. Excerpts of the protocol of Ben-Gurion's opening remarks at the meeting and Buber's statement (with Ben-Gurion's interlocutions) follow.

On the Moral Character of the State of Israel

Prime Minister David Ben Gurion (Opening Remarks):

Ladies and Gentlemen, I thank you in the name of the government of Israel for responding to our invitation and coming here. Welcome! You have been called here to discuss the participation of authors and intellectuals in the formation of our national character in the State of Israel. . . .

The formation of our national character, its spiritual and moral character, cannot be carried out by the government, although the government is not completely alien to spiritual matters. Out of necessity the principal concerns of the government will be concentrated in economic and political areas: the absorption of immigration, housing, settlement, labor regulations, taxation, services, security, our relations with our neighbors, with the U.N., and with the world powers. The resources of the state for spiritual needs—education, culture, art, literature, science—will necessarily be restricted and limited.

Until the present, the Prime Minister has had to concentrate mainly on building up the army and planning the war effort. From now on, I am convinced, he will have to concentrate on economic planning and settlement policy. While my colleagues and I consider political and economic matters to be those which, at this time, will determine our fate, many of us, and myself among them, do not see the historic task of the State of Israel in either its economy or its politics, but rather in its spirit.

The State of Israel will be measured not by its wealth, not by its military might, and not by technology, but rather by its moral character and its human values. . . .

What is the place of intellectuals in the process of consolidating the nation and uniting it, forming its tone and image, helping the immigrants strike roots in their new country and in the national past, letting them share in the riches of the human spirit and the Jewish spirit, encouraging their independent creativity? How will the author and the intellectual fit into the general endeavor of the state, and what will be his distinctive contribution? How will he give heart to the state and its actions? . . .

Professor Martin Buber:

Ladies and gentleman, first it is my heartfelt desire to congratulate the Prime Minister upon his excellent intention of making the contact between himself and intellectuals both permanent and continuing.[1] Let us not underestimate the importance of this matter. Generally intellectuals are called upon for ornament and decoration, whereas, in requesting permanent and continuous contact, the Prime Minister clearly has real collaboration in mind.

The Prime Minister, who reads the works of Plato in the original, does not need to be reminded of the words of that sage about the desirability of rule by philosophers, that is to say "intellectuals" in modern terms. The ideal has never been fulfilled, (Interjection by *Zwi Woislawski:*[2] "Marcus Aurelius." *Prime Minister David Ben-Gurion:* "He spent most of his time making war!") Although there have been a few rulers for whom philosophy was a sort of hobby, that is not what Plato had in mind. The ruler who is also a philosopher is a phenomenon which can be investigated in the history of ideas, but not found in the events of general history. More than two millenia after Plato, another thinker appeared, Kant, who in his book *Eternal Peace* nevertheless did not go so far as to demand that government be in the hands of intellectuals. He only asked that their words be heeded, and even that request was never honored. If only it would happen this time, and the good intentions of the Prime Minister could be realized.

The government has been charged with an awesome task, which it will be unable to accomplish without the cooperation of intellectuals. That task is what is called "spiritual absorption." I know of no task in

modern history as difficult as this one: absorbing the masses of immigrants who arrive daily in Israel, truly absorbing them, forming their
characters with the imprint of the nation.

In the invitation to this symposium, "the formation of the nation's
character" was mentioned. Now nothing can be formed except matter.
We must shape human material, the likes of which are unknown in the
history of recent generations, material that is far from easy to mold.
Let us state that this task is unprecedented. A great deal, a very great
deal, depends on the will, the energy, and the perseverance of those
very people who are able to shape matter, human material as well, and
to give it character—that is to say, the intellectuals. A great deal
depends on whether their contact with the masses is true contact, real
contact. For, in general, intellectuals do not have the power to act.

Men of action, the government and those who serve it, must give
full support to the intellectuals in their task. Of course, most of them
are "difficult" individuals, and almost every question is in dispute
among them. Perhaps it would be easier to unite the political parties
and their representatives than the intellectuals. Nevertheless, there is
one activity in which lies the possibility of uniting the intellectuals, and
that is education. It is possible to unite the intellectuals in an educational project which will serve as the true foundation of the enormous
task placed upon us.[3]

There is no way of accomplishing that task other than to establish a
great institution of popular education. In the middle of the last century, during the "cold and hot" war between the Germans and the
Danes, one intellectual arose, Sven Grundtvig,[4] and undertook the
great task of popular education. Thus he and his followers were able
to overcome the crisis which overcame the Danish people before and
after their defeat. It is marvelous how the development of that project
and its crucial success actually came after defeat. That project teaches
us one great general rule, which is: the education of the nation depends
principally upon the strong relationship between teachers and pupils
(in Denmark the students were farmers and farm-workers), and upon
the positive influence of the teachers, an influence not exerted mainly
through instruction, but rather through a spiritual stand and the whole
experience. And in addition, the learners became teachers, and the
process kept repeating itself infinitely. A dynamic connection was
established between the intellectuals and the people.

Only in that way can we set up groups of élite among the masses, not raised up over the people, permanently standing above them, but a dynamic link among those who rise up, who draw up others after them, new élites in an endless chain. Without the continuum, "forging tongs by means of tongs,"[5] there is no way to form the nation in this period of the absorption of immigration from all over the world.

Of course our historical situation is radically different from that of the Danes at the time of Grundtvig. We are living in the hour of victory, not of defeat. However, I fear that among us the crisis will arise out of victory. An internal crisis is taking shape already, in my opinion, and the order of the day is that we gird our loins and confront it. I do not underestimate the importance of our tasks in the fields of economics, politics, and national defence. However, greater than all those tasks, and also harder than them all, is the task of true absorption. What we must do will certainly not be similar to the project of Grundtvig. Naturally it will be consonant with our particular difficulties and needs. It will befit the human material which has come to us and which is yet to come to us, human material whose nature and circumstances are unparalleled in the world.

I heard one more important thing from the Prime Minister this evening. He said: "Not a *nation* like all the others." Might not one add, "Not a *state* like the rest either"? States generally act according to what is known as "raison d'état" whenever they must do anything or solve a problem. They choose the path in which the good of the state seems to lie at that moment, no less and no more. For us, that is insufficient. "Raison d'état" is not enough for this nation, for this state, at the moment in which we find ourselves.

One could well ask what can be done beyond "raison d'état." (*Prime Minister David Ben-Gurion:* "état de raison.") A fine expression, but I have a concrete instance in mind.

For the Prime Minister said one more thing, which also appears important to me. He used the word "morality" in describing the acts of the state. At this point I remembered that nearly seven years ago, during the time of the Biltmore Conference, you asked me, Mr. Ben-Gurion, in a private conversation, why I talk about politics and not about morality, for if I were to talk about morals, then you could prove to me that your position rests upon a moral foundation. (*Prime Minister David Ben-Gurion:* "Correct!") I do not intend to dispute the issue. God willing, we shall yet return to it. But in what way does a person exert moral influence on someone else? When that person is the

Prime Minister of a state? Only by his personal example, by serving as a model for the people.

I admit that when the government does this, it is apparently doing something unnecessary from the point of view of "raison d'état." However, it is just those "unnecessary" acts, acts with no apparent "explanation," that serve the true good of the state, the true good of the nation and of all nations.

For example, take the question of the Arab refugees. The possibility existed for the government, and perhaps it still does now, of doing a great moral act, which could bring about the moral awakening of the public, and its influence on the world would certainly not be bad. The government could have taken the initiative of calling an international, interfaith congress, with the cooperation of our people and the neighboring peoples—a congress which would have been unprecedented. I do not speak of concessions of one sort or another. The main point is that something be done on our own initiative. Were we not refugees in the diaspora?

This morning, while I was preparing to go to Tel Aviv, to take part in this symposium. I read in the newspaper that the Palestine Conciliation Commission,[6] which is presently in Beirut, intends to call an international meeting on the subject of the refugees. I hope that this information is false. They do not deserve that initiative. We deserve it. And if "raison d'état" argues against such an initiative, then it suffers from myopia.

Notes

1. In actuality, these colloquia took place only twice.

2. Zwi Woislawski (1889–1957), author of sociological and philosophical essays.

3. To this end Buber founded in 1949 the College for Adult Education Teachers, which sought to train teachers from among the new immigrants.

4. Ethics of the Fathers, 5:9.

5. Nikolai Frederik Severin Gruntvig (1783–1872), Danish educator who championed mass education, founded a system of "folk" high schools that continues to arouse world-wide interest.

6. Established by the U.N. in December 1948, the Palestine Conciliation Commission (consisting of representatives from the United States, France, and Turkey) was charged with assisting the countries involved in the Arab-Israeli conflict to negotiate a peace settlement, including repatriation or compensation for the Arab refugees from Palestine.

49

Should the Ichud Accept
the Decree of History?

(Spring 1949)

(Editor's prefatory note:)

After having resolutely defended itself against the invading Arab armies, the State of Israel was firmly established. It was clearly a victory for the votaries of the idea of a sovereign Jewish state, and, conversely, a defeat for the proponents of bi-nationalism. In the following article—an unpublished speech delivered at a meeting of the Ichud in the Spring of 1949—Buber addressed the question whether the Ichud should accept the decree of history, disband, and withdraw into silence. Buber proceeds to present a detailed survey of the events leading up to the defeat of the Ichud and its vision. He concludes that although the program of bi-nationalism may have been rejected by history, the cause of the Ichud still remains valid and urgent: to foster fraternal cooperation between the Jewish and Arab nations. The Ichud, Buber affirms, will continue to work for this cause, adjusting its program to the new situation.

SHOULD THE ICHUD ACCEPT THE DECREE OF HISTORY?

Not long ago I entered a certain Jerusalem shop, whose owner, in the past, often used to reveal to me his sympathy for our endeavors. This time he greeted me: "Oh! An utter political rout like the one your circle suffered is no common thing. It looks as if you'll have to face the facts and resign yourselves to total silence for the time being."

Ladies and gentlemen, it is a good thing that we have people like this, who do not watch their tongues, from whom we may learn what those who hide their opinions in their generous hearts think about us.

In any case, these words stimulated me to think about a question which had not yet concerned me, because I was in the habit of considering events in a completely different perspective. Now, since the question was raised before me by Public Opinion in person, as it were, and in such a forceful manner, I realized that it was worthy of reflection. It seems to me that this moment, the opening of our meeting, is a propitious one to present the results of my reflections to you. Indeed, I shall ask you, ladies and gentlemen, to regard these words simply as the fruit of my own reflections, and as my personal opinion alone.

The shopkeeper is mistaken in believing that a political defeat such as ours obliges us to keep completely silent. It was not on that question that I reflected. For if the cause we fought for is a good one, this is what obliges us to fight for it even more energetically, with perhaps a change in course according to the changed situation. That is to say, with a new program, new rallying cries, and new visions to fit the conditions of the new reality.

Who are greater than the Prophets of Israel, seekers and advocates of the truth? From them we hear that even God's plan progresses from failure to failure, until the terrible and glorious hour when His truth and His redemption will be revealed to all eyes. It is true that, unlike the prophets, we are not privileged to hear from time to time an affirmation of the truth and of the redemption from on high. Therefore we must carefully examine our actions after every failure to see whether we have erred in one detail or another in our conception of the good work or in our suggestions for accomplishing it, whether we were at fault and brought about our own failure. Even more so must we ask ourselves whether we have served the good cause to the best of our abilities, with all the necessary devotion. Perhaps we underestimated the task, which cannot be measured against ordinary standards, and which the routine course of history cannot contain. Therefore it requires that its proponents bear its yoke with a degree of earnestness and perseverence which was lacking among us. A number of us have asked questions like these, I among them. In brief, even if the cause that is so dear to us is defeated, we need not relegate ourselves to silence. On the contrary, we must continue to testify for it more readily and more forcefully.

Thus whether or not to keep silent is not our question. For this matter is now clear to us, although we have not yet paid sufficient attention to it because of the great difficulties we are encountering as we come together to act faithfully, under new conditions, in order to advance the vision of our spirit, that is to say, in order to find new paths towards its accomplishment under these new and wonderful circumstances.

Nevertheless we must also ask ourselves whether, and to what extent, we may speak of the defeat suffered by our *cause*. It is not the task which is being put to the test, for the task is not essentially influenced by changing historical events, but rather the *fact* which demands examination. This question troubled me after I heard from the lips of Public Opinion that we who always used to speak out the truth as we knew it, even at the moment when History was still veiling her face in the clouds of Biltmore—that we must now consign ourselves to silence, because History has made its pronouncement, and only History has the right to speak.

The answer at which I arrived is that, although there is good reason to speak of the failure of our group, of its lack of success, there is no reason whatsoever to speak of the defeat of our cause. While our hopes were raised for an agreement among the Western powers on the suggestions of the Anglo-American Inquiry Committee, I already dreaded the failure that threatened to come. It was clear to me that our plan of action would not be able to resist impending developments. For the fundamental historical fact, the mighty fact which alone allows one to evaluate the development of a situation, was the destruction of millions by Hitler, and the imprisonment of hundreds of thousands of the survivors in [displaced persons] camps. With regard to the horrible dynamic that sprang from this fact, there were two possibilities: either responding to it with real action, which would have released the tension of the Yishuv, a release which would have given us an opening to a solution based on a bi-national compromise or a confederation; or else the dynamic would become more powerful in the Yishuv, until it gained unbridled strength for the establishment of a state, as the only possibility for mass immigration.

It seemed as if fate had decreed that the three principal parties involved in the matter should have been struck with blindness, each one according to its own manner and circumstances. The name that stands for our blindness is "Biltmore." For the declaration of our claim on certain portions of the Land of Israel which are decidedly Arab was likely to arouse mistrust in the Arab world, and it did. I suspect that the war of seven Arab states against us was nothing but the first strong expression of that mistrust. Even if we should be fortunate, and our ideas will eventually exert their full influence both internally and externally, generations will pass before that ember [of mistrust] is extinguished which now smolders both visibly and invisibly. The name that stands for the blindness of the British, because of which they lost their naval base in Haifa, and the world lost the chance for a true and creative alliance between the two nations of the Near East, is "Exodus."[1] That is to say, repelling the refugees from Europe. In addition to our expansionist blindness and the British imperialist blindness, there is a third blindness which has repeatedly reinforced the first two, and that is the Arabs' blindness, their secludedness (and their separateness). Their blindness refuses to recognize that only by means of a great peace agreement with the Jews can the Near East, at this doubtful moment, and especially now, rise to new greatness. No well-known symbolic name is attached to that third form of blindness. However, a symbolic act which was not in the open, an act which was done here anonymously, was the murder of an Arab—although not a famous or representative man, he was a man of good will who was prepared to cooperate with us in preparing our great alliance of peace. His brothers rose up against him and slew him.[2] Out of the unconscious and harmful cooperation of these three forms of blindness, which feed each other and feed upon each other, rose the tide of History, which washed away all the possibilities of realizing our program at this moment.

Is the meaning of these events the failure of our cause? I cannot accept that assumption. I have heard it said that official Zionism has proven that it is more valid than our Zionism, for it has realized the Zionist ideal, whereas our Zionism did not so succeed. This claim is based on a fundamental misunderstanding. That which, in Zionism, deserves the name "ideal" is not the drive to bring masses of people to Israel, for immigration is only a means. Nor is it the desire for independence, for that too is only a means. It is the aspiration for national rehabilitation, regeneration. Now regeneration, both of an individual and of a people, is not a goal which one can reach by many different paths, according to the wishes of every individual. The goal itself sets the path which must be chosen by those who strive towards it. If one takes a path which does not indicate the character of the goal along every inch of its length, one may achieve one thing or another, but one will not achieve the rehabilitation of one's soul. One will not achieve regeneration. Recognition of that fact sustains the Zionist endeavor. It is the exalted opinion of many of its spiritual leaders, and it is the only living sentiment that guides the aspirations of every small group that has participated in that endeavor. The Zionist enterprise was built slowly, organically, by the efforts of workers, pioneers, and by people whose souls were bound up with it, by teams and groups, groups that were ennobled by the light of inner circles which drew them on, activated them, moulded their characters in their image and spirit—all this is part of the quality of that enterprise, and it is also the quality of its goal. And this too is part of the quality of the independence of the enterprise: it is a peaceful one. The builders and workers of this enterprise wish to develop the land hand in hand with their neighbors; they wish to build up shared interests. The truly daring are not those who dream of conquest and subjugation, but rather those who look to the future, when the two nations will together, in brotherhood, make the Near East flourish. They do post guards upon the walls of their endeavor, and the guards fight as they should. Guards who fight are not warriors, however.

Pedants might see self-contradiction here. We "conquer" work, and the worker from the outside is squeezed out. However, the "conquering" village helps its neighbor, guiding it, advising it, and teaching it. From the time when our group arose, speaking the explicit truth, announcing it openly, and advocating a "Covenant of Peace" (*Brith Shalom*) and a United Near East, our ideas have not penetrated men's hearts, and there have been those who find them repugnant—lest they lead to a weakening in the desire to settle the land; however, those who keep the straight path, those whom the suffering involved in construction has not confused, who have remained tolerant, they will admit, in quiet conversation, that this is the truth and this is the way.

In our neighbor nation, alongside resistance, both natural and artificial, despite growing nationalism, which grew in part out of the soil of reality, and in part was planted, there is no small measure of understanding and goodwill. There can be also found men whose hearts are open to understanding our great common task, and a person who has foreseen the coming hour, when the first brave mutual understanding will inspire opinion-makers both here and there, has had no vain vision. In this period of Grabsky[3] and Hitler, "History" has broken in and trampled all the tender shoots. The order of the day was to absorb immigrants, who are not internally connected to the land and the enterprise; the teams and groups radiating a vision and educating the people have been washed away in a torrent of morbidity, of masses struggling to make a living. Instead of an organic pace on our path, comes the pace of "History, holding a mountain over us like a wash-basin."[4] In our whole enterprise there is no hint of arbitrariness. *Necessity* is what determined our will and our desire. And now comes the reaction from the neighboring camp. Once again both natural fears and instigation have cut off the fruit. If at that time we had attempted to establish a great cooperative economic enterprise on a wide basis, this could have had great influence. Certainly it is not surprising that our leaders did not find sufficient courage and strength in their hearts for such an enterprise, especially during those days, the days of the deluge, which again inundated the world.

Now "History" has raised its arm for a final blow. The specter of the World War guides the hand that wrote the White Paper [of 1939]. And from the White Paper, in a period of death camps, terror arose. The three blindnesses have become stronger and reinforced each other. The end of the World War brought a constellation of events, which our side exploited. And how we exploited it! For it is the product of the great dynamic that impels mass immigration, and also the product of that blindness which locks the portals against immigration. Blindness responds to blindness. And now, events take over. The Israeli army, elements that are [physically *and* spiritually] rooted in the Land and those that are not, mingle with each other, stand up as a wall, conquer, vanquish.[5] But the cry of victory does not have the power of preventing the clear-eyed from seeing that the soul of the Zionist enterprise has evaporated. We stand at the threshold of the most bitter recognition of all.

We are told that the goal has been reached. Yes, a goal has been reached, but it is not called Zion. Not for that goal did Israel, yearning for Redemption, set its path. What sober and honest man, looking about himself in today's reality, could say that we are engaged in a process of regeneration?

They say "the ingathering of exiles."[6] It would be more apt to say, "the piecing together of exiles." Look how the different groups [of Jewish immigrants] are oppressing each other, struggling against each other to make a living. No spirit of brotherly love breathes among the different groups in the Land of Israel.

We have full independence, a state and all that appertains to it, but where is the nation in the state? And where is that nation's spirit?

Moreover, we have a fully Jewish economy. Instead of economic cooperation with the Arabs, we have an economy in which the Arabs are unemployed. We have just missed a great opportunity, and perhaps we have lost even more, something basic, which our economy will yet feel. There is nothing sillier than to be overjoyed because the Arab population has left. One day we will realize that the *fellah* is the caryatid that holds up the edifice of Eretz Israel.

No, I wouldn't say that all this adds up to the defeat of our cause. Our cause has lost its footing, its face has been sullied, but it has not been overcome. It would be overcome if the goal of Zionism had been achieved by taking the direction that has been taken. This was not achieved, and by taking that path, it cannot be achieved.

Thus, the question remains: is it at all possible for us to turn back from this fateful path, to stay this sentence, and to tread the true path?

No. There is no returning. Nothing remains to us except the hope of reaching, *via* deep disappointments and difficult trials, *via* serious self-examination and the destruction of illusion, *via* the recognition of the truth and our resolve to live a life of truth, to a new juncture of the true path, the path of our great task and of the great peace. How will that new juncture look? Today we cannot imagine it; we have no certainty of it, for from the point where we presently stand, it is much harder to get there than to any earlier point in the path. The day will yet come when the victorious march of which our people is so proud today, will seem to us like a cruel detour.

Among the past members of our faction, there are those who did not support the idea of "Brith Shalom" (a covenant of peace), of a binational state, or of a federal solution, only because they did not believe that we could win the war against the Arabs. They only learned one thing from human history: "God is always on the side of the big batallions," according to the epigram of Voltaire. They believed that our batallions were not sufficiently powerful. Their cause—if they had one—was, then, beaten by the other one, whose supporters were able to build up mighty batallions and use them effectively. We, however, without neglecting the superficial lessons of history, also learned the profound ones, that the might of batallions is only decisive temporarily, whereas the power of a creative accord among nations, is the only one which lasts for generations. We trembled and feared like every Jew for the outcome of the battles. However, we knew that even if success should favor our arms, the light of Zion would only seem to shine on the horizon of history. We, for whom the verse "Zion shall be redeemed in Justice"[7] is not simply a poetic phrase, and not an ideal-istic exaggeration, but a prophecy of truth—we await the day, amid acute pain because of what has happened and continues to happen, and with renewed faith in our cause, for a new stage in our mission. It is difficult for us to speak—and I confess that it was even difficult for me to begin speaking here to you this evening, my friends—but we are forbidden to keep silent. We must once again pronounce our mes-sage. In the new situation, and according to its conditions, as we are obliged to by our ideal.

We must condemn vanity, in accordance with our power of under-standing and description, whenever we encounter it. We must juxta-pose truth against lies, and against truth mixed with lies—for that is more dangerous than an open lie—human truth in all its frailty, the truth insofar as we recognize it. In every area where there is a need and a possibility of correcting some damage, and we know how it must be corrected, we must suggest the correction and execute it. Under these new conditions, which are so much more difficult from every point of view, we must teach the true goal of Israel and the renewed path towards it. We must show the way in which our efforts must be directed. The public's ears are still stopped. But everyday experience increases the number of those who are willing to listen, and of necessity it will continue increasing. Our throats still refuse to express the new words, and our hearts still flutter with pain—but the words press us, they exhort us to formulate and express them. Against our wills we must accede to theirs.

We have called this meeting, in order to fortify ourselves in our steadfastness. If it is common to us all, then so are our ways of express-ing it. The words I spoke came from within me, a spark of that torch by whose light we shall go on to search for the path we must now take.

Notes

1. In July 1947, a ship, "Exodus 1947," arrived in Haifa with 4,500 "illegal" Jewish immigrants, refugees from Nazi Europe. The Mandatory government forced the ship to return to Europe, where its hapless passengers were made to disembark in Germany. The "Exodus" affair had a profound affect on world public opinion.

2. On 11 November 1946 the League for Arab-Jewish Rapprochement signed an agreement with "Falastin al-Jedida" (the New Palestine), an Arab organization headed by Fauzi Darwish el-Husseini (1896–1946). The agreement signed by Fauzi and four other members of his organization endorsed the concept of a bi-national Palestine and

the right of "Jewish immigration in accord with the absorptive capacity of the country." Less than two weeks after the signing of the agreement Fauzi was assassinated by Arab nationalists. See Aharon Cohen, *Israel and the Arab World*, p. 303.

3. Wladyslaw Grabski (1874–1938) served in 1920 as Minister of Finance in several governments of Poland; from 1923 to 1925 he was Prime Minister. His financial policies and taxation system were prejudicial to Jewish merchants and shopkeepers. The resulting crisis in the economic life of Polish Jewry led to an increased emigration of Jews from Poland, 60,000 of whom went to Palestine. The Fourth Aliyah (wave of Zionist immigration to Palestine) of 1924–26 was thus popularly known as "the Grabski Aliyah."

4. A proverb referring to a Midrashic legend about the giving of the Torah on Mount Sinai, when God is said to have threatened to crush the children of Israel under the mountain unless they accepted the Torah.

5. Buber is here referring to the fact that the Defense Forces of the State of Israel were formed by uniting the Haganah—which drew its troops largely from the various Zionist movements devoted to the ideal of *halutziut* (pioneering) and communal settlement of the Land of Israel—and the Irgun with its very different view of Jewish renewal.

6. A rabbinic phrase, based on the Biblical prophecy of the return of the Israelites from captivity in the Diaspora. With the establishment of the State of Israel, the concept of the Ingathering of the Exiles was applied to the immigration of Jews "from the four corners of the earth."

7. Isaiah 1:27.

50

The Children of Amos

(April 1949)

(Editor's prefatory note:)

The reorientation of the Ichud to the new political reality created by the establishment of the State of Israel gained expression in the founding in April 1949 of a new Hebrew journal, *Ner (Light): Bi-Weekly for Political and Social Problems and for Arab-Jewish Rapprochement.*[1] This journal, as its first editorial underscored, was not animated by a spiteful negation of the state. Accepting the state, *Ner* would pursue constructive criticism in order

to clarify "the basis of the Jewish nation's existence *within* a state of its own."
Aware that the Jewish people *now* possessed the power to do justice, but also
evil, *Ner* would provide a vigilant, nonpartisan forum alerting the State of
Israel to the "evil" it might do and to the opportunities of promoting justice.

In the following article,[2] which was published as the lead article of the
inaugural issue of *Ner*, Buber acknowledges the State of Israel as fulfilling the
millennial longing of the Jewish people for independence. But, he asserts, a
Jewish state is not an end in itself. The purpose of independence is to enable
the people of Israel to realize its vocation to proclaim justice unto the world.
Being ultimately a political concept, justice requires that Israel, the exemplar
of justice, seek national independence. The pursuit of justice—in its laws and
institutions, and in its relations with other nations—is then the awesome burden of Jewish statehood. Those Jews who prod their people and state to recall
its prophetic vocation are "the children of Amos."

Notes

1. *Ner* had an English supplement, consisting largely of translations from the
Hebrew section. From April 1959 there appeared an Arabic edition of *Ner—al-Nur*.
The last issue of *Ner*, which at its height had 800 subscribers, was in 1965—appropri-
ately a memorial volume for Buber, who had died in June of that year.

2. Buber's article bears the date 29 April 1946, which is either a misprint (for 1949)
or indicates that the article was written in the anticipation that the Yishuv would be
bent on statehood.

THE CHILDREN OF AMOS

The yearnings of the People of Israel for a renewal of its independence
have been fulfilled in the form of a modern state. This historic fact
confronts Judaism with the gravest crisis of its history. Prevailing opinion maintains the opposite: many believe that precisely the establishment of part of the people within the framework of a state greatly
broadens the horizon for a soaring of the spirit of Judaism, and thereby
the way is paved for its "renaissance."

The power of a state, and the flowering of a culture, however, do
not always go hand and hand. Hence, even should the spiritual wealth
of the People of Israel residing in its own land greatly increase, it does

not necessarily follow that from this wealth will flower a new life for Judaism. For if we properly comprehend the uniqueness of Judaism, then it has but one content and purpose: a divine commandment that stands above the existence of the people as a people. It happened only once that a people, going forth on the road of its history, regarded that road as a path prescribed and commanded by God, a path which is a divine task given to the people to fulfil. Whenever the people's actual road through history deviated from the commandment, this deviation brought upon the people censure and rebuke. Every point of the actual road of the people through history was measured against that particular point of the way that had been commanded, "the way of the Lord," the way of justice. Unceasingly the people was called upon to "return." Unceasingly the vision of that one "way of the Lord" continued to be before its eyes. This—the relationship of the way of the people *qua* people to the way of Lord—this is Judaism, or else Judaism would never have existed.

Make no mistake as to the intent of these words! They do not aim at what usually is facilely called ethics. The Lord expects that Israel should live a life of justice before itself and the world—such is the content of its mission. The Lord demands not merely just institutions but rather just relationships, a system of life based on just relations in the sphere of economics, social affairs, and politics, and He demands just relationships between the people of Israel and other peoples.

This means that the Lord expects Israel to *begin* the realization of justice on earth. How great the danger! How great the promise!

The people has stumbled on occasion but it has never fallen prey to doubt. Not merely was there no doubt in its heart that the Lord, the Lord Himself, anticipates living justice from it, from Israel, but in all periods of the exile the people never wavered from the belief that it, Israel, would realize justice whenever it renewed its independence and its freedom to determine for itself its form of life. Now, after almost two millennia, Israel has regained the necessary premises for such a realization of justice. But Israel now seems to believe that, as a state, it has been granted the right and indeed the duty, like all modern states, to see in the demands dictated by its transient interests, that is, as understood by its leaders, the decisive and indeed the ultimate demand. The divine demand seems to have disappeared.

Formerly, in the days of the first Jewish state, there arose—in that place only and in that time only—prophets who reproached the people and its rulers and reminded them that whenever the interest of the moment, that is, what seemed at that moment to be the collective interest, was opposed to the unchanging will of the Lord, to the will of justice—that in any such event it is the duty of the people to pursue the will of the Lord and not its so-called interests, otherwise it would bring upon itself disaster and disintegration. Disaster and disintegration came. The great exile began. Today, when the wall of that exile has been extensively breached it seems that that situation of which the prophets spoke is likely to change. The change, however, is likely to be towards a situation even more difficult than that of ancient times because now some of the "spices" of the modern age have been added: the pseudo-wisdom known as "raison d'état" and the vain faith, presently at the height of its development, which proclaims that the achievements of the moment are what determines the course of history.

To be sure, we [in the State of Israel] do not dissociate ourselves from the prophetic tradition. We respect and venerate it, not, however, as a binding truth of life but rather only as a collective spiritual capital upon which one can draw easily and effectively for purposes of national propaganda. Yet there is no graver obstacle than this [use of the prophetic tradition] to the genuine expression of the word of God in the language of man.

The time has come for us to rescue the prophecy of Israel from the platitudinous. We should devote ourselves to understanding the real message of prophecy and place it, the true light in the world of man, over against the deceiving brilliance of what are called interests. The message of the prophets is Truth: only through justice can man exist as man, can the *human* nations remain *human*. On the other hand, anything human which can no longer exist as human, that is, in the reality of the spirit, has relegated itself to the fate of everything which is merely matter, that is, to rot.

It is true, to be sure, that we no longer have prophets who have the right to lend authority to their word by asserting: "Thus saith the Lord." Nonetheless every person who knows of the truth of prophecy is obligated today to raise his voice in this terrifying crisis. What was said in ancient times was said for this hour too, and perhaps it was intended for this hour more than for all times. For it is the very life of man which is bounded by the possibility that human existence may disintegrate if it is not founded on justice. We Jews, as in the past and forever, are merely the living archetype by which is explained what there is to explain—and the archetype is both sufficient for judgment and accustomed to such a role, for it is an archetype of salvation or disaster. What is said now of Israel is said of the miserable human race in its entirety. But the word is rightly spoken to Israel in particular for it is the one people which was sent on the road of its history by commandment of the Divine Power.

Love can be embodied only in the existence of individuals; justice cannot be embodied except in the life of a nation and in the lives of nations. Since the prophets sought a way that leads from *true* national existence to a *true* humanity, they held the demand for justice high above every other demand. Yet it is only a nation which is able to establish justice both among its various parts—individual and groups—and in its relations with other nations, for the sake of its own salvation and the salvation of humanity in the making. For this purpose a nation requires independence and self-dermination. There is need for the very things which Israel has now renewed. But what should be done with these new assets? That is the critical question.

When the prophets in ancient times promise "the Redemption" to Israel, and its release from the yoke of the Gentiles, they did not promise this for the people's own sake but for the sake of that task which it is its duty to undertake. Do not, however, imagine that the task to be undertaken is a mere "national culture"! Israel has no living culture without the desire for justice. And the matter does not change if we term the task now incumbent upon Israel "religious renewal," for Israel has no living religion without the desire for justice. What is meant is not simply just laws and just institutions, no matter how indispensable these are. What is meant is a sincere desire for the existence of justice in each and every thing we undertake, both in our relations with individuals and in our relations with other communities. What is meant is a *direction* which shall determine the course of collective and individual life. What is meant is the establishment of the rule of justice, the hallowed rule of justice. Hence, every Jew, both in the State of Israel and in the Diaspora, who has knowledge of the truth of prophecy, is duty bound, to the full measure of his influence upon his friends, the members of his circle, and those in association with him, to call and awaken them to this truth.

This is not an issue of a party or an organization but a shared service, the service of truth, both within each political party and organization and outside parties and organizations: to share in seeing the eternal prophetic truth as a binding obligation; to help each other to return to the truth and acknowledge it as a binding obligation in terms of the realities of each hour; to return to it and emphasize its character as a binding obligation upon themselves and upon Israel, in each hour according to its demands, to the extent of their understanding and their capacity.

Let this circle or association increase and go forward here and in the whole world, quickly and slowly, either in conquering the soul of many or in persuading the hearts of the few, as the Lord may wish. And to this circle let there be given the name Children of Amos.

51

"Preface" to a Projected Volume on Arab-Jewish Rapprochement

(*circa* 1950)

(Editor's prefatory note:)

Buber and his friends in the Ichud feared that the "intoxication of victory" over the Arab "enemy" might totally vitiate the pristine moral and spiritual motives of Zionism. To help reverse this tendency, they contemplated the publication of a volume of essays on Arab-Jewish understanding by individuals prominently associated with Zionist settlement in Palestine from the period of the First *Aliyah*—before the turn of the century—to the establishment of the State. The project never came to fruition; Buber did, however, write a draft of the preface to the projected volume. This "preface," which he wrote in about 1950, follows. Here he argues that the so-called practical Zionists, who emphasized settlement on the land and the upbuilding of the

Jewish community of Palestine in a gradual and organic fashion, increasingly realized the necessity for Arab-Jewish cooperation. This process was frustrated, he contends, by the sudden influx into Palestine in 1924–28 of 60,000 immigrants fleeing anti-Semitism in Poland, and by the 160,000 German Jews who sought refuge in Palestine between 1933 and 1936. Most of these "middle-class" immigrants had no desire to change their way of life and thus settled in the towns. As a result of these—and later—unanticipated developments the nature of the Zionist endeavor in Palestine was radically altered. Thus historical circumstance undermined the conditions favoring Arab-Jewish rapprochement. Buber, however, remained sanguine.

"PREFACE" TO A PROJECTED VOLUME ON ARAB-JEWISH RAPPROCHEMENT

This book contains a collection of characteristic utterances by a small, but slowly growing circle which, from the very beginnings of Jewish settlement in Palestine to this day, held and expressed the conviction that the precondition for genuine and enduring success of this endeavor is full cooperation with our Arab neighbours. But the members of this circle have always been fully aware of the fact that the future of the Near East—whether it is approaching a new golden age or whether, despite all efforts to the contrary, it is doomed to decline— depends on the realization of Jewish-Arab collaboration. Elsewhere it may suffice to strive for the "coexistence" of two diametrically opposed social systems, but here it can and must be a matter of nothing less than an intensive and far-reaching cooperation. The situation of latent or actual conflict can and must be resolved here by nothing less than an active community of interest between the peoples concerned. The members of this small circle have come to understand this more and more profoundly.

Without being expressed in so many words, this tendency was the basis of the modern "Zionist" settlement venture from its very beginning. The great epoch of this settlement, which lasted until shortly before the Second World War, had a selective and evolutionary character. The settlers were generations of pioneers, individuals who were constantly augmented by similar-minded immigrants and their descendants, whose chosen purpose in life was to rebuild with their own hands this country, the Biblical "Land of Israel," as the objective basis for the rebirth of the Jewish people. The work, which was to provide the nucleus of large-scale concentrated settlement, proceeded at an organic pace. This implicity required the acquisition of what would be indispensable for the future collective life [of Jewry in Palestine]: the trust of the indigenous Arab population. Through friendly contacts with the Arabs and through benevolent and helpful neighborliness, they sought to obtain their trust. In this the settlers were not always successful, through their own and the other side's faults, yet there were many and increasingly numerous successes. Then, however, so-called world history intervened, first in the guise of the persecutions of the Jews in Poland [in the 1920s], and then, in far greater dimensions, in Germany. Jewish masses were forced to migrate, and for the masses Palestine—though it had remained holy to them by virtue of tradition—was not "the" land which they wanted to rebuild, but just a country that did not refuse to receive them. The selective-evolutionary principle and the organic pace were subverted by the inrush of these masses. The suspicions of the Arabs, which had hitherto found sporadic expression only, were aroused in a mighty wave. This happened even before there had been time to win their trust. The official representatives of the Zionist cause were unable to allay these suspicions by a programmatic declaration of conciliation and planned cooperation. The masses needed political security; the establishment of a state was no longer simply expected as a future outcome of the work of settlement, but now appeared to be the order of the day. As against the resulting demand for a "Jewish State" our small circle proposed the alternative of a bi-national state and, later, of a Near East federation which the new state should join as a full member and whose national interests would be guaranteed. This demand, based on the belief in the possibility of new, higher forms of national coexistence, was not accepted by public opinion. It was repeatedly stated that this group of "idealists" took no account of the reality of this situation. Some of those who then made this charge are today beginning to doubt the correctness of their judgment—at least, as far as the past is concerned.

Today, when a necessary condition for a Near East Federation— that is Arab unity—no longer exists, such a peace seems to have become unattainable. But an end of the "Cold War" might make it again possible. Be this as it may, there is a good chance for the realization of peace between Jews and Arabs on the basis of an incipient cooperation: thus and only thus could the historic situation of *both* peoples decisively improve.

52

A Protest Against Expropriation of Arab Lands

(March 1953)

(Editor's prefatory note:)

The hundreds of thousand of Arabs who fled what was to be the State of Israel left huge property holdings. In 1950, the government of Israel appointed a custodian to handle the absentee property, authorizing him to transfer some of this property to the state for purposes of settling Jewish immigrants and the founding of new settlements and towns. There were, however, many ambiguities with regard to the definition of an absentee owner. In 1953, a Land Acquisition Law was drafted to remove these ambiguities. As the government acknowledged in the proposed legislation, the requisition of absentee properties often included plots also belonging to "non-absentee Arabs," especially in agricultural areas. The right of ownership to these plots, the government held, was not sufficiently clear, and moreover, it was emphasized, it was not now possible to restore these lands to their owners for reasons of security and because development projects were being implemented. The draft law proposed indemnification instead. The Ichud construed this legislation as an unjust endeavor to divest the Israeli Arabs of their lands. Buber was one of the three signatories to the following letter, dated 7 March 1953, to Joseph Sprinzak, Speaker of the Knesset, protesting the porposed law. The law was adopted on 10 March 1953.

A PROTEST AGAINST EXPROPRIATION OF ARAB LANDS

7 March 1953

Dear Mr. Sprinzak:

The draft legislation entitled "Expropriation of Land" will be placed this week before the Knesset for a second and final reading. The legislation will legalize an existing fact, namely the expropriation of land belonging to Arab subjects living in Israel by right and not on sufferance (i.e., not *refugees!*).

We fail to understand why, according to press reports, hardly a single Jewish Member of the Knesset has raised his voice against a law intended to give the stamp of legality to acts and deeds which he would consider a grave injustice if they were directed against himself or against Jewish property.

We understand that real security requirements may make it necessary to expropriate land in certain places. We refer specifically to real security requirements, in distinction to those in which the word "security" conceals the true purposes. Even then, such expropriation should be possible with two reservations: (a) that the property be affected only as secruity requirements dictate, that is, only for the duration of the emergency (this excludes any definite and permanent expropriation); (b) that the rightful owners be entitled to appeal to court demanding an inquiry into the question whether such expropriation was really taken for reasons of security.

We know well, however, that in numerous cases land is expropriated not on grounds of security, but for other reasons, such as expansion of existing settlements, etc. These grounds do not justify a Jewish legislative body in placing the seizure of land under the protection of the law. In some densely populated villages two-thirds and even more of the land have been seized.

As Jews and citizens of the State of Israel, we find it our duty to cry out against a proposed law which will add no honor to the Jewish people.

In general terms we propose:

(a) The Defense Minister (or any other Minister the law may specify) shall be empowered to take over any land for reasons of security, subject to the two reservations previously made, namely, only for as long as security considerations make it necessary and without prejudice to its legal ownership.

(b) Even when land is taken over as under (a), the owners should be left enough land to support themselves by cultivation, as set down in the "Land Tenants Defense Ordinance." It is understood that even in such cases the owners are entitled to compensation.

(c) In any other case in which land has been seized, but not for security requirements as previously mentioned, such land shall be fully returned to its owners within a maximum term specified by law, on condition that the owner may apply to court for a return of his land before the expiration of the term.

We beg you to consider our proposal and to pass it on to the Members of the Knesset, so that it may save and prevent the Jewish legislative body from enacting a law which is in conflict with the principles of Judaism and all the solumn pledges given by the Government of Israel at the founding of the State.

Faithfully yours,

Martin Buber et al.

53

We Need the Arabs, They Need Us!

(January 1954)

(Editor's prefatory note:)

In the last decade of his life, Buber—now a venerated sage especially beloved by progressive youth—gave frequent interviews to the Israeli press. The following interview appeared in a Tel Aviv weekly on 21 Janaury 1954.

WE NEED THE ARABS, THEY NEED US!
An Interview

*Professor Buber, in view of the fact that mutual enmity between
Israel and its Arab neighbors is increasing, do you believe that a peace
accord between them is still possible?*

In my opinion, the time is near when it will be possible to reach an
agreement, resulting in cooperation between Israel and the Arab states.
This would, in my opinion, involve Israel's participation in some kind
of federation of Near Eastern states. For years, I have been a proponent
of such a federation. Naturally the federation would have to be established in such a way that the majority could not impose its will on the
minority, otherwise our national existence would be endangered. That
is to say, the federation's charter would have to be some sort of international Magna Carta [guaranteeing the rights and integrity of the
smaller states].

*Do you mean a federation in Palestine only, or do you refer to the
whole region, to the entire Near East?*

I am not interested in Palestine alone. Our problems are intricately
bound up with those of the whole region and no real separation can be
made between them. This became manifest to me when I first became
involved with the so-called Arab question in 1917, at which time [the
Balfour Declaration] confronted [the Zionist movement] with an
entirely new situation. Since then I have given this matter much
thought, and it is on the establishment of such a federation that I pin
my hopes.

For the whole area?

Yes. I have seen that the fate of the Near East depends on the coop-
eration of all the peoples who live in the region. Neither we nor the
Arabs will succeed alone. They need us just as much as we need them.
And the region needs both peoples, cooperating.

*Do you think we [in Israel] have done enough in the past to promote
this cooperation?*

I believe our principal error was that when we first came here we
did not endeavor to gain the Arabs' trust in political and economic
matters. Thus we gave cause to be regarded as aliens, as outsiders who
were not interested in befriending the Arabs. To a large measure, our

subsequent difficulties are a consequence of this initial failure to achieve mutual trust.

Is it not correct that you and your friends warned us about the dangers entailed in such a failure?

We made certain declarations but no attention was paid to them. In politics one is judged by one's successes. With the establishment of the State of Israel some of our followers deserted us. They believed the problem to have been solved. Alas, I did not make any public reply; I was gripped by anxiety. But in the present state of affairs everyone devoted to our cause must express himself openly.

Do you believe that the situation is more grave than it was ten years ago?

The most opportune time to have tried to come to an agreement with the Arabs was immediately after our victory [in the War of Independence]. Clever, farsighted people did indeed perceive this. Thus they sought to hold talks with King Abdullah of Jordan.[1] I do not wish to go into details, but I believe that with certain concessions an agreement might have been reached.

Why did the discussions fail?

Our envoys evidently thought that should we hold out we would attain more favorable terms. They forgot that men die, that sons do not always follow in their father's footsteps. Nevertheless, it is almost certain that following a change in world politics another propitious moment will arrive. Everything depends on whether or not we will know how to make good use of it this time, that is to say, if we prepare for it right now.

Disregarding this possibility [of a change in world politics favoring Arab-Israeli repprochement] do you believe time is against us?

I do not. May I reiterate, we need to be ever alert. Three years ago some other people and I were invited to meet with one of Israel's leaders. We spoke about shaping the nation's character. I was asked: "How can the government shape the spiritual and moral character of the nation?" I replied that the government could not determine the people's character by laws and regulations, but the government could do something which would arouse the people's conscience, namely, by taking the initiative and inviting the interested states to a convention to decide the problem of the Arab refugees.[2]

What was the response of that leader to your proposal?

In a private talk we had later he told me: "Don't think I don't agree with what you said. But in history, time is either too early or too late." That is true. What you possess now may be out of your hands a little later. Only a few days after [our meeting] the United Nations called for mediation talks. We lost the initiative.

What political proposal would you make today?

Politics worthy of its name is not simply a matter of decisions and deeds. First of all, direction—a policy—is needed, a policy from which decisions and deeds, made according to ever changing conditions, emanate. I believe our political policy regarding the Arabs was mistaken and misleading, and the first step we must now take is to change the direction of our policy.

Who do you expect will initiate this new direction?

It is almost certain that for some time the matter will be unpopular. In a democratic state every political party eagerly awaits its opponent's failure [to gain popular support]. Much courage is needed to bring about a change in policy.

Is a new personality needed?

A general reform is the important thing, not a new personality. But the individual who will fearlessly do what the moment demands will be the *true* hero of the nation. We must all pave the way for this individual who has yet to arrive on the political scene. I have the impression that some important people already have seen the light but are afraid to come out in the open.

Professor Buber, is your outlook political or moral?

I do not make a basic distinction between what is right morally and what is right politically. Something immoral may be of temporary benefit, but it cannot benefit generations or even one generation. The basic outlook of the prophets was politically realistic. They were not defeatists. In the final analysis there is no contradiction between realistic politics and moral politics. One has to sacrifice temporary benefits for future existence.

Do you, then, seek a spiritual renewal?

Correct. A political act will not in itself help. If indeed the new policy to which I alluded is eventually adopted, it will necessarily influence the spiritual life [of the country]. Mutual effect exists here. But spiritual, moral renewal is the main factor.

In your opinion, Professor Buber, what will be the essence of this renewal?

At present we are experiencing a profound spiritual and moral breakdown. But I have not given up hope. We must return to our people's unique truth, national universalism; the geo-political situation also demands it of us. This has always been the view of authentic Zionism, of a Zionism worthy of the name "Zion." National universalism will ensure a sound basis for the nation to realize its part in the establishment of a true humanity. We were Zionists because we wished to take this idea from the realm of discussion and put it into practice. Returning to national universalism means to struggle against the obstacles placed in our way by chauvinism.

Would you say that the State of Israel is the realization of the dream you had fifty years ago?

Others like myself have never looked upon the achievement of national independence as an end in itself but rather as a basis on which it would be possible to bring about the rebirth of the [Jewish] nation. We looked forward to the opportunity of fostering the organic development of the Yishuv as a healthy political and social entity.

Were these hopes thwarted?

No one can be blamed that these hopes were not realized. The tragic history of our people, which enveloped us in clouds of terror and pogroms, put us on the wrong track. Psychological pressure was created by the hordes of homeless and displaced people, pressure that Zionism was not only unable to withstand but that some of the world's leading statesmen deemed to be a historical verdict. Thus as a result of the hour's need the State of Israel came into being. Deeds were done at the time which were too hasty and which unwittingly injured the future progress of the State.

Professor Buber, did your group want another kind of state?

Most Zionists wished first to obtain a [sovereign Jewish] state, but our group believed it was more important how we obtained it. We wanted to see an organic development in the Yishuv which would finally emerge as a state that would be the [moral] center of the Near

East. We believed this state would be established on the basis of general trust, of the mutual trust [between the peoples] of the region.

Would you say we [in Israel] are in need of cultural renewal?

We must first realize that we do not yet have a living qualitative culture. We have a great heritage, people endowed with talent and ability, authors, poets, artists, philosophers, scientists, and research workers. We also have excellent educational and cultural institutions. But a culture whose influence is felt in all facets of the nation's life— that we do not have.

Do you believe a new culture is developing here?

All great cultures, especially Oriental cultures, are built on the decisive order of justice and truth. The same is true of Greek culture, which was also born in the Near East, in Asia Minor. The common belief in the whole West was that Truth was ordained by the gods and had to be accepted by man here on earth. The ancient Chinese, Hindus, Persians, and later our people believe so. Justice might be monotheistic or not, but there could be no true justice as long as there was no decisive order of justice which determined the course of life.

In what manner can this spiritual renewal be brought about?

I do not know, nor do I believe that anyone can mark the path beforehand. There may be a great change at any moment. If you look back into history you will see that many such changes came suddenly. Historians have traced these changes, and have offered various explanations. But history has no verdict which man was unable to rend and change. I am thus continually looking forward to the changes I know must come.

Notes

1. Abdullah ibn Hussein (1882–1951), the first king of the Hashemite Kingdom of Jordan. His attempts to reach a negotiated settlement with the State of Israel were cut short by his assassination in Jerusalem on 20 July 1951.

2. Cf. selection 48.

54

Instead of Polemics

(November 1956)

(Editor's prefatory note:)

A speech by Rabbi Benjamin[1]—the intensely idealistic president of the Ichud and editor of *Ner*—prompted Buber to write the following essay, published in the November 1956 issue of *Ner*. When addressing political issues, Buber argues, the declaration of abstract moral principles—of which Rabbi Benjamin was apparently guilty—is by its very nature polemical and politically sterile. The demand of the Ichud on Israel's leadership, Buber avers, is not that it embrace abstract moral principles and abandon politics, that is, that it cease to attend to the needs of the moment. On the contrary, the Ichud appreciates the alertness of Israel's leaders to the exigent needs of the Jewish people; it merely urges them also to maintain a moral, universal perspective so as to minimize the harm done to the Arabs through their efforts to meet these needs.

Note

1. Pseudonym of the prolific Hebrew essayist Yehoshua Radler-Feldmann (1880–1957). An observant Jew, he passionately devoted himself after settling in Palestine in 1906 to the cause of Arab-Jewish understanding, being among the founders of almost every endeavor in the Yishuv promoting this goal.

INSTEAD OF POLEMICS

Rabbi Benjamin's important words, which were spoken at the [recent] meeting of Ichud, have stimulated me to return to a matter which has concerned me repeatedly on many occasions during my life. I refer to the relationship between practical politics and general moral principles.

Politicians believe that they must only strive towards what is, in their opinion, the good of the state at a given moment. It is not that they intend to rebel against morality. On the contrary, if someone were to tell them that their behavior was immoral, they would protest that it is precisely morality which dictates their endeavors and their behavior, since they further the life of the nation, as if egoism on behalf of a collective were more moral than individual egoism. In contrast to the politicians stand the men of principle. They come forward in the name of general assumptions which determine what is justice and what is iniquity, and from these principles they draw conclusions concerning the present moment. They do not attempt to verify each day what is possible to accomplish under the conditions of that particular day, without causing harm to the life of the nations. Such verification would have to combine two factors: a conscience that cannot be misled and a trustworthy insight into reality.

Politicians have no orientation beyond politics. But only such an orientation could show them, beyond the petty considerations of the moment, what the truly vital interest of the nation is for the coming generations. Conversely, principled individuals have only a sense of orientation with no sense of proportion or a sense of what can and should be done at any given time. They perceive the politician as a kind of despot, drunk with power, who knows no direction above his own will. Politicians in turn see them as ideologues enslaved to high-flown talk, living in the clouds, and not on an earth full of contradictions.

Between these two camps any chance of doing that degree of right and correct action which reality permits to be done is lost. It is extremely difficult to decide what that degree is in our present moment. But it is possible to decide if men of good will join together, men to whose minds "garden variety" politics is shortsighted, and the strict observance of moral principles is too abstract. I refer to those people who speak and act in a way that shows that they have taken responsibility upon themselves for the decisions that will come today and tomorrow. All true human responsibility is dual: directed towards heaven and towards the earth. Such dual responsibility is not to be unifed by means of principles, but rather by means of examination and restraint constantly renewed. Man, in that he is man, cannot be entirely without sin, and the same is true of a nation in that it is a nation. How then will men or nations act in accordance with their conscience. The main point is to examine oneself at all times to ascertain whether one's guilt is not greater than the amount necessary to carry on living. This is not simply the commandment of pure morality: because of their excessive guilt both men and nations are wiped off the face of the earth. Great statesmanship, which is directed by the true interest of coming generations is a policy that ensures that the nation does not heap upon itself too great a degree of guilt. Clearly one does not administer such a policy on the basis of generalizations and principles. We must take upon ourselves repeatedly and continuosly the hardest task: responding to both demands at the same time, the demand of the moment and the demand of truth.

In the period of settlement, which in effect was a conquest by peaceful means, the finest people among us did not pretend to remain guiltless and unsullied in our national struggle for survival. Inasmuch as we came here to ensure a place for our future generations, we were perforce reducing the space for future generations of the Arab nation. Yet our intention was to sin no more than was absolutely necessary in the endeavor to obtain our objective. At the same time that history forced us to replace the system of careful selection and training of immigrants, or rather *halutzim*, with an [urgent] program of mass immigration, and afterwards to strive for international security [for the newly established State of Israel], it was still within the power of our political leadership to participate in determining the form of that security. It was incumbent upon us to seek the maximum degree of justice compatible with the exigencies of life. (This was the fundamental intention of our program for a bi-national state and later the suggestion for a federation of Near Eastern countries.) Since that hour passed and nothing was done in that direction, the ground was prepared for the [Arab] refugee program and thus for an enormous increase in our objective guilt.

The small circle called *Ichud* has always regarded this issue as central and has demanded of the political leadership of the Zionist movement and the State of Israel that it also consider the issue thus and to treat it as such an issue merits. Our position on this matter remains resolute. Accordingly, as opposed to the exclusively political outlook of the leaders of the state, which is, for that reason, a faulty one from the political point of view as well, we propose a moral-political outlook.

Nevertheless, beyond this point there is an evident division in our camp. Some of us declare a moral principle and demand its realization.

That realization, if we comprehend it consistently, would force us to accept not only the cessation of immigration but also the deportation of Jews in their hour of need. As opposed to them, some of us do not appear in public as innocent men before sinners. They do not propose purely principled behavior to the people, and they do not demand that the people obey pure principles. They wish to repair what can be repaired under the given circumstances, and no less than that. These circumstances must be scrupulously examined, and on the basis of such an examination one must work out a settlement program that is well founded. In that program we must make clear how many refugees it is possible to settle, what kinds, and where, and how. This program is likely to be accepted as a single chapter, that is to say, the one we are writing, in a general program for the resolution of the refugee problem. That general program cannot arise except with the cooperation of all the interested parties. For such cooperation, and first of all for consultation and preparation, we must take the initiative. We can do so only if we decide to make our own contribution to the project and prepare a program for it.

I already advocated such an initiative during the first years of the state.[1] I repeat that demand in the present situation, and in any case the demand for a change in the direction of Israeli policy is included in my first demand. We do not ask the state to practice a moral principle just because it is moral, but we do ask of it that degree of justice which is necessary so that the future of our nation will be ensured, not in a vision or in imagination, but in actual fact.

Note

1. See selection 48.

55

An Outrage

(November 1956)

(Editor's prefatory note:)

At the outbreak of the Sinai Campaign on 29 October 1959 a tragic incident occurred. A strict curfew was suddenly imposed on the Arab villages bordering Jordan, and forty-three villagers—men, women, and children—returning from the fields to their villages of Kfar Kassim after the start of the curfew, were shot and killed by a Border Police patrol. When reports of this outrage and similar incidents reached the Jewish civilian public, the Council of the Ichud held an extraordinary meeting to review the events. At the conclusion of the meeting Buber and three other members were charged with composing the following letter to Prime Minister David Ben-Gurion.

AN OUTRAGE

Jerusalem
15 November 1956

The Prime Minister
Mr. David Ben-Gurion
Jerusalem

Dear Sir,

The Council of the Ichud passed at its meeting on 15 November 1956 a resolution to turn to you in the following matter:

At the Council Meeting reliable persons reported about the dreadful deeds committed by members of the Border Police force in Kfar Kassim and other places. According to these reports curfew was proclaimed on the 29 October 1956 beginning at 5 o'clock P.M. in the villages of the Arab districts. The Mukhtars (village heads) were informed about the curfew only a short time before it came into force. When they asked what would happen to the tens of workers who would return from their working places only after the curfew had come into force, they received the answer that everything will be all right. When buses full with men and women workers arrived at the outskirts of the villages, the passengers were told to get out from the buses, to stand at the side of the road, and were killed by machine-gun fire. As reported, the number of killed is very high. During the hours of curfew also women and children who left their houses were wounded or killed.

The Council certainly hears also other tales, but these seemed to us not well enough founded and were therefore not accepted. The Council noted with appreciation the Government's action in appointing a special inquiry commission which came to certain conclusions. Considering the prevailing tension among the Jewish and Arab population in connection with the latest events and the possible danger of renewed outbreaks the Council of Ichud resolved to demand from the Government

(a) to bring before a court all those guilty of having committed murder. Not to be satisfied with the prosecution of any local commander but to demand that legal steps are taken against all responsible whoever and wherever they are,

(b) to arrange for court proceedings in public and not behind closed doors, and

(c) to pay full compensation to the families of the killed and the wounded in the manner usual when Jewish citizens are concerned.[1]

We are drawing your attention to the terrible impression the said action made in wide circles in this country and abroad. We express our hope that you will act energetically and effectively to cleanse the name of the State of Israel in the eyes of the public.

Yours truly,

Martin Buber et al.

Note

1. Compensation, in fact, was paid to the families of the victims, and the soldiers responsible were placed on trial. At a special session of the Knesset on 12 December

1956, Ben-Gurion expressed "profound concern at the fact that such an act had been possible—an act which strikes a blow at the most sacred foundations of human morality. . . ." In 1958 a military court sentenced the eight soldiers involved to periods of imprisonment ranging from seven to fourteen years. By the end of 1959, however, all had been granted clemency.

56

Socialism and Peace

(1956)

(Editor's prefatory note:)

To Buber the moral and spiritual significance of Zionism did not lie in the creation of a state, but in the effort of the *halutzim*, the pioneers of Jewish settlement in Palestine, to evolve radically new forms of social life, preeminently the *kibbutzim*. Despite all the difficulties that have overtaken the Zionist endeavor—the mass immigration of Jewish "refugees" who were for the most part not *halutzim*,[1] the conflict with the Arabs, and the ambiguities of statehood—these efforts to create a truly just society are still the vibrant core of Zionism. In the following article—an excerpt from Buber's contribution to a volume entitled *Israel: Its Role in Civilization* (New York, 1956)—Buber affirms Israel's communitarian socialism to be the basis of the Jewish state's auspicious role in the world, especially in the Near East.

Note

1. Buber elaborates this point in selection 49.

SOCIALISM AND PEACE

The new social life that has evolved in Palestine has a significant bearing on the relations between Israel and the outside world, and espe-

cially on Israel's relationship to the other people of the Near East, particularly the Arabs. I am a member of a group that once sought a
solution for the isolation of Israel in the Near East by seeking a way of
cooperation between Israel and the Arabs. There were friends of mine
who thought a bi-national state the best form for such cooperation. I
was inclined toward a federation. This question is now an academic
one since history has decided against either solution. But the basic
problem remains: What will be the relation between our people in
Israel and their neighbors? This is the essential question both for Israel
and for her neighbors. There cannot, in my opinion, be any rebuilding
of the Near East adequate to the great task of modern times without
the real cooperation of all these peoples. But how can this cooperation
come into being?

Most of us are so accustomed to political thinking that we view our
era as one in which hot war has been succeeded by cold war and
believe that on a certain day the cold war will cease too and there will
be peace. I think this is a great illusion. A peace that comes about
through cessation of war, hor or cold, is no real peace. Real peace, a
peace that would be a real solution, is organic peace. A great peace
means cooperation and nothing else. What is less than this is nothing.
How can such an organic peace be brought about? It seems to me a
terribly difficult thing to do, I must confess, and I do not see that it can
be done by political means alone. Political action must be preceded by
a revolutionary change in the peoples of the Near East. By revolutionary I do not mean the influence of certain systems which call themselves "socialist." On the contrary, I see a great danger in these systems.
The only thing, in my opinion, that could bring about real peace, real
cooperation, is the influence of the best that Israel has produced, the
new social forms of life, on the Arab people. The Arabs need this influence. They need a great agrarian reform, a just distribution of the soil,
and the formation of small communities which would be the organic
cells of this new economy and this new society.

Do not think that I have in my pocket a blueprint of how this ultimate solution can be brought about! I do not know how we can accomplish it, but I see the direction. There is no other direction. Through a
renewed and ever more intensive development in our new social forms,
through a renaissance of these social forms in spite of all difficulties
that now attend them, we can bring about another kind of revolution
than what is generally called by that name.

In a chapter in my book *Paths in Utopia*,[1] I have dealt very imperfectly with some of these problems. At the conclusion of this chapter I opposed Jerusalem to Moscow, each standing for a particular type of socialism. Is it proper, asks a rather sensible critic, that I allow Jerusalem to stand for the "utopian socialism" with which it has had so few historical ties? (A statement which is, in fact, historically inexact.) What does the community of communities mean in concrete terms, he asks, and what level or levels of social reality will bring it to life? Finally, he asks whether it is right for me to put before mankind a choice between two types of socialism at a time when far more serious and demanding issues confront the world? Even in Israel, he asserts, the socialist impetus and the faith in the *kibbutzim* are largely exhausted. This last statement is not at all exact. It is a boundless exaggeration of a crisis that really exists and that must be recognized and overcome as such. Such crises are part of the life of man and the life of society.

Actually, I doubt if there is anything more important today than the choice between two types of socialism. What matters most is that we know that there are two possibilities and that we are called upon to choose between them. One is a so-called socialism that is imposed from above, allowing people to live only one way and not otherwise; the other is a socialism from below, a socialism of spontaneity arising out of the real life of society. In this new form of society, men live a just life with one another, not because such a life is imposed on them, but because they want to live in this way. A part of this socialism of spontaneity is the possibility of living in one or another type of settlement, but all types have in common just this living together in real community.

I believe that the decision between these two types of society and socialism is the most important decision confronting the next generations of mankind, and I think that the coming stage of humanity that will emerge from this great crisis of man depends in great measure on just this decision. It depends on whether it will be possible to set up over against Moscow another, spontaneous kind of socialism, and I venture even today to call it Jerusalem.

Note

1. *Paths in Utopia*, trans. R. F. C. Hull (Boston: Beacon Press, 1958).

57

Active Neutralism

(October 1957)

(Editor's prefatory note:)

Upon his election to the presidency of the World Zionist Organization in 1956, Nahum Goldmann (1895–1982) called upon the government of the State of Israel to pursue a policy of nonalignment with the major power blocs. Neutralism, he contended, would help isolate the Arab-Israeli conflict from the confounding effects of cold war politics. In the following article, a circular from October 1957, Buber and two of his colleagues from the Ichud endorse this position, adding that to be credible neutralism must be "active."

ACTIVE NEUTRALISM

It is known that especially among the peoples of Asia the tendency prevails to declare themselves neutral in the cold war between the Western and Eastern blocks, not to identify with and not to commit themselves to any of them. This tendency found many sympathizers also in Israel, especially in connection with views expressed by Dr. Nahum Goldmann, the President of World Zionist Organization.

We agree in principle with all those who demand the neutralization of the Middle East, but we believe that Israel should not be satisfied with a passive role, a policy of "Wait and See," in the struggle of the powers. On the contrary, Israel should choose the way of *"active* neutralism" by calling on all nations of the world, East and West, to join in exploring ways and means for the solution of a problem endangering the peace of the Middle East and the world, which can only be solved when *all* the peoples of the region and all the great powers combine in a constructive effort: the problem of the Arab refugees.

We propose that the Israeli Government should make a solemn declaration that it is prepared to allow the return to its territory of Arab refugees—without fixing any definite figure—and to pay compensations under the condition that all the interested parties (the Arab states, the refugees, the U.N. and the great powers) will cooperate with Israel in the discussion and the execution of plans for the resettlement of the refugees in Israel and the Arab states.

Such a declaration will surely find a sympathetic response in the whole world, in the Arab, the Eastern, and the Western countries. Instead of the request for the supply of arms will come the demand for an immediate *common* peaceful action. The Arab refugees, now rotting in an atmosphere of poverty, bitterness, and hatred, will wake up from their lethargy. Cooperation between Jews and Arabs will start, in "Mixed Refugee Commissions" and other places. Capital from different sources, Jewish and non-Jewish, will flow into the region, where the states in the course of time will become able to reduce their present defense expenditure and to divert the sums thus saved to positive constructive purposes.

In a time when the world is obsessed by the idea of impending war and destruction, from Jerusalem, the "City of Peace," will emanate a new call for peace, understanding and cooperation in constructive work.

We turn to you with the hope that the above-explained idea of "active neutralism" will find your support. We would be pleased if you would write to us how you stand in relation to it and what suggestions you have to make in order to put such a plan into practice.

Yours truly,

Martin Buber et al.

58

Letters from Arabs to Buber

(1958–1965)

(Editor's prefatory note:)

Buber's presence was felt and appreciated by many individual Arabs, as is witnessed by the following selection of letters to him. The first (written originally in English) is from Farid-Wajdi Tabari, who at the time was a lawyer in the Muslim religious court in Nazareth and currently is the Qadi of Jaffa and Jerusalem; the second (written in Hebrew) is from Atallah Mansour, then a reporter for the anti-establishment journal *Ha-Olam Ha-Zeh*, and today a columnist for the Tel Aviv daily *Ha-Aretz*; the third letter (written originally in English) is from a Palestinian refugee who in print remains anonymous.

LETTERS FROM ARABS TO BUBER

7 February 1958

My dear Professor Buber:

On the eve of your eightieth birthday permit me to express my sincerest wishes for a very happy, productive, and peaceful life. . . .

Although we sat together very few times, and though we had few personal contacts, you always made a deep impression on me. I even felt, in spite of the great difference of rank, experience, culture, and age, that you are close to my soul.

It is my humble wish that, before you feel too old to express yourself on these matters, you should point out to the Israeli government the need to grant more justice, greater democracy, and fuller rights to the Arab citizens of this country. The Israeli Arab could easily serve as a bridge for peace between this dear state of ours and the neighboring countries. . . . Our government in my humble opinion does not even have a policy for the Arabs of this country. I have spoken at length with the authorities on this and related subjects, but a word or action by you might do much more, and do it better.

It is my hope too that you will draw the attention of Jewish public opinion [to the plight of Israel's Arabs] so as to make the required task of the government easier.

May I close with sincere prayers that God may keep you and yours happy and blessed. I am

Yours cordially and respectfully,

Farid-Wajdi Tabari

4 May 1958

The distinguished Martin Buber, Shalom!

I hope you will forgive me for intruding upon you with this letter. I am a young man who was born in this country and I hold an Israeli identity card which designates me as an Arab. I was born of Catholic parents. I do not intend to give you a long account of my experiences and theirs, and I only mention these facts in this manner because my own feeling is that I am simply a human being. I am writing you, sir, not as a professor, not as a Jew, but as a person whom I consider to be nothing else but a great man.

I had the privilege of meeting you once at a memorial service one evening in honor of the late Rabbi Benjamin.[1] I was the young man who translated Bishop Hakim's[2] address into Hebrew.

I work for the newspaper *Ha-Olam Ha-Zeh*, as a reporter on Arab affairs. The job barely allows me to make a living, but I have no complaints, thanks and praise be to God. But I do cry, every day and night I cry because I fail to see anything decent. Every day and at every turn I encounter evil deeds by all sorts of people and institutions. I wonder whether I am supposed to understand that this world of ours is evil. Is not there any possibility that one fine day I will wake up and everything will be good and decent?

Is Jewish-Arab enmity something eternal? Is there no possibility that this world of ours will change for the better? I ask you—not as a journalist now but as a human being—would not I be committing a crime against my conscience if I, a young bachelor, were to marry and bring children into the world who would have to live under these conditions?

Why do I address these questions to you? Because I believe that a great man can give me advice and help, and indeed I shall be grateful for your advice and help, sir, my revered teacher.

With deepest respect and gratitude,

Atallah Mansour

Notes

1. See page 269, note 1.

2. Archbishop George Hakim of the Greek Catholic diocese of Haifa, was one of the leading spokespersons of the Christian Arab community of Israel. His eulogy for Rabbi Benjamin is published in English translation in *Ner* 9, nos. 5–7 (February–April 1958), pp. 58–62.

January 1965

Dear Professor Buber:

I am a Christian Arab, who, born in Haifa in 1930, had taken refuge in Lebanon in 1948. Very much on my mind lately has been the necessity of preparing grounds for peace between the Arab countries and Israel.

Having come upon a reprint of the address you gave on September 27, 1953, when you were awarded the Peace Prize of the German Book Trade at Frankfurt am Main, in the Paulskirche,[1] I am moved to present myself to you, in the belief that it is more than probable, you and I can initiate the dialogue, in your own words, so urgently needed as a first step, across the political barbed wire that divides us. Not overlooking the division, but with the determination to bear it in common.

Both our peoples have suffered, and he who has had a taste of suffering knows how bitter and hard it can make one. But for those of us who have survived the souring poison of pain, it hurts that the Jew had been exterminated in a German concentration camp in 1945. It hurts that the Palestinian still huddles homeless in a Middle-Eastern refugee camp in 1965. The Jew in search for identity has found it as an Israeli—at the expense of the Palestinian and the annihilation of his identity. This is simply a statement of fact—the barbed wire that divides us.

I shall be going back from America to Beirut, where I will pursue the planting of seeds of peace that I wholeheartedly believe in. I am not too sure how to go about it as yet, but that will solve itself in its time.

In trust,

[Anonymous]

Note

1. See "Genuine Conversation and the Possibility of Peace," in Martin Buber, *A Believing Humanism: My Testament*, trans. and intro. by Maurice Friedman (New York: Simon and Schuster, 1967).

59

Memorandum on the Military Government

(February 1958)

(Editor's prefatory note:)

With the conclusion of Israel's War of Independence, a military government was imposed on predominantly Arab areas close to the border and in sections of the country considered strategically important. Movements in these areas were restricted and special passes had to be obtained from the military government for travel to other parts of the country, whether for business, for work or study, or for short visits. This system, which caused deep resentment among the Arabs, was gradually curtailed (and eventually abolished in December 1966) as security improved and opposition to the system grew within the Jewish community. On 24 February 1958 Prime Minister Ben-Gurion received a three-man delegation of the Ichud headed by Buber. After their audience with the Prime Minister they submitted the following memorandum to him, demanding a radical revision of the military government and the redress of other grievances of the Arab population of the state.

MEMORANDUM ON THE MILITARY·GOVERNMENT

I. Military Government

We ask you, Mr. Prime Minister, to re-examine the possibilities of restricting both the scope of military government and the areas under its jurisdiction. Although we are in principle for the outright abolition of military government, we realize that it would involve difficult security problems, but it is with deep concern that we discern, among the public, what might be termed a "military government ideology" which takes it for granted that part of the population of the State of Israel—the Arab minority—is deprived of the rule of civil law that applies to the rest of the population.

In keeping with your statement that military government should concern itself only with military and security questions in border areas, we ask that military rule be lifted from all areas which are not in proximity to the frontier and that in border areas all residents be treated equally, without discrimination.

Since such questions as work permits, building permits, and marriage licences should be outside the jurisdiction of military government, we also suggest that the implementation of all matters that are not closely tied up with security needs be entrusted to civil authorities and civilian officials. This will incidentally make it possible to introduce suitable elements among the educated Arabs into the ranks of officials, something which is understandably impossible under military government as it exists today.

Freeing the military administration of such civil functions can only redound to the benefit of all sides and will do away with such situations as having to grant travel permits to students, which you yourself have termed "absurd" but which have complicated the life and the studies of Arab students at the Hebrew University for the past ten years.

II. The Condition of the Moslem and Christian Religious Communities

We suggest the establishement of a Supreme Religious Council for Moslems and one for Christians. The Moslem Council will be made up of the High Qadis of Nazareth, Acre, and Jaffa, and the Christian Council of the heads of the Christian communities. These supreme councils, as well as the local religious councils, will operate without any interference. We oppose all Jewish trusteeship over the religious life and institutions of other communities. These councils must be entrusted with all the functions with which their religion invests them, including religious education, the establishment of religious and social welfare institutions such as orphanages and old-age homes, etc.

These activities will be financed from Waqf funds[1] and state aid, under government guidance and supervision, as is the case with other institutions in Israel. The councils will have specialized departments for finance, construction, education, etc. which will deal with these matters and be responsible for their execution.

The shortage of religious Moslem literature can be solved by contacts with such Moslem countries as Tunisia and Persia. The councils and their departments will employ Arab specialists, officials, and laborers and this too will help solve one of the most difficult questions of the Arab minority: the problem of the Arab intelligentsia.

III. The Arab Intelligentsia

The educated Arab classes are confused and perplexed, for they have been deprived of suitable fields of activity which would incidentally integrate them into the life of the state. The fact that many educated Arabs belong to the Communist Party does not mean that they are ideologically close to it, but springs primarily from their having been accepted in the party, and being accepted there to this day, under conditions of complete equality.

Generally speaking, the Jewish population is not prepared to treat
the Arab intellectuals as equals, either because it does not know
them—a great many Jews have never met an educated Arab—or
because it suspects them of being a "fifth column." This is a most complex psychological problem which we will be able to solve only with a
great deal of patience and understanding on both sides. In any case,
we cannot afford to let it fester perpetually.

We note with regret that the government does not seem to have a
consistent and above-board policy toward the Arab minority, and the
activities of various bodies in this field are sometimes at variance with
each other. This is why the fine achievements of the Ministries of Education, Agriculture, Social Welfare, Labor, Interior, and Health among
the Arab population have not met with the recognition and the
response that they deserve. It might perhaps even be indicated to concentrate all the government work among the Arab population in one
special and separate ministry with various departments, which would
do away with the present fragmentation. In such a ministry too some
of the educated Arabs would find jobs and proper fields of activity,
working in cooperation with Jewish officials.

We feel this particular opportunity is specially worth exploiting in
view of the fact that until now the young Arab who finishes his studies
in secondary school or at the Hebrew University has found it impossible to get a position in a public or private institution or organization.
This casts a shadow over his entire life and leads him to actions which
can be neither for his own good nor for that of the state. It is with great
satisfaction, Mr. Prime Minister, that we welcome your statement that
Arab teachers ought to be taken on as teachers of Arabic in Jewish
schools and that Solel Boneh and other firms should hire Arab engi-
neers.[2] We also thank you for abolishing the limitations on travel by
Arab students that resulted in such hardship for them for a number of
years. We are convinced that the Arab public will greatly welcome
these new measures.

IV. The Arab Refugee Problem

The problem of Arab refugees is made up of two separate issues: the
uprooted refugees within the boundaries of the state and the Arab refugees in the Arab states. As for the former, we welcome the govern-

ment's declaration that it is ready to get on energetically with a solution to this painful problem and to allocate substantial funds to it. We are well aware of the great difficulties that will stand in the way of the government, but we still believe that a quick start in impementing this program with goodwill and without discrimination can do a great deal to bring about a change of heart among the uprooted refugees and among the Arab population in general and move them to participate of their own free will in this rehabilitation project that will turn them into a productive element. We ask you, Mr. Prime Minister, to bring your great influence into play with all the parties entrusted with the drafting and implementation of this program so that they will carry it out with speed and determination.

With regard to the refugees in the Arab states too we feel that the Government of Israel now has an opportunity to change the situation radically, raising at the same time the prestige of the State of Israel and the Jewish people. Now that the Arab world is in the throes of national unification, we ask ourselves with concern whether it is set on peace or on war. Yet Israel can now test the Arabs before the whole world and force them to declare their true intentions.

We suggest that the Government of Israel request the U.N. to undertake an immediate and comprehensive program for solving the problem of the Arab refugees, and that the Government further declare that Israel is ready to do its part for world and regional peace by agreeing to settle a certain number of refugees within its borders, this, however, under one condition: that all the interested parties—the Arab States, the U.N., the refugees, and the Great Powers—sit down together with Israel to discuss this major project and to begin its implementation. At the General Assembly of the United Nations, the Government will solemnly invite the entire world to send experts and specialists to the Middle East to help work out a practical solution of the Arab refugee problem by settling them in Israel and in the Arab states.

All the details of the implementation of the program, including the numbers of refugees to be settled in each country, would be left to the discretion of committees to be made up of these world experts. We do not believe that any individual can quote any preliminary figures, large or small, in this respect, without a thorough investigation of conditions on the spot in Israel, in the refugee camps and in the Arab countries. The ultimate answer to this question as well as to the various technical, security, economy, psychological, and human issues involved will be provided by Israel, Arab, and world experts working in collaboration.

We want the initiative for such a project to come from the Government of Israel. We want to be able to boast that in a world of conflict and disunity with its madness and fear, the call for an endeavor of construction and peace such as this will come from Israel and Jerusalem, the city of peace. We want to make it impossible for any man in the world to say that Israel is an aggressor and "opposes any peaceful solution." We want to move the Arab states, which have consistently refused to sit down together with us even at world conferences on purely scientific or cultural issues, to work together with our experts in a great constructive enterprise. We want such a common international endeavor to provide the opportunity for renewed collaboration and interaction between Jews and Arabs as well as between East and West. In our opinion this is far more important than any peace treaty, which will always remain only a scrap of paper unless there is a "state of peace," unless hearts are prepared for a real peace.

We beg you, Mr. Prime Minister, to take the initiative in proposing such a project, and the peace lovers of the world will bless you and the State of Israel and the Jewish people.

Notes

1. Waqf funds are endowments in the form of real estate, given to Muslim religious foundations in accordance with the laws of Islam.

2. "Solel Boneh" is the construction company of the Histadrut, Israel's Federation of Labor.

60

Israel and the
Command of the Spirit

(April 1958)

(Editor's prefatory note:)

On the occasion of a visit to the United States in 1958, Buber gave the following address to the American Friends of the Ichud in New York City. Here he offers a new formulation to his familiar theme that the genuine work of Zionism—namely, *halutziut*, pioneering or the renewal of Jewish settlement in Palestine in a deliberate, organic fashion by an idealistic elite—was overwhelmed and diverted by historical forces. These forces bore with them the pernicious belief that power—and not fidelity to the "command of the spirit"—rules the social and political destiny of humanity. This celebration of power, Buber laments, has taken hold of Zionism, indicatively leading to the most demonic aberrations of the pristine Zionist ethos. Nonetheless, in order to dispel any misunderstanding on this score, Buber concludes with an affirmation of the factual reality of the State of Israel. The command to serve the spirit—foremostly to work for Arab-Jewish rapprochement—must be fulfilled from within the new situation, by "starting from it."

ISRAEL AND THE COMMAND OF THE SPIRIT

When I entered the Zionist movement more than sixty years ago, I very soon saw myself compelled to take sides in the conflict between the "political" and the "practical" tendencies within the movement. I decided without hesitation for the latter, and have remained faithful to it, manifold as have been its forms in the course of time. One can find in my writings from 1901 on, and in much stronger form after 1917, programmatic and concrete expressions of this trend.

What is at stake here is not usually understood with sufficient seriousness and depth. It is not basically a question of which activity was more urgent, the attainment of political concessions or the factual work of settlement. The "practical" tendency to create a reality first and then aspire to legal rights for it afterwards did not stem from tactical considerations. It stemmed from the insight that the tremendous double work of completing the rebirth of the Jewish people and of its becoming a member of the world of the Near East could not be accomplished through a sudden, insufficiently prepared mass settlement but only through the preparatory activity of generations in the Land.

We by no means sought a small center, as the *Chovevei Zion*[1] formerly did; we wanted to establish a great productive Jewish community. But we recognized as the way to it a pioneering stage of work and peace, a selective organic principle of development that would take several generations. That meant, first, that an élite of workers who saw their future and that of their children in the building of just this land should realize this in as many generations as might be necessary until the core of a Jewish community able to serve as the base for a completed rebirth should be created, a community that would then be entitled to an autonomous government and could accordingly demand it from the world. Secondly, our principle of development meant that in cooperative living together with our neighbours, in helpful participation in their economic life, a relationship of solidarity should be made possible out of which a comprehensive working together of both peoples might then arise. This second meaning of the selective organic principle must be explained more exactly here because of its importance for our subject.

We had recognized early that a new, aspiring factor among the already existing peoples of the Near East could not establish itself and hold its ground as an enclave of the Western world, that a genuine, and not just a tactical, understanding with the surrounding peoples was therefore needed. It could by no means suffice to win the trust of the Arabs merely in order that they later should not oppose our desire for autonomy; not seeming, but real, objectively founded, comprehensive solidarity was meant. Only such solidarity could withstand the shocks coming from the outside for which one had to be ready. Thus it happened that more than forty years ago many of us recognized the incipient world crisis in which the Near East was to play an even greater part as an essential element. An element in either a great construction or a great disintegration. If we were genuinely to enter into the life of the Near East, we could earn an important share in the decision between these alternatives.

The political side of this postulate was expressed by us wherever this matter was discussed, particulary by me in 1921 in the political committee of the Zionist Congress where, in opposition to what I stressed as the possibility of a federation of Arab states, I put forward the idea of a Near Eastern federation in which we should participate.[2] But the indispensable presupposition of political activity in this direction was the creation of a common consicousness of solidarity.

In the age of the beginning world crisis, *halutziut* had realized a substantial part of the first postulate—the creation of the core of a community, without being able as yet to bring it to completion. The second postulate in contrast, that of awakening a Jewish-Arab consciousness of solidarity, has been realized only fragmentarily in sporadic, locally limited undertakings of good neighborliness; neither an organized work of this kind nor even a practical program of comprehensive cooperation has arisen.

In that hour our work of settlement, as well as the principle on which it was based—the principle of selective, organic development—found itself overrun by the consequences of the most frightful happening of modern history, the extermination of millions of Jews by Adolf Hitler. The harrassed, tormented masses crowded into Palestine. Unlike the *halutzim* for whom no sacrifice toward building the land of Jewish rebirth was too great, they saw in this land merely safety and security (even though the tradition of the Messianic promise still lived on in them). Who would have taken it on himself to obstruct this onrush of the homeless in the name of the continuation of the selective method! The masses came at a time when the first postulate had not yet found sufficient fulfillment and the second had not gone beyond isolated attempts. The first task produced manifold difficulties, but the effects of the second were disastrous. Since a Jewish-Arab solidarity had not been instituted, either in the form of facts or even in an announced program of cooperation, the Arab people received the mass immigration as a threat and the Zionist movement as a "hireling of imperialism"—both wrongly, of course. Our *historical* re-entry into our land took place through a false gateway.

But that hour in world history in which evil seemed to have become all-powerful, able to extirpate everything odious to it with impunity, also exercised a harmful inner influence. The most pernicious of all false teachings, that according to which the way of history is determined by power alone, insinuated itself everywhere into the thinking of the peoples and their governments, while faith in the spirit was retained only as mere phraseology. What we experience today, the universal accumulation of power of destruction in opposition to every command of the spirit, was only made possible through this inner disintegration, although since then it has been learned many times anew.

In a part of the Jewish people that was most cruelly afflicted through that victory of the subhuman over the human, the false teaching continued to prevail even when the subhuman was overthrown. And here, in Jewry, in an altogether special way, it meant the betrayal of faith. By means of the spirit this people had been preserved unbroken through the ages despite the most wretched of fates. By means of the spirit alone the Zionist movement established its position in Palestine and wrested for itself the first legal title of a political nature. Only if it preserved the spirit as it guide could it hope to bring forth something greater than just one more state among the states of the world. He who was here unfaithful to the spirit was also unfaithful to a great task.

How deep the evil had penetrated into a part of the people was first recognized by us when the fact could no longer be overlooked. Meanwhile, in opposition to the proposals for a bi-national state or a Jewish share in a Near Eastern federation, the unhappy partition of Palestine took place, the cleft between the two peoples was split wide asunder, the war raged.[3] Everything proceeded with frightening meaningfulness. It happened one day, however, that outside of all regular conduct of the war, a band of armed Jews fell on an Arab village and destroyed it.[4] Often in earlier times Arab hordes had committed outrages of this kind and my soul bled with the sacrifice; but here it was a matter of our own, or my own crime, of the crime of Jews against the spirit. Even today I cannot think about this without feeling myself guilty. Our fighting faith in the spirit was too weak to prevent the outbreak and spread of false demonic teaching.

All this concerns the past, a never-to-be-forgotten past. But I must say a few words more about something that has remained present, something present in the most actual sense, in order that where I stand and where I do not stand may become clearer.

I have accepted as mine the State of Israel, the form of the new Jewish Community that has arisen from the war. I have nothing in common with those Jews who imagine that they may contest the factual shape which Jewish independence has taken. The command to serve the spirit is to be fulfilled by us in this state, by starting from it. But he who will truly serve the spirit must seek to make good all that was once missed: he must seek to free once again the blocked path to an understanding with the Arab peoples. Today it appears absurd to many—especially in the present intra-Arab situation—to think now about Israel's participation in a Near East federation. Tomorrow with an alteration in certain world-political situations independent of us, this possibility may arise in a highly positive sense. Insofar as it depends on us, we must prepare the ground for it. There can be no peace between Jews and Arabs that is only a cessation of war; there can only be a peace of genuine cooperation. Today, under such manifoldly aggravated circumstances, the command of the spirit is still to prepare the way for the cooperation of peoples.

Notes

1. *Chovevei Zion*--"Lovers of Zion," adherents of the *Chibbat Zion* (Love of Zion), a "Zionist" movement among the Jews of Russia and Rumania which preceded the founding by Herzl of the World Zionist Organization. Their practical activities were limited to small-scale settlement in Palestine during the period of the First Aliyah (1882-1903).

2. Cf. selection 5.

3. [Buber's note:] "I must add here a personal remark because on this point I can speak for most, to be sure, but not for all of my closest political friends. I am no radical pacifist: I do not believe that one must always answer violence with non-violence. I know what tragedy implies: when there is war, it must be fought."

4. On 9 April 1948, during the seige of Jerusalem, a combined force of the Irgun and the Stern Gang attacked Deir Yasin, an Arab village commanding the road to Jerusalem, reportedly killing 254 of its inhabitants—men, women, and children. The Jewish Agency denounced the action.

61

Letter to Ben-Gurion on the Arab Refugees

(October 1961)

(Editor's prefatory note:)

On 11 October 1961 Prime Minister David Ben-Gurion gave a speech in the Knesset defending the Government's policy on the problem of the Arab refugees, in which he said *inter alia* that:

> Israel categorically rejects the insidious proposal for freedom of choice for the refugees, for she is convinced that this proposal is designed and calculated only to destroy Israel. There is only one practical and fair solution for the problem of the refugees: to resettle them among their own people in countries having plenty of good land and water and which are in need of additional manpower.

In response, Buber in the name of the Ichud wrote the following open letter to Ben-Gurion.

LETTER TO BEN-GURION ON THE ARAB REFUGEES

Jerusalem
15 October 1961

Dear Prime Minister,

. . . a. The Ichud expresses its deep sorrow at the Prime Minister's statement of 11 October 1961, in which he firmly rejects "the insidious proposal for freedom of choice for the refugees" between returning to Israel and accepting compensations and resettlement elsewhere.

b. The Prime Minister's stand contradicts not only the repeated resolutions of the General Assembly of the United Nations, but also all the principles that the civilized world has come to accept out of humanitarian considerations as well as the Declaration of Rights of Man, as a result of which a vast number of refugees, among them many Jews, have returned to their former homes.

c. The Ichud is not unaware of the numerous difficulties and severe problems, particulary concerning security, which are involved in the solution of the Arab refugee problem. However, we believe that, given a sincere desire on the part of all concerned to have hundreds of thousands of refugees transferred to a productive way of living as peace-loving citizens in the Arab states and in the State of Israel, the means to have these problems peacefully solved will be found.

d. The solution of the Arab Refugee problem can only be brought about by full cooperation of all parties: Israel, the Arab states, the refugees, and the U.N. This cooperation should start with the setting up of joint committees of experts who should together discuss projects for rehabilitation of the refugees and methods of carrying them out "in a constructive spirit and with a sense of justice and realism" (U.N. General Secretary Hammarskjöld), taking into account the economic, demographic, humanitarian, and, particularly, security conditions involved in this operation. It will be their special task to ensure that the choice of the refugees will really be a free one, based on objective information of the conditions prevailing in Israel and in the Arab states.

e. The Ichud therefore addresses:

1. Both the State of Israel and the Arab states with an appeal to change their present stands as expressed in repeated declarations and to agree to a solution of the Arab refugee problem through cooperation and mutual understanding;

2. All the nations of the world with an appeal to extend their help to the parties concerned with all the means at their disposal for the achievement of an agreed solution of the Arab refugee problem as a first step towards a real peace in the Middle East. . . .

Respectfully yours,

M. Buber

62

Ben-Gurion and
Israel's Arabs

(January 1962)

(Editor's prefatory note:)

During an official visit to France, Prime Minister David Ben-Gurion gave an exclusive interview to the Parisian newspaper *Le Figaro*. The interview, which appeard on 4 January 1962, was entitled "Israel, Ben-Gurion, and the Arabs." With regard to the 240,000 Arabs remaining within the borders of the State of Israel, Ben-Gurion offered the following observations:

> The Arabs in Israel enjoy economic, social, and educational conditions superior to those in any Arab country, yet they are discontented or hostile towards Israel. Not that they wish for quicker material or social advancement, but it is a question of sentiment and solidarity—they are imbued with Arab nationalism. While highly appreciating their material benefits they personally derive from Israel's development, most would prefer this country to be an Arab country. And if given the opportunity [Israeli Arabs] would help destroy Israel.[1]

Appalled by what they deemed to be the biased assumptions of this statement, Buber and two associates issued in the name of the Ichud the following protest.

Note

1. "Israël, Ben-Gourion et les Arabes." Interview by Serge Groussard, *Le Figaro*, 4 January 1962, p. 5.

BEN-GURION AND ISRAEL'S ARABS

In an interview which he gave to a reporter of *Le Figaro*, Prime Minister Ben-Gurion also expressed his views on the Arabs of Israel. The

Prime Minister declared that the Arabs of Israel "enjoy economic, social, and educational conditions superior to those in any Arab country, yet they are discontented or hostile toward Israel."

Mr. Ben-Gurion has, apparently, forgotten what we have learned from the history and ideology of the Zionist movement, namely, that one should not forego a life of equality and dignity—personal and national—for the sake of superior economic, social, and educational conditions. When the State of Israel was established, the Arab population was promised full equality, without discrimination. During the last thirteen years, however, the government of Israel has neglected many opportunities [to improve the civic and political situation of the Arabs] and has committed acts which have engendered in the Arab inhabitants of the State a feeling that they are but second-class citizens.

Accordingly, the *Ichud* calls upon the government to do all that is in its power to fulfill its commitments to the Arab citizens of the State, and to rescind all current discriminatory practices taken against them, foremostly by the Military Government.

63

We Must Grant the Arabs Truly Equal Rights

(January 1962)

(Editor's prefatory note:)

In January 1962, a mass rally of Jews and Arabs protesting the institution of the Military Government was held in Tel Aviv. Buber was unable to attend but he sent a recorded speech. Abdul Aziz Z'uabi, an Israeli Arab who was at the time a member of the Knesset and a participant in the rally, recalled how moved he was by Buber's words: "I remember that I then said [to myself] that it is a great honor for me to live in a country of which Martin Buber is a citizen."[1] Buber's speech follows.

Note

1. Proceedings of Martin Buber Memorial Seminar for Jewish-Arab Understanding, Tel Aviv, 4 September 1966, *New Outlook*, 9, no. 8 (October–November 1966), p. 12.

WE MUST GRANT THE ARABS TRULY EQUAL RIGHTS

A few days ago Prime Minister Ben-Gurion said, at a meeting with journalists, that you cannot ask people to be angels, and that the members of the Arab nation, who hear incitement against Israel from Arab radio stations every day, would have to be angels not to be influenced by that propaganda.[1] In this way the Prime Minister attempted to explain that we must maintain the military government in the future, although with some limitations.

To my mind that way of thinking is mistaken and misleading. Especially if we are speaking of the national minority in our country. When such a national minority hears, day in and day out, that the ruling nation hates it, the imperative of political wisdom is to contradict propaganda with facts. Here, as in every area, and every time when we must work for long-term results, the decisive word must be dictated not by political tactics but by political strategy. Tactics say that, if there is a reason for suspicion, we must do everything that suspicion obliges us to do. Whereas the point of departure for political strategy in a case like this is that unbridled suspicion is likely to strengthen what gives rise to suspicion, and even create new reasons for it. It is true that blind faith causes damage both to individuals and to nations, but an open-eyed faith, a faith in the possibility of influencing someone else by one's own positive and constructive behavior, justifies itself more and more. The validation of this faith, however, is not instantaneous; its efficaciousness will not be immediately evident to everybody.

If we apply this insight to the field of our relations with the Arab minority in our land, it means that we are obliged to grant that minority truly equal rights to the degree permitted to us by the conditions of our security. No more, but also no less. The main point here is to determine with extreme precision and at frequent intervals what is the positive and constructive maximum that we can offer at any time, and to offer it.

In my opinion, we have not acted in that manner.

It seems to me that in the foreign policy of our Prime Minister, strategy has not, for the time being, reached the high level of his marvelous tactics. This is apparently linked to his pessimism, which he made clear recently in a meeting with army officers. He told them— not in a tone of conjecture, but as if he were defining the future—that Israel must expect a difficult campaign, both militarily and politically. Politically? Fine. But also militarily?

Today whoever considers war to be inevitable collaborates, willingly or unwillingly, consciously or unconsciously, in bringing about war. Here I must remind you that in the words of the Prime Minister, the campaign will take place in two circles: the smaller circle of the Middle East, and the wider circle of the globe. On the other hand, whoever refuses to believe that we cannot prevent the outbreak of war—that is to say, under today's technological conditions, which bring such widespread destruction and killing—such a person does his part to advance the cause of peace.

Note

1. The reference is to an interview Ben-Gurion gave to the Paris newspaper *Le Figaro* on 4 January 1962. See introduction to selection 63.

64

On the Development of the Galilee: An Exchange between Buber and Levi Eshkol

(October 1964)

(Editor's prefatory note:)

In October 1963 Levi Eshkol (1895–1969), who succeeded Ben-Gurion as Prime Minister in June of that year, dedicated the new town of Carmiel. Built in an area of almost exclusively Arab farming villages, Carmiel was part of the Central Galilee Development Project, initiated in 1963. Buber was deputized by the Ichud to write a letter to Eshkol, indicating its concern about the allegedly wanton confiscation of Arab farming lands in connection with the construction of Carmiel. Buber's letter and Eshkol's reply follow.

ON THE DEVELOPMENT OF THE GALILEE:
AN EXCHANGE BETWEEN BUBER AND LEVI ESHKOL

Jerusalem
26 October 1964

Dear Prime Minister Eshkol,

I would like to inform you personally of a position adopted last night at a meeting of the committee of the "Ichud" Association held in my home.

We decided unanimously to make public our view on the worsening of relations between Jews and Arabs in the country as related to the confiscation of lands near Carmiel.

Together with the entire community, we too welcome and extol a development plan for the Galilee, but stress the vital need to implement this plan for the benefit of Jews and Arabs alike. To that end a comprehensive plan will have to be proposed which from the outset takes into account the needs of both groups of citizens.

If that direction is taken, the impression will not be created here and abroad that Arab farmers are being ousted from their ancestral lands, but rather are being included in a joint development program.

Please permit me to add a personal note. Ever since you have assumed the premiership a marked change in tone, and to a certain extent even a change in policy has been discernible in certain fields, including the attitude towards Israel's Arab citizens. This has been all to the good. I am hopeful that you will have the strength to continue on this course precisely at a time that may well be fateful.

With sincere greetings,

Martin Buber

4 November 1964
Jerusalem

Dear Prof. Buber,

I thank you for your letter of 26 October 1964, and for the way you formulated your comments. I hope that in the future, too, you will not hesitate to send me your reservations and comments, should you find that necessary or useful.

The decision of the committee of the "Ichud" Association accords with everything I said in the Knesset (and elsewhere) about the development of the Galilee. In my view this project will benefit all its inhabitants, the old and new alike.

You have no doubt already acquainted yourself with what I said at the Carmiel opening ceremony last Thursday and could have noted that we do not disagree about the objectives of the development. But there is nothing better than seeing for yourself. When I was on the site, it increasingly became apparent to me that the development policy I announced is in fact being implemented.

It is a fact that Carmiel, the youngest of our development towns, has already brought benefit to the Arab inhabitants nearby. Witness to that are the many dozens of workers from the nearby villages who today are already employed there and no longer have to travel long distances, the pipeline bringing drinking water and irrigation to the nearby villages, and the electric power line that is approaching their doorstep.

It should also be known that 90 percent of the lands designated by the planners for construction of the city is rock-covered and cannot be cultivated. Only 500 of a total of 5000 dunam[1] are classified as agricultural land. It is a pity that you do not have the opportunity to see these lands before they are developed and built up and to see the envisioned city once it is constructed.

As someone who has worked in agriculture for many years, I, perhaps more than many others, feel the pain of the loss of many dunam of government agricultural land, private Jewish land, and superb Jewish National Fund land which has been "chewed up" around our large cities in the development boom of the last fifteen years. As of now I do not see any way of avoiding this, although it is always necessary to try to limit the damage as much as possible. The owners of the land have been guaranteed compensation in land, wherever possible, or in money.

The people at work implementing the project in Carmiel are also involved in negotiations for suitable and fair compensation for the lands expropriated and it is quite likely that we could have proceeded in this at a faster pace had it not been for the organized incitement against all settlement and development activity in the Galilee conducted by hostile elements and misguided individuals.

The "Luddite" opposition to the development plans reminds me of Jewish wagon drivers in the towns of the Pale[2] who said that the railroad would pass through their town over their dead bodies, and, whips in hand, stretched themselves out on the ground in order to delay the construction. The railroad was built—and they adjusted to the new era, to their own benefit and well-being. The same will no doubt happen

here. I cannot help being amazed that people whose thought is anything but primitive saw fit to identify with this kind of backwardness.

Your kind personal words pleased me very much and I thank you
for them.

With friendship and esteem,

Levi Eshkol

Notes

1. Metric surface measure equal to 1,000 square meters, or roughly one-fourth of
an acre.

2. Reference is to Pale of Settlement, or the provinces in Czarist Russia where Jews
were permitted permanent residence. Permission to live outside its confines was
granted on an exceptional basis only. Because of its restrictive nature, "the Pale" is
frequently used as a term equivalent to the Ghetto.

65

The Time To Try

(February 1965)

(Editor's prefatory note:)

In December 1964, the Tunisian weekly *Jeune Afrique*, a leading forum on
Afro-Arab affairs, published a dramatic editorial by its editor Bashir Ben-
Yahmed in which he appealed to the Arab world to reconcile itself to the
reality of the State of Israel:

The State of Israel, however unfortunate its creation may have been,
is a reality which cannot be eradicated short of a war whose only cer-
tainties are the suffering and destruction that will follow. . . . The real

solution, therefore, does not lie either in the consolidation of Israel—a Sisyphean labor—or in its destruction. It could lie in the disappearance of all the states in the region, their fusion in a Federation of the States of the Middle East, in which Israel, having taken back part of the Arab refugees and compensated the others, would no longer be a sovereign and hostile state, but, like Texas or California, a Federal State linked with the others within a framework which could be that of the U.S. of the Middle East,[1]

New Outlook, an English-language Israeli journal devoted to Arab-Jewish rapprochement, invited leading Israeli public figures to share their reaction to Ben-Yahmed's editorial. The eighty-seven-year-old Buber's response was his last published essay before his death on 13 June 1965.

Note

1. *Jeune Afrique*, 27 December 1964.

The Time To Try

At this hour I can only make a few preliminary remarks on the problems raised by the gratifying article in *Jeune Afrique*.

1. Undoubtedly the fate of the Near East depends on the question whether Israel and the Arab peoples will reach a mutual understanding before it is too late. We do not know how much time is given us to try.

The call to strive for such an agreement—the first call coming now to us from an Arab land—may obtain historical significance if it will awaken an echo in the Arab nation.

2. It is equally certain to me that an understanding between the Arab peoples and Israel must mean a federative union or rather a confederative one—the latter denomination meaning a considerably larger national autonomy for every part (such a union has already been advocated by some friends of mine and myself some time before the State of Israel came into being). We may compare the present situation of our peoples to the world situation of today; the decay of mankind will be inevitable if the cold war is replaced only by non-war; what

should come in its place must be not less than a true cooperation in dealing with the great common problems of humanity.

In October 1960, I received a questionnaire from the Novosti Press Agency in Moscow. The subject was: What will the world be like in twenty years?"

In my answer I wrote: "Everything depends on what the word peace means here, mere cessation of the war or true co-existence."

3. It is indeed indispensable to clarify first of all what is the meaning of the federative union we have to strive for. The author of the article in *Jeune Afrique* means by it a relation as between Texas and California. But the premises here and there are essentially different. In all parts of the U.S.A. there is the same population, an equally mixed one; in the Near East two different nations—related but different—are living. The situation here may rather be compared to that of Switzerland. The basis on which a federative union can be established is, by necessity, so that for each of the two partners the full national autonomy is preserved; neither one should be allowed to injure in any point the national existence of the other. (Therefore the Jews must not criticize the national movement of the Arabs nor should the Arabs criticize that of the Jews. It is, by the way, to be regretted that the author of the article himself speaks in such a manner of Zionism.)

4. In order that so immense a work, an unprecedented work in fact, may succeed, it is indeed necessary that spiritual representatives[1] of the two peoples enter into a true dialogue with one another, a dialogue based on shared sincerity and mutual recognition alike. Only such a dialogue can lead to a purification of the atmosphere, and without such a precedent of purification the first steps on the new way are bound to fail. These spiritual representatives must be independent in the full sense of this word; they must be individuals whom no consideration of any kind hinders from serving the right cause without reservation. If here and now a dialogue between such persons will come about, its significance will spread far beyond the boundaries of the Near East; it may show whether in this late hour of history the spirit of humankind can influence our destiny.

Note

1. That is, intellectuals, the custodians of culture and the spirit, as opposed to politicians.

Sources

Abbreviations:

Der Jude	Der Jude: Eine Monatsschrift, Vols. 1–4 (1916–19), Berlin/Vienna: R. Löwit; vols. 4–8 (1920–24), Berlin: Jüdischer Verlag. Founded and edited by Martin Buber.
Die Jüdische Bewegung	Martin Buber, Der Jüdische Bewegung: Gesammelte Aufsätze und Ansprachen. Zweite Folge: 1916–1920. Berlin: Jüdischer Verlag, 1920.
Kampf um Israel	Martin Buber, Kampf um Israel: Reden und Schriften. 1921–1933 Berlin: Sclocken, 1933.
Der Jude und sein Judentum	Martin Buber, Der Jude und sein Judentum: Gesammelte Aufsätze und Reden; with an introduction by Robert Weltsch. Cologne: Joseph Melzer Verlag, 1963.
Briefwechsel	Martian Buber, Briefwechsel aus sieben Jahrzehnten, 3 vols. edited and introduced by Grete Schaeder, in collaboration with Ernst A. Simon and assisted by Rafael Buber, Margot Cohen, and Gabriel Stern. Heidelberg: Verlag Lambert Schneider, 1972–75.
Martin Buber Archive	Martin Buber Archive, Jewish National and University Library, Jerusalem.

1. *A State of Cannons, Flags, and Military Decorations?*
   Correspondence: Martin Buber to Stafen Zweig, 4 February 1918, in *Breifwechsel*, 1: 525f.; Martin Buber to Hugo Bergman, 3/4 February 1918, in *ibid.*, 1: 526f. Translated by Itta Shedletzky.

2. *Toward the Decision*
  "Vor der Entscheidung," *Der Jude,* 3, no. 12 (March 1919):
  541–46; also in *Die Jüdische Bewegung,* 189–204; and *Der
  Jude und sein Judentum,* 508–14. Excerpts translated by Jeffrey M. Green.

3. *At This Late Hour*
  "In später Stunde," Der Jude, 5, no. 1 (April 1920): 1–5; also in
  Die Jüdische Bewegung, 205–16; and *Der Jude und sein
  Judentum,* 515–19. Excerpts translated by Jeffrey M. Green.

4. *Nationalism*
  "Nationalismus," *Wiener Morgenzeitung,* 3 September 1921;
  also in *Kampf um Israel,* 225–42; and *Der Jude und sein
  Judentum,* 309–19. English translation by Olga Marx, in Martin Buber, *Israel and the World; Essays in a Time of Crisis,*
  New York: Schocken Books, 1963, pp. 214–26. Reprinted by
  permission of Schocken Books Inc. Copyright © 1948 by
  Schocken Books Inc. Copyright renewed © 1976 by Schocken
  Books Inc.

5. *A Proposed Resolution on the Arab Question*
  "Rede auf dem XII. Zionistenkongress in Karlsbad, 2 September 1921," *Kampf um Israel,* 337–41; also in *Der Jude und
  sein Judentum,* 473–75. Excerpts translated by Paul R.
  Mendes-Flohr.

6. *Resolution on the Arab Question of the Twelfth Zionist Congress*
  Stenographisches Protokoll der Verhandlungen des XII. Zionistenkongresses in Karlsbad, 1. bis 14. September 1921, Berlin:
  Jüdischer Verlag, 1922, p. 769. Translated by Paul R. Mendes-Flohr.

7. *Notes from the Congress Concerning Zionist Policy*
  "Kongressnotizen zur zionistischen Politik," *Der Jude,* 6, no. 1
  (April 1921): 1–9; also in *Kampf um Israel,* 342–60; and *Der
  Jude und sein Judentum,* 476–87. Excerpts translated by Jeffrey M. Green and Paul R. Mendes-Flohr.

8. *Sidelights*
  "Streiflichter," *Der Jude,* 7, no. 7 (April 1922): 393–96; also in
  Kampf um Israel, 370–77. Excerpts translated by Jeffrey M.
  Green.

9. *Responsa on Zionist Policy*
  "Frage und Antwort," *Der Jude,* 6, no. 12 (March 1922): 713;
  also in *Kampf um Israel,* 382. Translated by Jeffrey M. Green.

10. *Brith Shalom*

   Martin Buber Archive, ms. varia 350, vav 5.

11. *Soul-Searching*

   "Selbstbesinnung," *Jüdische Rundschau* (Berlin), 31, nos. 29–
   30 (16 April 1926); also in *Kampf um Israel*, 393–412. Excerpts
   translated by Paul R. Mendes-Flohr.

12. *No More Declarations*

   From an address, *Protokoll der Verhandlungen des XVI. Zionistenkongresses und der konstituierendes Tagung des Council
   der "Jewish Agency" für Palästina, Zürich, 28. Juli bis 14.
   August 1929*, London: Zentralbureau der Zionistischen Organ-
   isation, 1929, pp. 203–8; also in *Kampf um Israel*, 423–31; and
   Der Jude und sein Judentum, 520–26. Excerpts translated by
   Paul R. Mendes-Flohr.

13. *The National Home and National Policy in Palestine*

   "Jüdisches Nationalheim und nationale Politik in Palästina,"
   lecture held at the Berlin chapter of Brith Shalom, 31 October
   1929, unpublished manuscript, *Martin Buber Archive*, ms.
   varia 350, vav 14. Translated by Gabrielle H. Schalit. (A revised
   and abridged version of this lecture was published, under the
   same title, in *Kampf um Israel*, 432–51; also in *Der Jude und
   sein Judentum*, 330–42.)

14. *The Wailing Wall*

   Excursus extracted from *ibid.*, *Martin Buber Archive*, ms. varia
   350, vav 14. Translated by Paul R. Mendes-Flohr.

15. *Hans Kohn: "Zionism Is Not Judaism."*

   Unpublished letter, Hans Kohn to Berthold Feiwel, 21 Novem-
   ber 1929. *Martin Buber Archive*, ms. varia 350, chet 376.
   Translated by Gabrielle H. Schalit and Paul R. Mendes-
   Flohr.

16. *And If Not Now, When?*

   "Wann denn?" *Jüdische Rundschau*, 37, no. 71 (6 September
   1932): 343; also in *Kampf um Israel*, 452–60; and *Der Jude
   und sein Judentum*, 343–47. English translation by Olga Marx
   in M. Buber, *Israel and the World: Essays in a Time of Crisis*,
   New York: Schocken Books, 1963, pp. 234–39. Reprinted by
   permission of Schocken Books Inc. Copyright © 1948 by
   Schocken Books Inc. Copyright renewed © 1976 by Schocken
   Books Inc.

17. *Mohandas K. Gandhi: The Jews.*
   M. K. Gandhi, "The Jews," *Harijan,* 26 November 1938, pp. 352–53.

18. *A Letter to Gandhi*
   Two Letters to Gandhi: From Martin Buber and Judah L. Magnes, pamphlets of the Bond, Jerusalem: Rubin Mass, 1939, pamphlet no. 1, pp. 1–22. (Excerpts of this letter were previously published in Martin Buber, *Israel and the World,* 227–33.)

19. *Keep Faith!*
   "Keep Faith!" *The Palestine Post* (Jerusalem), 18 July 1938, p. 6. Translation of article, "Al Ha-Begida" (On Betrayal), published on the same day in the Tel Aviv Hebrew daily, *Davar,* p. 2.

20. *Our Pseudo-Samsons*
   "Ha-Shimshonim," *Davar,* 5 July 1939, p. 5; also in *Neged Ha-Terror (Contra Terrorism): A Collection of Articles,* eds., Rabbi Benjamin (Y. Radler-Feldman) and Y. Peterzeil, Jerusalem, August 1939, pp. 25–29; and in Buber, *Te'uda Ve-Ye'ud (Destiny and Mission): Collected Writing on Jewish Affairs,* 2 vols., Jerusalem: Ha-Sifria Ha-Zionit, 1964, vol. 2, pp. 330–33. Translated by Deborah Goldman.

21. *And Today?*
   "Ve-Ha-Yom?" *Al Parshat Darkenu (At the Crossing of Our Ways). A Collection of Articles on the Problems of Zionist Policy and Arab-Jewish Cooperation,* eds., Rabbi Benjamin (Y. Radler-Feldmann), R. Weltsch, A. Lichinger, H. Margalit-Kalvarisky, E. A. Simon, and Y. Peterzeil, Jerusalem, March 1939, p. 136. Translated by Carol Bosworth Kutscher.

22. *Concerning Our Politics*
   "Al Ha-Politiqa Shelanu," *Darkenu (Our Way): A Collection of Articles on the Problems of Zionist Policy and Arab-Jewish Cooperation,* eds., Rabbi Benjamin (Y. Radler-Feldmann) *et al.,* Jerusalem: League for Arab-Jewish Rapprochement and Cooperation, August 1939, pp. 3–5. Translated by Jeffrey M. Green.

23. *False Prophets*
   "Neviei Sheqer," *La-Mo'ed* ("a one-time publication" issued by the editorial board of *Be'ayot Ha-Yom*), April 1940, pp. 9–

10. English translation in M. Buber, *Israel and the World: Essays in a Time of Crisis*, New York: Schocken Books, 1963, pp. 113–18 (excerpts). Reprinted by permission of Schocken Books Inc. Copyright © 1948 by Schocken Books Inc. Copyright renewed © 1976 by Schocken Books Inc.

24. *Let Us Avoid Provocations!*
"Iggeret El Ha-Mosadot" (A Letter to the Institutions [i.e., the governing bodies of the Yishuv]), *La-Mo'ed*, April 1940, p. 7. Translated by Deborah Goldman.

25. *The Ichud*
"Declaration of the Association 'Union' (Ichud)," in English-language supplement to *Be'ayot Ha-Yom*, 3, no. 1 (September 1942): 12.

26. *In the Days of Silence*
Foreword to *Bi-Yemei Elem (In the Days of Silence): Essays*, by M. Smilansky and S. Zemach, Jerusalem: Ichud Association, 1943, pp. 3–5. Translated by Michael Plotkin.

27. *Do Not Believe It!*
"Al Taamin!" *Be'ayot*, 1, no. 3 (June 1944): 136–37. Translated by Carol Bosworth Kutscher.

28. *Nathan Rotenstreich: "I Believed—Too Hastily?"*
"Heëmanti—Ha-im Beḥefzi?" *Be'ayot*, 1, no. 5 (August 1944): 228–29. Translated by Carol Bosworth Kutscher.

29. *An Additional Clarification: A Reply to Nathan Rotenstreich*
"Berur Nosaf: Teshuva Le-Natan Rotenstreich." *Be'ayot*, 1, no. 5 (August 1944): 229–30. Translated by Carol Bosworth Kutscher.

30. *Dialogue on the Biltmore Program*
"Du-Siaḥ Al Biltmor," *Be'ayot*, 1, no. 6 (September–October 1944): 241–43. Translated by Deborah Goldman.

31. *A Majority or Many? A Postscript to a Speech*
"Rov O Rabbim? Beshulei Neum Eḥad," *Be'ayot*, 1, no. 2 (May 1944): 52–54. Translated by Deborah Goldman.

32. *Politics and Morality*
"Mediniut U-Musar," *Be'ayot*, 2, no. 3 (April 1945): 110–13. Translated by Jeffrey M. Green.

33. *Our Reply*
"Teshuvahteinu" *Be'ayot*, 3, no. 1 (September 1945): 1–4; "Our Reply," in *Towards Union in Palestine: Essays on Zionism and Jewish-Arab Cooperation*, ed. by Martin Buber, Judah L.

Magnes, and Ernst A. Simon, Jerusalem: Ichud Association, 1945, pp. 33–36.

34. *The Meaning of Zionism*
Buber's testimony before the Anglo-American Inquiry Commission 14 March 1946, in Judah L. Magnes and Martin Buber, *Arab-Jewish Unity: Testimony Before the Anglo-American Inquiry Commission for the Ihud (Union) Association*, London: V. Gollancz, 1947, pp. 44–48.

35. *A Tragic Conflict?*
Unpublished (untitled) manuscript, *Martin Buber Archive*, ms. varia 350, vav 58. Translated by Arnold Schwartz.

36. *It Is Not Sufficient!*
"Lo Dai!" *Ha-Aretz*, 26 July 1946, p. 1. Translated by Deborah Goldman.

37. *A Plea for Clemency*
Letter to High Commissioner for Palestine, 21 August 1946, signed by Martin Buber, Chaim Kalvarisky, Leon Roth, Ernst Simon, Werner D. Seantor, Moshe Smilansky. *Martin Buber Archive*, ms. varia 350, chet 306b.

38. *Two Peoples in Palestine*
"Shenei Amim Be-Erez Yisrael," *Be'ayot*, 6, nos. 3–4 (February 1948): 200–208. Translated by Deborah Grenimann. (Lecture originally delivered in German on Dutch radio, June 1947.)

39. *Can the Deadlock Be Broken?*
"Palestine: Can the Deadlock Be Broken?" Symposium with Richard Crossman, Thomas Reid, Martin Buber, and Edward Atiyah, *Picture Post* (London), 36, no. 2 (12 July 1947): 22–25.

40. *The Bi-National Approach to Zionism*
"The Bi-National Approach to Zionism," in *Towards Union in Palestine: Essays on Zionism and Arab-Jewish Cooperation*, ed. by Martin Buber, Judah L. Magnes, and Ernst A. Simon, Jerusalem: Ihud Association, 1947, pp. 7–13.

41. *Let Us Not Allow the Rabble To Rule Us!*
"Al Niten La-Rehov Lehishtalet Aleinu!" *Ha-Aretz*, 29 January 1948, p. 12, letter to the editor signed by Martin Buber, J. L. Magnes, and D. W. Senator. Translated by Deborah Goldman.

42. *A Fundamental Error Which Must Be Corrected*
"Ta'ut Yesodit Sheyesh Lesalqah," *Be'ayot Ha-Zman*, 7, no. 9 (1 April 1948): p. 3. Translated by Carol Bosworth Kutscher and Paul R. Mendes-Flohr.

43. *Zionism and "Zionism"*
   "Zionut Ve-'Zionut.'" *Be'ayot Ha-Zman*, 7, no. 8 (27 May 1948): 3–5. Translated by Jeffrey M. Green.

44. *On the Assassination of Count Bernadotte*
   Unpublished manuscript (untitled, incomplete), *Martin Buber Archive*, ms. varia 350, vav 78. Translated by Arnold Schwartz.

45. *Let Us Make an End to Falsities!*
   "Nasim Qez Le-Petumei Ha-Millim" *Be'ayot Ha-Zman*, 7, nos. 23–25 (1 November 1948): 1; "Let Us Make an End to Falsities," *Freeland: Periodical of the Freeland League for Jewish Territorial Colonization* (New York), 5, no. 1 (1 February 1949): 30.

46. *Gideon Freudenberg: War and Peace: An Open Letter to Martin Buber*
   "Milḥama Ve-Shalom: Michtav Galui Le-Martin Buber," *Be'ayot Ha-Zman*, 8, no. 3 (17 December 1948): 3. Translated by Michael Plotkin.

47. *Facts and Demands: A Reply to Gideon Freudenberg*
   "Uvdot Ve-Drishot: Teshuva Le-Gideon Freudenberg," unpublished manuscript, *Martin Buber Archive*, ms. varia 350, vav 77. Translated by Michael Plotkin.

48. *On the Moral Character of the State of Israel*
   Protocol (in Hebrew) of a meeting between Prime Minister David Ben-Gurion and Israeli intellectuals, 27 March 1949, Tel Aviv: Government Printing Office, 1949, pp. 5–6. Translated by Arnold Schwartz.

49. *Should the Ichud Accept the Decree of History?*
   Unpublished manuscript (untitled), *Martin Buber Archive*, ms. varia 350, vav 80. Translated by Jeffery M. Green.

50. *The Children of Amos*
   "Benei Amos." *Ner*, 1, no. 1 (February 1950): 3–4. Translated by Paul R. Mendes-Flohr.

51. *"Preface" to a Projected Volume on Arab-Jewish Rapprochement*
   "Vorwort," unpublished manuscript (in German), *Martin Buber Archive*, ms. varia 350, vav 58a. Translated by Gabrielle Schalit.

52. *A Protest Against Expropriation of Arab Lands*
   Letter, dated 7 March 1953, to Joseph Sprinzak, Speaker of the

Knesset, Signed by M. Buber, E. Simon, and S. Shereshewsky. English translation in *Ner*, 4, nos. 5–6 (March 1953): 13–14.

53. *We Need the Arabs, They Need Us!*

"Anu Zequqim Le-Aravim, Ha-Aravim Zequqim Lanu!" *Ha-Olam Ha-Zeh*, 17, no. 848 (21 January 1954): 12–13. Translation by Paul R. Mendes-Flohr.

54. *Instead of Polemics*

"Bimkom Vikuach," *Ner*, no. 1 (September–November 1956): 7–8. Translated by Paul R. Mendes-Flohr.

55. *An Outrage*

Letter to Prime Minister David Ben-Gurion, dated 15 November 1956, English translation in *Ner*, 7, nos. 2–3 (November–December 1956): 36–37 (letter signed by Martin Buber in the name of the Ichud.)

56. *Socialism and Peace*

"Character Change and Social Experiment in Israel," in Moshe Davis, ed., *Israel: Its Role in Civilization*, New York: Seminary Israel Institute of the Jewish Theological Seminary of America, 1956, pp. 204–13 (excerpts).

57. *Active Neutralism*

"Active Neutralism," English translation in *Ner*, 9, nos. 1–2 (October–November 1957): 50 (circular signed by M. Buber, Rabbi Benjamin, and S. Shereshewsky).

58. *Letters from Arabs to Buber*

Farid-Wajdi Tabari to M. Buber, 7 February 1958, *Martin Buber Archive*, ms. varia 350, chet 802a (English); Attalah Mansour to M. Buber, 4 May 1958, *Martin Buber Archive*, ms. varia 350, chet 474a (translated from the Hebrew by Michael Plotkin); Anonymous Arab Palestinian Refugee to M. Buber, c. January 1965, *Ner*, 15, nos. 6–8 (Fe'   1965): 33 (English).

59. *Memorandum on the Military Government*

Memorandum submitted by Central Committee of the Ichud to Prime Minister David Ben-Gurion, 24 February 1958, signed by M. Buber, E. Simon, S. Shereshewsky, English translation in *Ner*, 9, nos. 5–7 (February–April 1958): 49–52.

60. *Israel and the Command of the Spirit*

"Israel and the Command of the Spirit," translated by Maurice Friedman in *Congress Weekly*, 25, no. 4 (September 1958): 10–

12; republished in Martin Buber, *Israel and the World: Essays in a Time of Crisis*, New York: Schocken Books, 1963, pp. 253–57 (exerpts). Reprinted by permission of Schocken Books Inc. from *Israel and the World: Essays in a Time of Crisis*, by Martin Buber. Copyright © 1948 by Schocken Books Inc. Copyright renewed © 1976 by Schocken Books Inc.

61. *Letter to David Ben-Gurion on the Arab Refugees*
    Open Letter in name of Ichud to Prime Minister David Ben-Gurion, 11 October 1961, translated in *Ner*, 13, nos. 1–2 (September–October 1961): 2.

62. *Ben-Gurion and Israel's Arabs*
    Statement to the Press on behalf of the Ichud, signed by Professor M. Buber, Professor E. A. Simon, and Dr. S. Shareshewsky, *Ha-Aretz* (26 January 1962), p. 5. Translated by Paul R. Mendes-Flohr.

63. *We Must Grant the Arabs Truly Equal Rights*
    "Yesh Latet Le-Miut Shivyon Zekhuyot Amiti," *Ner*, 13, no. 5–6 (February 1962): 7. Translated by Jeffrey M. Green.

64. *On the Development of the Galilee: An Exchange between Buber and Levi Eshkol*
    Correspondence, Buber to Prime Minister Levi Eshkol, 26 October 1964; Levi Eshkol to Buber, 4 November 1964, *Martin Buber Archive*, ms. varia 350, chet 197c. Translated from the Hebrew by Arnold Schwartz.

65. *The Time To Try*
    "The Time To Try." *New Outlook*, 8, no. 1 (January–February 1965): 13–14.

Index

Transliteration of Hebrew terms follows, with some adaptations, the principles of the Israel Academy of Sciences and Humanities. Exceptions, however, have been made for terms which have an established spelling in the literature on Israel and Zionism.